No. 1643
$19.95

8-BIT & 16-BIT
MICROPROCESSOR
COOKBOOK

BY JOSEPH J. CARR

TAB BOOKS Inc.
BLUE RIDGE SUMMIT, PA. 17214

FIRST EDITION

FIRST PRINTING

Copyright © 1983 by TAB BOOKS Inc.

Printed in the United States of America

Library of Congress Cataloging in Publication Data

Carr, Joseph J.
  8-bit and 16-bit microprocessor cookbook.

  Includes index.
  1. Microprocessors. I. Title. II. Title: Eight-bit
and sixteen-bit microprocessor cookbook.
TK7895.M5C365 1983   001.64   83-4959
ISBN 0-8306-0643-2
ISBN 0-8306-1643-8 (pbk.)

Contents

Introduction

This book is a technical catalog of available microprocessor chips and certain special purpose accessory chips. Of course, with the immense proliferation of available devices, it is in no way intended to be comprehensive. Thus, the chips represented here are selected on a sampling basis to give you an overview of the market. The most popular chips are included (Z80, 6502, 6800, and so forth), as well as widely used obsolete chips such as the 8080A. Each chip is covered sufficiently to allow you to make wise choices with regards to interfacing, assembly/machine language instruction sets and so forth.

The first chapter of this book introduces you to microprocessors and defines many of the terms that you will encounter in this field. The next two chapters take a detailed look at two of the most popular eight-bit microprocessor chips, the Z80 and the 6502. These chapters are included in order to give you an explanation of the terms, control signals, and other functions of microprocessor chips. Both chapters detail the internal organization of their respective chip. These chapters will enable you to understand the material in the later chapters of the book.

Chapters 4 through 10 of this book are a catalog of microprocessor specification sheets. All of these are the manufacturer's original data sheets, and are published here with the permission of the copyright owners. These data sheets give the original manufacturer's own claims regarding each device, hence they are viewed as the most accurate source of information.

The last part of the book consists of appendices that contain information of interest to circuit and interface designers. These appendices give examples about the generation of device-select pulses, address/port decoders, I/O port design and so forth. The limited space available in this book makes it necessary to abbreviate this treatment somewhat. In the event additional information is needed, I suggest my book *Microprocessor Interfacing*, TAB book number 1396.

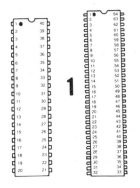

Introduction to Microprocessors

It is unlikely that anyone would contradict me if I made the claim that the microprocessor chip has revolutionized the electronics industry. The giant leap forward made by the industry more than a decade ago with the invention of the first microprocessor is at least as startling as any previous grand scale advance—perhaps on a par with the transistor itself, as some have claimed. In the late seventies, some of the more forward looking engineering professors were telling their students that an E.E. would be unemployable in ten years if he or she did not learn microcomputer technology. In truth, that prediction was wrong by almost half—five years was nearer the truth. The time has now arrived where skill in applying microprocessors and/or microcomputers is a must for all engineers, not just the electronic engineers.

The microprocessor is a large integrated circuit (typically 40 pins) that contains all of the circuitry needed to make the central processor unit (CPU) of a programmable digital computer (some provide memory and I/O functions as well). Most microprocessors, especially the earlier designs, required at least a few additional external chips in order to make a real computer, but still others contain all the necessary computer stages. The 8048 by Intel, for example, contains all the normal CPU functions found in a microprocessor plus a limited amount of internal random access memory (RAM), 2K worth of programmable read only memory (ROM), and a pair of input/output ports. That chip is not merely a microprocessor, but is actually an example of a single-chip computer.

The purpose of this book is to introduce you to several of the most popular forms of microprocessor, explain their similarities and differences, and generally provide you with enough information to intelligently make a choice from among them. We will also discuss certain related matters regarding microcomputer interfacing. The appendices are concerned with such esoteric topics as address decoding methods, generation of device select pulses, I/O port design, and simple dc power supplies for microcomputers. These topics are not as "neat" as some others that computerists could consider, but they are absolutely essential for the person who wishes to completely understand how to apply microcomputers/microprocessors. In this chapter, we are going to deal with vocabulary matters so that you will understand the differences between what appear to be similar terms. An introductory chapter should *introduce!*

THE MICROPROCESSOR: SOME BACKGROUND

Intel Corporation is usually credited with the invention of the microcomputer back in 1972. The story usually told is that Intel was contracted to build a four-bit programmable digital "controller" that would allow the user to control traffic lights. That unit supposedly became the now-obsolete 4004 four-bit microprocessor. Oddly enough, the original contractor did not want the device so Intel went on the market with it. The next unit was the 8008 device, which was an eight-bit version of the 4004 device. Later, the now-famous 8080A device was invented. Next came the Z80 device by *Zilog, Inc.* This device used the same basic philosophy of design as the 8080A, and many of the same instructions. In fact, the Z80 instruction set used all of the 8080A instruction and added quite a few more. We next saw the *Motorola* 6800, which used a slightly different design philosophy than the 8080A/Z80 machines. The *MOS Technology, Inc.* 65xx family of devices (of which, the 6502 is the most famous) was next on the scene and became immensely popular. The *Apple II*, for example, uses the 6502.

Currently, almost every semiconductor company makes at least one microprocessor or single-chip computer. Some of these are copy-cats of more popular machines, second-sources and the like, while others are entirely new and unique circuits.

My own involvement with microcomputers came about in the mid-seventies. The first I heard about the machines was on an amateur radio two-meter repeater in the Washington, DC area. Two amateurs who were among the new "in-crowd" were discussing the machines which they had recently purchased from *Altair* (the *original* S-100!), so I interrupted the conversation and asked for some additional information. Later that same month I was entering Ross Hall, the building for the George Washington University Medical School in Washington, DC, with Chuck McCullough (a colleague and fellow hospital Bioelectronics Laboratory employee). The university security service was pretty lax in those days, so guards tended to "do their own thing" while on duty. For most, that meant sleep or read questionable trash novels, but for this one chap it meant building his own computer. The guard on after-hours duty that evening was a graduate student who had just purchased an Altair S-100 computer and was assembling the kit on the guard desk! Being a couple of electronics hackers, Chuck and I stopped and asked a few questions and both of us were hooked by the computermania bug. It wasn't long before Chuck bought a Digital Group, Inc. Z80-based machine, and I followed along a few months later.

In order to illustrate how *new* this whole area was to us, let me tell a little story about a friend of mine and our mutual advisor in Engineering Graduate school. Gene Banasiak was a Radiology Engineer in the hospital, and he designed an X-ray anode-heat calculator based on the *KIM-1* microcomputer. The advisor, however, was skeptical that it was suitable for a Master's Thesis project because he thought that Gene was going to merely mount a programmable calculator on a box and make it work the equation with pushbutton inputs. In actuality, however, it was a sophisticated instrument that would keep track of the heating of the anode, and thereby indicate to the user when a dangerous operating region was reached. Because people weren't thinking in terms of microprocessors in those days, the professor did not understand the project at first and was unaware that Gene was developing a sophisticated electronic instrument.

SOME TERMINOLOGY

The terminology of microcomputers/microprocessors is on everyone's lips these days, so I suppose this section might be a waste of space for most readers. On the pure off-chance that there are those among you who are not totally familiar with the microprocessor field, let's first discuss some of the terminology that will be used in this book and by your fellow microcomputerists.

Programmable Digital Computer

A programmable digital computer contains a "memory" section that is used to *store* both data and *instructions*. The central processing unit (CPU) in a programmable digital computer responds to a certain set of binary numbers that it recognizes as "commands" or "instructions." These binary numbers are stored in the memory. The job the computer will perform is determined by these instructions and the order of their use. Since the operator can insert any of these instructions that he/she wants in memory, and can determine the order, the computer is said to be *programmable*. It is "digital" because it works with binary devices such as electronic switches that can implement base-2 (binary) arithmetic. The alternative to programmable is non-programmable or fixed-programmed computers, while the alternative to digital computers are the analog computers. These latter forms were once used extensively, and consisted of amplifiers, integrators, differentiators and a lot of other linear electronic circuits.

Bit

A "bit" is a *bi*nary dig*it*, either 1 or 0 (the only two digits permitted in the binary base-2 arithmetic system). These digits are represented in digital computers by discrete voltage or current levels. For example, in the popular TTL logic system of devices, logical-0 is represented by a *low* voltage of 0-volts (actually 0 to 0.8 volts), while logical-1 is represented by a *high* voltage of +2.4 to +5 volts.

Byte

A "word" consisting of bits; e.g., 11010011 is an example of an eight bit, or "one byte" binary number.

Microprocessor

A microprocessor is an *integrated circuit* that contains all of the necessary components to form the central processor unit of a programmable digital computer. The microprocessor is not to be confused (as it often is) with the microcomputer. The latter term (defined below) is a programmable digital computer that uses a microprocessor as the CPU. Thus, a microcomputer will contain a microprocessor plus additional circuitry that makes it operate as a fully qualified digital computer.

Microcomputer

A *microcomputer* is the smallest element that is truely identifiable as a full-fledged programmable digital computer. It is, by definition, built around a microprocessor CPU rather than other chips. It will, in addition to the microprocessor, contain other chips to fill out the functions of the computer. For small single-board computers, these extra chips might be only two or three LSI special purpose chips that contain a small amount of RAM memory, perhaps some ROM memory, and the I/O functions. On larger machines, the additional chips may number 40 to 100 or more. Just what comprises a microcomputer varies. For example, a small single-board computer without any input or output devices sold as an O.E.M. (i.e., a component used by other manufacturers in a larger electronic instrument) is certainly a microcomputer. So is the *Timex T/S-1000* microcomputer, as is the *Apple II.* Yet, at the same time, we find large tabletop and rack-mounted computers that are based on the microprocessor chip—and they are still called "microcomputers."

Minicomputer

The minicomputer has traditionally been a scaled-down mainframe (large data processing) computer. Examples of true minicomputers are the obsolete Digital Equipment Corporation (DEC) PDP-8 and the newer PDP-11 machines. These machines have not in the past used microprocessor chips in the CPU, but rather discrete logic elements, mostly TTL. It is not unlikely that a minicomputer required 35 to 40 amperes of current at +5 volts dc.

In the past, minicomputers have been more powerful than microcomputers. They would, for example, be found with data bus lengths of 12 to 32 bits rather than 4 or 8 bits common in microcomputers. Also, the minicomputer operated at fast clock speeds of 6 to 12 MHz rather than the 1 to 3 MHz of the microcomputer.

Today, the difference between minicomputers and microcomputers is hazy—almost indistinct. We now see microcomputers that are housed in rack-mounted cabinets and minicomputers that are in desk-top cabinets. The minicomputers may now also use an LSI chip that looks suspiciously like the microprocessor. The DEC PDP-11 format was implemented in the LSI-11 microprocessor chip and wound up in computers such as the Heath H11. It is now quite difficult to draw the line of demarcation between the minicomputer and microcomputer.

Mainframe Computers

The big horse used in the data processing department of a large company or university is called a mainframe computer. The *IBM 370* is an example of a mainframe computer. These computers are derisively called dinosaurs by the elitist-minded among the micro-computer fraternity. Be well aware that this dinosaur is not about to become extinct like its reptilian namesake. If the mainframe computer is a dinosaur, then the microcomputer is but a mere lizard!

Interfacing

Interfacing is the art of taking a microcomputer and wedding it to other circuits and equipment in order to solve some particular problem. At least one author has defined interfacing as the art of replacing hardware logic with software, and that is a reasonable explanation. It is interesting to note that interfacing is a relatively simple process, and normally not requiring large amounts of smarts, yet it is in interfacing that technicians, engineers and other assorted hackers make their reputation among the non-technical. In a university research setting, for example, one can make large strides up the respect ladder by being able to work the black magic that makes a microcomputer control an experiment or improve an instrument.

SELECTING A MICROPROCESSOR

The gut-feeling selection of a microprocessor will usually lead us to the chip with the greatest amount of capability, the longest data bus length, and the best instruction set. But that might also be the least economic choice! The selection of a microprocessor chip should be made with regard to the application at hand (seems reasonable, huh?) and not on an emotional level. If a brand new 16-bit microprocessor chip seems exciting, then take a second look at the situation before becoming committed. If, for example, an 8-bit microprocessor would do the same job, just as well, then why go to the trouble and expense of a 16-bit machine? After all, your memory and I/O costs will almost double when a 16-bit machine is selected over an 8-bit machine. On the other hand, if an 8-bit machine is used where a 16-bit machine is needed, then the operation will not be a success.

Proper regard must also be given for expansion of the system. If you lock yourself into a machine that does not operate fast enough, for example, you will be hard pressed to make the machine deliver more when additional software must be added. Also consider the matter of memory size. It turns out that one never has enough memory. Some of this problem is due to the natural tendency of programmers to use up the entire memory of the computer. In fact, one computer designer I know claims that it is wise to tell the programmer about only half of the memory provided! That way, the programmer will scale the program to fit the memory, rather than take it all with an "elegant" program. If the programmer genuinely needs more, then the computer designer can suddenly make the "change" without bloodletting.

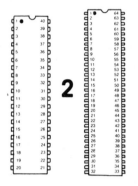

The Z80

The Z80 microprocessor chip was invented by Zilog, Inc. and originally second-sourced by Mostek, Inc. Today, the Z80 is available from a variety of sources and is widely used in microcomputers. National Semiconductor markets a version that is a low-power CMOS Z80 replacement.

The Z80 device grew out of the 8080A designed by Intel, so it is one of the earliest eight-bit microprocessor chips on the market. One may think of the Z80 as a second-generation 8080A that uses an improved and expanded instruction set, simplified clock signals, and a simplified control signal. Except for those that generate timing loops or otherwise depend on chip timing, programs written for 8080A will generally also run on Z80 machines. The subset of Z80 instructions that matches the 8080A instructions use the same op-codes—a remarkably farsighted design decision on the part of Zilog.

There are several features of the Z80 which made it more popular than certain other microprocessors. For one thing, the Z80 is heavily register-oriented. There are a total of twenty-two registers in the Z80 organized as follows: Two accumulators, two Flag registers, twelve general-purpose registers, and six special-purpose registers. Not all registers can be accessed at the same time, however, but are instead arranged into two banks as shown in Fig. 2-1. Each bank consists of an accumulator or "A-register," a Flag ("F") register and six general-purpose registers that are de-

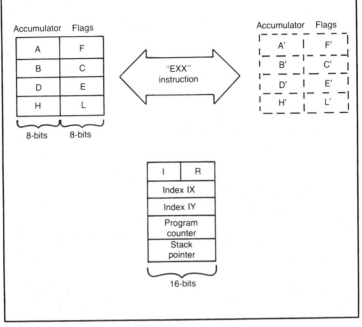

Fig. 2-1. Z80 registers.

signed B, C, D, E, H, and L. The main registers are accessible as soon as power is applied or a *reset* signal is received. The other bank of registers that are not accessible at this point and are designated by a prime sign: A′, F′, B′, C′, D′, E′, H′, and L′. These registers are switched with the main bank by executing an *exchange* (EXX) instruction.

In each bank, main or primed, the six general-purpose registers are grouped into three two-register pairs (BC, DE, and HL) which can be manipulated as if the Z80 were a 16-bit machine. Although the data bus to and from the outside world is still 8-bit, double-precision 16-bit arithmetic/logic instructions can be handled internally; several "double-register" instructions are available. The resistors of each bank, plus the non-banked registers, are described below:

General Purpose Registers (B, C, D, E, H, L). These registers are 8-bit registers used for temporary data storage within the Z80. These registers are essentially extra memory locations located inside the Z80 chip, rather than externally. The "addressing" of these registers is implied by the instruction used. The general purpose registers are grouped into register pairs (BC, DE, and HL) in order to handle 16-bit words.

Accumulator (A-register). The accumulator is the main data-handling register of the Z80. Most of the data handling instructions are used with this eight-bit register. Unless otherwise specified, all instructions refer to operations with respect to the accumulator. There are two accumulators in the Z80, one in each bank of registers. The A and A' registers are reversed when the EXX instructions is executed.

Flag (F and F') Registers. This eight-bit register serves as a processor status register, and its bits will indicate the status of the Z80 after the execution of the previous instruction. Each bit of the flag register is called a *condition bit*, and will *set* (i.e., 1 or HIGH) or *reset* (i.e., 0 or LOW) depending upon the condition being denoted. Figure 2-2 indicates the functions of each condition bit, which are also partially summarized below.

☐ C-flag: C=1 if there is a carry from the high-order bit of the accumulator (B 7), otherwise C=0

☐ Z-flag: Z=1 if result is zero, otherwise Z=0

☐ S-flag: S=1 if result is negative (i.e., B7 is 1), otherwise S=0

I-Register (Interrupt Vector). The I-register is used to point to the location in memory of an interrupt subroutine program. The I-register contains the high-order eight bits of the subroutine address, while the peripheral device initiating the request supplies

Flag Bit	Designation	Use
0	C	Carry flag
1	N	BCD Subtract flag
2	P/V	Parity/Overflow
3	—	Unused
4	H	BCD half-carry
5	—	Unused
6	Z	Zero flag
7	S	Sign flag

Fig. 2-2. Status register flags.

the low-order eight bits of the subroutine address. The actual address if the first instruction in the interrupt service subroutine is the *sum* of the 8-bits supplied by the peripheral and the 8-bits supplied by the I-register.

R-Register (Memory Refresh). The R-register is used to aid in refreshing dynamic memory. During the period when the Z80 is decoding and executing the instruction fetched from memory, a refresh signal goes active and the contents of the R-register are placed on the lower eight bits of the Z80 address bus (A0-A7), and the contents of the I-register are placed on the upper eight bits (A8-A15) of the address bus. The lower 7-bits of the R-register are incremented during each *instruction fetch* cycle. The eighth bit (B7) of the R-register is set using the LD, R, A instruction.

Index (IX & IY) Registers. The index registers are each 16-bits long and are used to point to an external memory address during indirect addressing mode instruction execution. The actual address of the external memory location is computed as the sum of either IX and IY contents and an integer *d* that is the second byte of the instruction.

SP Register (Stack Pointer). The external "stack" is a sequential series of memory locations used by the Z80 for certain "housekeeping" chores. For example, Z80 responds to an interrupt request, it saved the address of the current instruction on the stack so that it will know where to return after the interrupt program is completed. The Stack Pointer is a 16-bit register that contains the current address of the *last-in-first-out* (LIFO) stack. In addition to automatic data handling on the stack, it is also possible to send data to and from the stack via PUSH and POP instructions.

PC-Register (Program Counter). The *program counter* holds the address of the instruction being fetched from memory. Thus, the PC is a 16-bit register because the Z80 address bus is sixteen bits in length. The PC register is incremented a number equal to the number of bytes in the instruction. Thus, a one-byte instruction increments the PC by one, a two-byte instruction increments PC by two, and a three-byte instruction increments PC by three:

☐ one-byte instruction   PC   PC + 1
☐ two-byte instruction   PC   PC + 2
☐ three-byte instruction   PC   PC + 3

A JUMP instruction works by causing the contents of the PC register to change.

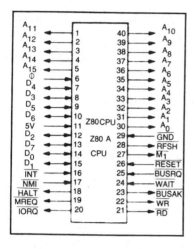

Fig. 2-3. Z80 package (courtesy of Mostek).

Z80 PIN-OUTS

The Z80 microprocessor chip is packaged in a standard 40-pin DIP integrated circuit package. Figure 2-3 shows a standard Z80 package with pin designations. The functions of the pins are described below.

A0-A15   Address Bus (16-Bits). During memory operations the Z80 will output the address on all 16-bits of the address bus. Possible combinations are from 0000 to FFFFH. Thus, a total of 2^{16}, or 65,536 different memory locations can be addressed. During input/output (I/O) operations, the 8-bit address of the selected port passes over the low-order 8-bits of the address bus (A0-A7), while the 8-bit data from the address bus (A8-A15). The Z80 uses an 8-bit I/O port address, so can uniquely address 2^8, or 256_{10}, different I/O ports numbered 000_{10} to 255_{10}. All bits of the address bus are active-HIGH (i.e., HIGH = 1, LOW = 0).

D0-D7   Bidirectional Data Bus (8-Bits). Main data path into and out of the Z80 chip. Like the address bus lines, D0-D7 are TTL-compatible, active-HIGH. During *write* operations, the data bus direction is out of the Z80, and during *read* operations it is into the Z80. The data bus can be tri-stated during some operations so that the Z80 merely "floats" at high impedance across the bus.

M1   Machine Cycle-1. Active-LOW output that tells the outside word when Z80 is in the "op-code fetch" portion of the instruction-execution cycle.

MREQ   Memory Request. Active-LOW output signal that tells the outside world that either a *memory read* or *memory write* operation is taking place. This signal is taken with either $\overline{\text{RD}}$ or $\overline{\text{WR}}$ in memory device select pulse generation.

$\overline{\text{IORQ}}$ Input/Output Request. Active-LOW output signal that tells the outside world that either *input* (read) or *output* (write) operation is taking place. This signal is taken with either $\overline{\text{RD}}$ or $\overline{\text{WR}}$ in I/O port device select pulse generation. The $\overline{\text{IORQ}}$ also becomes active to acknowledge an interrupt request. This signal is thereby used to signal the interrupting device to place the interrupt vector on the data bus.

$\overline{\text{WR}}$ Write Signal. This active-LOW tri-state output signal indicates that a *write* operation to either memory or an I/O port is taking place.

$\overline{\text{FRSH}}$ Refresh Signal. Active-LOW tri-state output that indicates that the refresh address is present on the lower 7-bits of the address bus (A0-A6).

$\overline{\text{HALT}}$ Halt. Active-LOW output that indicated that the Z80 CPU executed a HALT instruction. The Z80 will continue to execute NOP instructions while in the *halt* state, and is awaiting an *interrupt request*.

$\overline{\text{WAIT}}$ Wait. This active-LOW input causes the CPU to idle, and is used to allow slower peripherals or memory devices to get ready to transfer data to the data bus.

$\overline{\text{INT}}$ Maskable Interrupt Request. Active-LOW input that tells the CPU that an external device wants to interrupt the processor. This interrupt request can be disabled by software instruction which resets the interrupt flip-flop in the Z80.

$\overline{\text{NMI}}$ Nonmaskable Interrupt Request. This active-LOW interrupt request input acts like $\overline{\text{INT}}$, except that it cannot be masked.

$\overline{\text{RESET}}$. This active-LOW input *clears* the Program Counter (i.e. PC+ 0000H) and both I and R registers. In essence, the $\overline{\text{RESET}}$ line is a hardware "JUMP to 0000H" instruction.

BUSRQ Bus Request. This active-LOW input forces the Z80 data bus, address bus and control signal outputs to go to "tri-state" condition (high impedance) so that some other device can take control of those busses. $\overline{\text{BUSRQ}}$ takes priority over both $\overline{\text{INT}}$ and $\overline{\text{NMI}}$.

$\overline{\text{BUSAK}}$ Bus Acknowledge. Active-LOW output that tells the outside world that the Z80 has responded to a $\overline{\text{BUSRQ}}$ request, and indicates that the Z80 outputs are in the tri-state condition.

Clock Input. TTL-Compatible clock signal into the Z80.

GND. Ground.

+5. Dc power supply connection for +5 Vdc (regulated).

Z80 TIMING AND CONTROL SIGNALS

Any programmable digital computer works magic wonders because it is a *synchronous* device. That is, it operates in step with a *clock* signal. In a digital circuit, the "clock" is a chain of pulses. For example, in the Z80, which uses TTL-compatible inputs and outputs, the clock pin sees a train of pulses that transition from 0-volts to +5-volts at a frequency of no more than 2.5 MHz for the Z80 and 4 MHz for the Z80A. Some Z80 variants (e.g., Z80B) operate to 6 MHz.

The programmable digital computer operates in cycles determined by the clock. Figure 2-4 shows the *instruction fetch* cycle for the Z80. Each of the pulses shown (T_1-T_4 repeated) are *clock* pulses. The instruction cycle is broken into three subcycles designated M1 through M3. The M1 cycle occupies four clock periods (called T-Periods or T-cycles), while M2 and M3 occupy three. The three M-subcycles are used for the following purposes:

- ☐ M1   Op-Code Fetch
- ☐ M2   Memory Read
- ☐ M3   Memory Write

The M1 cycles is also called the *machine cycle*. A pin on the Z80, designated $\overline{M1}$, drops LOW whenever the computer is in the machine cycle, i.e., when it is fetching the op-code for the next operation from memory.

The M1 cycle is a busy time, as shown by Fig. 2-5. During the first half of the M1 cycle, i.e., during T_1 and T_2, the Z80 is in the op-code fetch mode. Since these op-codes are stored in memory,

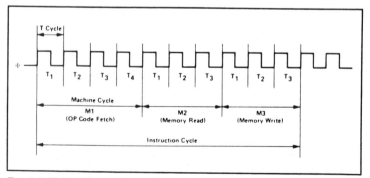

Fig. 2-4. Timing diagram for instruction cycle (courtesy of Mostek).

14

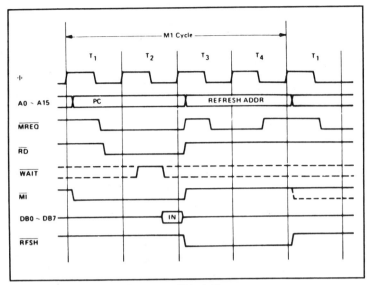

Fig. 2-5. M1 cycle timing (courtesy of Mostek).

the op-code fetch is essentially a memory read. Thus, during T_1-T_2, both the $\overline{MREQ}$ (memory request) and $\overline{RD}$ (read) lines are LOW, in addition to M1. Also during T_1-T_2, the Program Counter (PC) contents are passed along the address bus to designate the memory location of the op-code being fetched. The data (i.e., op-code) from that location is passed over the data bus to the Z80 (see "IN" on DB0-DB7 in Fig. 2-5) during the last quarter of the T_1-T_2 period.

The second half of the $\overline{M1}$ cycles consists of period T_3-T_4. This period is used to operate the refresh system for dynamic memory. Such memory devices decay rapidly unless refreshed, so the Z80 provides the ability to refresh such memory. During the T_3-T_4 period of the M1 cycle, the refresh address is output to the address bus; the $\overline{M1}$ signal goes HIGH (i.e., inactive) and RFSH line drops LOW (i.e., active). The MREQ signal also goes active for a portion of T_3-T_4.

The input/output cycles are shown in Fig. 2-6. On the Z80, the inputs are treated as *read* operations, while outputs are treated as *write* operations. The $\overline{RD}$ signal indicates reads, while the $\overline{WR}$ signal indicates a write. In order to distinguish inputs from memory reads, the $\overline{IORQ}$ signal will go LOW simultaneously with $\overline{RD}$. Similarly, an output is distinguished from a memory write by having $\overline{IORQ}$ simultaneously LOW with WR. During equivalent memory operations, $\overline{MREQ}$ is active rather than $\overline{IORQ}$.

Figure 2-6 shows I/O timing. During both input read and output write cycles the eight-bit port address is placed on the lower-order byte of the address bus (A0-A7). Also active (i.e., LOW) during these operations is the $\overline{IORQ}$ line. During the read cycle (an input operation) both $\overline{RD}$ and $\overline{IORQ}$ are LOW. Data applied to the input port is gated onto the data bus (and hence into the Z80 accumulation) during the last portion of the third T-Period. Input data must remain stable for at least this period.

During the output write cycle (also shown in Fig. 2-6), $\overline{IORQ}$ and WR are simultaneously active. The output data from the Z80 accumulator is placed on the data bus immediately following T_2, and remains stable for the entire period T_1-T_3. The control signals ($\overline{IORQ}$ & $\overline{WR}$) do not become active until the beginning of T_2, so is assured stable data.

Memory read and write operations are similar to I/O operations, except that all sixteen of the address bus bits are used (A0-A15), so 65,536 locations can be accessed; also, the $\overline{MREQ}$ replaces $\overline{IORQ}$. Both memory read and memory write cycles require three clock cycles (T_1-T_3). Figure 2-7 shows the memory read/write cycle timing diagrams. Note that, with the exception of the $\overline{IORQ}/\overline{MREQ}$ switch, these two cycles are essentially similar to the I/O cycle.

During the memory read cycle, shown in the left side of Fig. 2-7, the $\overline{MREQ}$ and $\overline{RD}$ control signals drop LOW, and the sixteenth-bit memory address appears on A0-A15. The read cycle

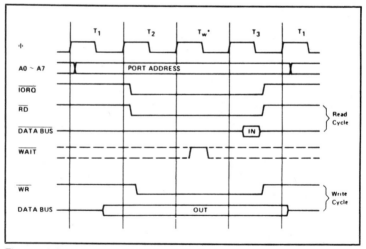

Fig. 2-6. I/O cycle timing (courtesy of Mostek).

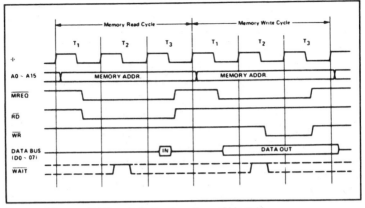

Fig. 2-7. Memory R/W cycle timing (courtesy of Mostek).

takes three clock cycles, and the data memory will appear on the bus during the last part of T3.

During the write cycle, the $\overline{\text{MREQ}}$ and $\overline{\text{WR}}$ control signals become active (i.e., LOW). The data from the accumulator is placed on the data bus at the end of T_1, and will remain stable for T_2 and T_3 (see Fig. 2-7). Thus, the data being written to memory will be stable during the period when $\overline{\text{WR}}$ is active. Like the read operation, the memory element being addressed is selected by a sixteen-bit address code on A0-A15.

Z80 INSTRUCTION SET

One measure of the microcomputer's power is the nature and extent of the machine-code instruction set. Compared to the 8080A, which was the Z80 predecessor, the Z80 has an almost awesome instruction set. The instructions are blocked into the following groups:

1. Load and exchange
2. Block transfer/search
3. Arithmetic and Logical
4. Rotate and Shift
5. Bit manipulation
6. JUMP, CALL, RETURN
7. I/O
8. CPU control

According to the official Zilog count, there are 158 distinct Z80 instructions, almost twice the 8080A count. But when you break apart grouped instructions according to bit or register operated on (for example), the 158 expands to well over 400!

Load and Exchange Instructions

These instructions are used for data movement both within the CPU and between the CPU and the rest of the "world." Amongst the load instructions there are two basic forms. One type involves purely internal Z80 data moves, i.e., between registers. The other type involves data moves between the Z80 CPU and external memory. The load instructions are further subdivided into 8-bit and 16-bit groups. Although the Z80 is an 8-bit machine, there are instructions that permit the transfer of two bytes of data into and out of Z80 *register pairs*. For the purpose of these instructions, internal Z80 registers are grouped AF, BC, DE and HL. The 8-bit load group instructions are shown in Fig. 2-8, while the 16-bit are in Fig. 2-9.

The exchange instructions are used to swap the contents between analogous register pairs. For example, "EX DE, HL" swaps the contents of register pairs DE and HL. These instructions include the following:

> EX AF, AF'
> EX DE, HL
> EX (SP), HL
> EX (SP), IX
> EX (SP), IY
> EXX

The EXX instruction swaps the entire main bank with the prime bank.

Block Transfer and Search Instructions

This group of instructions permit the computer to either transfer (in one operation) an entire block of data, or, to search a block for specific data. The sixteen-bit register pairs are used to designate the starting locations of the origin and destination addresses, as well as a byte counter (which specifies the number of bytes to be transferred). Members of this group are LDI, LDIR, LDD, LDDR (all transfer instructions), API, CPIR, CPD, and CPDR (search instructions) for all of these instructions, the sixteen-bit register pairs are used as follows:

> HL source address
> DE destination address
> BC Byte counter

SOURCE / DESTINATION matrix (8-bit load group)

DESTINATION	IMPLIED I	IMPLIED R	REGISTER A	REGISTER B	REGISTER C	REGISTER D	REGISTER E	REGISTER H	REGISTER L	REG INDIRECT (HL)	REG INDIRECT (BC)	REG INDIRECT (DE)	INDEXED (IX+d)	INDEXED (IY+d)	EXT ADDR. (nn)	IMM. n
A	ED 57	ED 5F	7F	78	79	7A	7B	7C	7D	7E	0A	1A	DD 7E d	FD 7E d	3A n n	3E n
B			47	40	41	42	43	44	45	46			DD 46 d	FD 46 d		06 n
C			4F	48	49	4A	4B	4C	4D	4E			DD 4E d	FD 4E d		0E n
D			57	50	51	52	53	54	55	56			DD 56 d	FD 56 d		16 n
E			5F	58	59	5A	5B	5C	5D	5E			DD 5E d	FD 5E d		1E n
H			67	60	61	62	63	64	65	66			DD 66 d	FD 66 d		26 n
L			6F	68	69	6A	6B	6C	6D	6E			DD 6E d	FD 6E d		2E n
(HL)			77	70	71	72	73	74	75							36 n
(BC)			02													
(DE)			12													
(IX+d)			DD 77 d	DD 70 d	DD 71 d	DD 72 d	DD 73 d	DD 74 d	DD 75 d							DD 36 d n
(IY+d)			FD 77 d	FD 70 d	FD 71 d	FD 72 d	FD 73 d	FD 74 d	FD 75 d							FD 36 d n
(nn) EXT. ADDR.			32 n n													
I	ED 47															
R		ED 4F														

8-bit load group instruction table

Mnemonic	Symbolic Operation	Flags S Z H P/V N C	Op-Code Hex	No. of Bytes	No. of M Cycles	No. of T States	Comments
LD r, r'	r ← r'	• • • • • •		1	1	4	r, s Reg.
LD r, n	r ← n	• • • • • •		2	2	7	000 B
LD r, (HL)	r ← (HL)	• • • • • •		1	2	7	001 C
LD r, (IX+d)	r ← (IX+d)	• • • • • •	DD	3	5	19	010 D
LD r, (IY+d)	r ← (IY+d)	• • • • • •	FD	3	5	19	011 E
LD (HL), r	(HL) ← r	• • • • • •		1	2	7	100 H
LD (IX+d), r	(IX+d) ← r	• • • • • •	DD	3	5	19	101 L
LD (IY+d), r	(IY+d) ← r	• • • • • •	FD	3	5	19	111 A
LD (HL), n	(HL) ← n	• • • • • •	36	2	3	10	
LD (IX+d), n	(IX+d) ← n	• • • • • •	DD 36	4	5	19	
LD (IY+d), n	(IY+d) ← n	• • • • • •	FD 36	4	5	19	
LD A, (BC)	A ← (BC)	• • • • • •	0A	1	2	7	
LD A, (DE)	A ← (DE)	• • • • • •	1A	1	2	7	
LD A, (nn)	A ← (nn)	• • • • • •	3A	3	4	13	
LD (BC), A	(BC) ← A	• • • • • •	02	1	2	7	
LD (DE), A	(DE) ← A	• • • • • •	12	1	2	7	
LD (nn), A	(nn) ← A	• • • • • •	32	3	4	13	
LD A, I	A ← I	↕ ↕ 0 IFF 0 •	ED 57	2	2	9	
LD A, R	A ← R	↕ ↕ 0 IFF 0 •	ED 5F	2	2	9	
LD I, A	I ← A	• • • • • •	ED 47	2	2	9	
LD R, A	R ← A	• • • • • •	ED 4F	2	2	9	

Notes: r, s means any of the registers A, B, C, D, E, H, L. IFF the content of the interrupt enable flip-flop (IFF) is copied into the P/V flag.

Flag Notation: • = flag not affected, 0 = flag reset, 1 = flag set, X = flag is unknown, ↕ = flag is affected according to the result of operation.

Fig. 2-8. 8-bit load group (courtesy of Mostek).

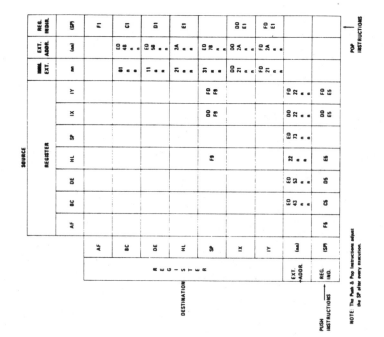

Fig. 2-9. 16-bit load group (courtesy of Mostek).

Notes: dd is any of the register pairs BC, DE, HL, SP. qq is any of the register pairs AF, BC, DE, HL.
$(PAIR)_H$, $(PAIR)_L$ refer to high order and low order eight bits of the register pair respectively. e.g.
$BC_L = C$, $AF_H = A$
Flag Notation: • = flag not affected, 0 = flag reset, 1 = flag set, X = flag is unknown, ↕ flag is affected according to the result of the operation.

The block transfer instructions will transfer an N-byte long block of data stored in sequential locations. The definitions of LDI, LDIR, LDD, and LDDR follow:

☐ LDI *(Load and Increment)*. Transfers one byte of data from the memory location specified by (HL) to the locations specified by (DE). This instruction will then *increment* both DE and HL, *decrement* BC.

☐ LDIR *(Load, Decrement and Repeat)*. Same as LDI except that it repeats until finally BC is decremented in 00H. By loading the initial source and destination addresses in HL and DE, respectively, and the number of bytes to be transferred into BC, an entire block of data can be transferred.

☐ LDD and LDDR. Identical to LDI and LDIR, except that HL and DE are decremented instead of incremented.

The *Block Search* instructions compare the contents of the accumulator with the contents of a memory location specified by (HL). The result of the comparison is indicated by the flag register (F). The following are block search instructions: CPI, CPIR, CPD, and CPDR.

☐ CPI *(Compare and Increment)*. Single operation comparison instruction. Following SPI, (HL) is incremented and (BC) is decremented.

☐ CPIR *(Compare, Increment and Repeat)*. This instruction repeats the CPI operation until one of two conditions exists: 1) the contents of BC are 00H, or, 2) the contents of the memory location pointed to by (HL) exactly matches the data in the accumulator; (HL) is incremented.

☐ CPD/CPDR. Same as CPI and CPIR, except that the contents of HL are decremented instead of incremented.

Arithmetic/Logical Instructions

This group of instructions performs the *computing* function of the computer. There are two groups of arithmetic and logical instructions: 8-bit and 16-bit. In the 8-bit arithmetic group are the addition (ADD) add with carry (ADC), subtract (SUB), and subtract with carry (SBC). The 8-bit logical group consists of AND, OR, or XOR instructions. Also included in this 8-bit classification are compare (CP), increment (INC), and decrement (DEC) instructions.

The same basic set of ADD, ADC, SBC, INC, and DEC instructions are used in the 16-bit arithmetic/logical group, but instead of the 8-bit registers (A, B, C, D, E, H, and L), and single memory locations, they use the register pairs (HL, IX, IY, BC, DE, and SP).

There is also a series of instructions that decimal adjust the accumulator data (DAA). These can be used to allow multiprecision BCD numbers, signed or unsigned binary numbers, or two's complement signed numbers.

There are four additional instructions in the arithmetic/logic group: *complement accumulator* (CPL), *negate accumulator* (NEG), *complement carry flag* (CCF), and *set carry flag* (SCF). The CPL instruction causes the number in the accumulator to be complemented. This means that the 1's become 0's and the 0's become 1's. The NEG instruction causes the contents of the accumulator to be expressed in two's complement form. The CCF instruction causes the carry flag to be complemented. If the carry flag is 1, then it will become 0, and if it is 0 it will become 1. The SCF instruction will cause the carry flag to be set (i.e., made 1).

Rotate and Shift Instructions

The rotate and shift group instructions include RLC, RRC, RL, RR, SLA, SRA, SRL, RLD, RRD, RLCA, RRCA, RLA, and RRA. These instructions move specified bits left or right.

Bit Manipulation Instructions

One of the things that make the Z80 one of the better μP chips is the existence of the bit manipulation instructions. We can test a bit 1 or 0, we can reset a bit (RES), and we can set (SET) a bit. The particular bit tested, set, or reset can be in any specified register (A, B, C, D, E, H, and L), or any memory location. In the latter case, we may use either indexed or register indirect addressing of the selected memory location. There are quite a large number of individual instructions in this group, because we can select any of eight bits (0-7), seven different registers, or memory locations specified by HL, IX, and IY register pairs.

JUMP, CALL, and RETURN Instructions

A digital computer executes instructions in a sequential manner. In the ordinary course of events, the program counter is incremented one to several counts every time an instruction is executed. The number of counts incremented is determined by the number of bytes required for the particular type of instruction.

Although this sequential execution is one of the powerful aspects of digital computers, it would also limit the range of possible problems that could be solved to those amenable to direct sequential processing. It would be impossible to perform most operations requiring even the simplest decision. Even the simple matter of inputting data would become impossible. In those operations, an input port is connected to a keyboard. We create a loop, using a JUMP instruction that tests the strobe bit (usually B7), and if none is found, jumps back to the beginning of the loop. If a strobe is found, on the other hand, the program is allowed to fall through to the next instruction (usually an input instruction). But this is merely a trivial example. Most problems requiring decision logic on the part of the computer could not be performed without the use of the JUMP, CALL, and RETURN instructions. The instructions in this group include JP, JR, CALL, DJNZ, RET, and RETN.

A JUMP (JP mnemonic) instruction is a branch to a subroutine at some address other than the next address in sequence. The address at which the next instruction (i.e., the first instruction of the subroutine) is to be found is loaded into the program counter (PC). We may use either of three addressing modes; immediate extended, register indirect, and relative.

Each of the different types of JUMP instructions are keyed to certain conditions that are reflected by the status bits of the flag (F) register. The conditions that may be specified by the selection of the op-code include carry, noncarry, zero, nonzero, parity even, parity odd, sign negative, sign positive, and unconditional.

The conditional JUMP instructions look for the status of the appropriate bit of the flag register. If the condition is met, then the JUMP operation occurs.

In immediate extended addressing, the JUMP occurs to a 16-bit memory address specified by the two bytes following the JUMP instruction. If the condition called for is met, then the program control will be shifted to the location specified by the following two bytes.

Register indirect addressing allows us to store the 16-bit address of the first instruction in the subroutine we wish to execute in one of the three double registers. Either the HL, IX, or IY register pairs can be specified by appropriate selection of the op-code. The register indirect JUMP instructions are all unconditional.

A relative addressing JUMP (JR mnemonic) instruction exists for each of the following conditions: carry, noncarry, zero, nonzero, and unconditional. In this type of JUMP instruction the next instruction for the program to execute (i.e., the first instruction op-code in the subroutine) is specified by the current contents of the PC added to a displacement integer e. The value of e can be anything in the range -126 to $+129$, as measured from the address of the instruction op-code (rather than the location of the displacement integer.)

In the case of one of the unconditional JUMP instructions (all forms of JUMP used in the Z80 will recognize an unconditional "condition"), the program counter is loaded immediately with the two bytes immediately following the op-code for the jump. The second byte of these three-byte instructions becomes the low-order byte of the RC address, while the third byte of the instruction becomes the high-order byte of the PC address. Since the contents of the PC are now changed, program control is transferred to the instruction located at a memory location specified by the PC.

There is also one special form of JUMP instruction that is very useful: DJNZ. This stands for decrement register B and jump if it is nonzero. This instruction allows us to use the B register as a byte counter. We load register B with an integer equal to the number of times that we wish to execute a subroutine. The program control will transfer to the subroutine specified by a displacement integer e (this is relative addressing) as soon as the jump occurs again. This will continue until B counts down to zero. If B was preloaded with zero, then the program will jump and loop through all 256 integers before terminating when zero is again encountered.

An example of a possible application of this type of instruction is signal averaging. If we want to average 100 data points, then we can nest an input instruction inside a DJNZ loop. The B register is loaded with 100, and is decremented with each execution. When all 100 data points are input, then the B register decrements one more time to zero, terminating the operation. The program then falls through to the next instruction in sequence. Note that the relative displacement integer e is expressed in the form of a two's complement number.

The CALL instruction is a special case of the JUMP instruction. If the CALL is used, then the address of the memory location immediately following the CALL instruction is loaded into an external memory stack (pointed to by the SP register contents). This allows us to branch to a subroutine, and then return to the main program sequence.

The return (RET) instruction is a reverse CALL instruction,

and is used to return to the main program once the subroutine jumped to by the CALL instruction is finished. The RET instruction is usually the last instruction in the subroutine. When this instruction is encountered, the program counter is loaded with the contents of the external memory stack (again, pointed to by SP). This will be the address of the first instruction that instigated the subroutine branch.

There are two specialized RETURN instructions, RETI and RETN. These are for returning to main program control after the servicing of an interrupt and a nonmaskable interrupt, respectively.

Input/Output Instructions

Input/output instructions cause data to be input to, or output from the CPU. The Z80 uses several different registers, and has I/O instructions allowing direct use of these registers without first requiring the programmer to transfer the contents of the accumulator. In addition, there are several block I/O instructions.

Immediate addressing is available to the accumulator (i.e., register A), while the B, C, D, E, H, and L registers use register indirect addressing. The block I/O instructions are also register indirect.

Perhaps the most common I/O instructions are the immediate input and immediate output instructions (IN A, n, and OUT A,n). In these instructions, the operand n is the eight-bit address of one of 256 (000-255) possible ports. This address will appear on the lower eight bits (A0-A7) of the address bus, while the contents of the accumulator appear on the upper eight bits of the address bus (A8-A15). The input or output data are passed over the eight-bit data bus to, or from, the accumulator, respectively.

In the case of register indirect addressing, the contents of the C-register specify the eight-bit address of the selected port. This address (i.e., contents of C) are passed over the lower byte of the address bus to signal the device being selected. Also at this time, the contents of the B register are passed over the high-order byte of the address bus. This is analogous to the immediate I/O instructions, except that the sources of the data passed to the address bus are different.

The block input instructions include INI, INIR, IND, and INDR. The block output instructions include OUTI, OTIR, OUTD, and OTDR. They are analogous to the memory block transfer instructions, except that they use the contents of register pair HL to point to an eight-bit I/O address at an external memory location. In these instructions, register B is used as a byte counter. As in the register indirect case above, the contents of the C-register hold the address of the I/O port. Note that this means that the contents of register pair HL point to a location in external memory. The contents of this location are then loaded into register C. When the actual transfer takes place, the contents of C are then placed on the low-order byte of the two-byte address bus. Also, as in other register indirect I/O instructions, the contents of the B-register (i.e., byte counter) are placed on the high-order byte of the address bus.

CPU Control Instructions

There are seven instructions in the Z80 set that are used exclusively for the control of the CPU: NOP, HALT, DI, EI, IM0, IM1, IM2.

The NOP instruction is a "no operation" instruction. During the execution of the NOP, the CPU will do absolutely nothing. The HALT instruction causes the CPU to cease operations until an interrupt is received. The DI instruction disables the interrupts, while EI enables interrupts.

The IM0, IM1, and IM2 instructions will allow the programmer to set any of three interrupt modes. The zero-mode (IM0) causes the Z80 to think that it is an 8080A. The IM1 causes program control to transfer automatically to location 00 38 (hex) when an interrupt is received. Interrupt mode 2 (IM2) allows indirect call to an interrupt service subroutine at a location specified by two bytes: the contents of the I-register and the 8-bit word received from the interrupting device. This feature allows vectored interrupts serving several peripheral devices whose subroutines may be different.

INTERRUPTS

An interrupt is a process in which your computer stops executing the main program, and begins executing another program located somewhere else in memory. This is not a mere "JUMP" or "CALL" operation, but a response to an external stimulus.

There are several reasons why an interrupt capability may be required. One of these is the case of an alarm condition. We could, for example, use a computer in an environmental control system, and use the interrupt capability to allow response to alarm situations (e.g., smoke detector, liquid level, burglar alarm, oven-temperature, etc.). The computer would ordinarily go about some other chore, perhaps the business of controlling the system. But once during the execution of each instruction of the program, the

CPU will interrogate the interrupt system. It is, then, monitoring the alarm status while executing some unrelated program. When an interrupt is received, indicating an alarm status, the computer would jump immediately to the program that services the interrupt—rings a bell, calls the fire department, turns on a light, sighs heavily.

Another application is to input data that occurs only occasionally, or whose periodicity is so long as to force the computer to do nothing for an inordinate amount of time. A real-time clock, or timer, for example, might want to update its input to the computer only once per second or once per minute. An analog-to-digital converter (ADC) might have a 20-millisecond conversion time. Even the slower version of the Z80 CPU chip (using a 2.5-MHz clock) can perform hundreds of thousands of operations while waiting for that ADC to complete its conversion job. Since the ADC will not provide valid data until after the conversion time expires, waiting for those data would be a tremendous waste of CPU time.

Another use is to input, or output, data to/from a peripheral device such as a line printer, teletypewriter, keyboard, terminal, etc. Those electromechanical devices are notoriously slow to operate. Even so-called "high-speed" line printers are considerably slower than the Z80 CPU. A classic example is the "standard" 100-word-per-minute teletypewriter. A "word", in this case, is five ASCII characters, so we have to output 500 characters per minute to operate at top speed. This is a rate of 8 characters per second, so each character requires ⅛ of a second, or 125 milliseconds, to print. The CPU, on the other hand, is a trifle faster. It can output the character to the input buffer of the teletypewriter in something like 3 microseconds. The Z80 can execute almost 42,000 outputs in the time it takes the teletypewriter to print just one character.

There are at least two ways to handle this situation, and both involve having the peripheral device signal the CPU when it is ready to accept another character. This is done by using a strobe pulse from the peripheral, issued when it is ready to receive (or deliver) another data byte. One way to handle this problem is have the programmer write in a periodic poll of the peripheral. The strobe pulse is applied to one bit of an input port. A program is written that periodically examines that bit to see if it is HIGH. If it is found to be HIGH, then the program control will jump to a subroutine that services the peripheral. But this approach is still wasteful of CPU time, and places undue constraints on the programmer's freedom.

A superior method is to use the computer's interrupt capability. The peripheral strobe pulse becomes an *interrupt request*. When the CPU recognizes the interrupt request, it transfers program control to an interrupt service subroutine (i.e., a program that performs some function required for the operation of the peripheral that generates the interrupt). When the service program is completed, then control is transferred back to the main program at the point where it left off. Note that the CPU does not recognize an interrupt request until after it has finished executing the current instruction. Program control then returns to the next instruction in the main program that would have been executed had not interrupt occurred.

TYPES OF Z80 INTERRUPTS

There are two basic types of interrupt recognized by the Z80 CPU: nonmaskable and maskable. The nonmaskable interrupt is executed next in sequence regardless of any other considerations. The maskable interrupts, however, depend upon the condition of an interrupt flip-flop inside of the Z80. If the programmer wishes to mask, i.e., ignore, an interrupt, then the appropriate flip-flop is turned off.

There are three distinct forms of maskable interrupt in the Z80, and these take the designations mode-0, mode-1 and mode-2. There are two interrupt input terminals on the Z80 chip. The $\overline{\text{NMI}}$ (pin 17) is for the nonmaskable interrupt, while the $\overline{\text{INT}}$ is for the maskable interrupts.

The nonmaskable interrupt $\overline{\text{(NMI)}}$ is much like a restart instruction, except that it automatically causes program control to jump to memory location 00 66 (hex), instead of to one of the eight standard restart addresses. Location 00 66 (hex) must be reserved by the programmer for some instruction in the interrupt service program, very often an unconditional jump to some other location higher in memory.

The mode-0 maskable interrupt causes the Z80 to pretend that it is an 8080A, preserving some of the software compatibility between the two CPUs. During a mode-0 interrupt, the interrupting device places any valid instruction on the CPU data bus, and the CPU executes this instruction. The time of execution will be the normal time period for that type of instruction, plus two clock pulses. In most cases, the interrupting device will place a restart instruction on the data bus, because all of these are one-byte instructions. The restart instructions transfer program control to one of eight page-0 locations.

Any time that a $\overline{\text{RESET}}$ pulse is applied (i.e., pin 26 of the Z80 is brought LOW), the CPU automatically goes to the mode-0 condition. This interrupt mode, like the other two maskable interrupt modes, can be set from software by executing the appropriate instruction (in this case, an IM 0 instruction).

The mode-1 interrupt is selected by execution of an IN1 instruction. Mode-1 is totally under software control, and cannot be accessed by using a hardware action. Once set, the mode-1 interrupt is actuated by bringing the $\overline{\text{INT}}$ line LOW momentarily. In mode-1, the Z80 will execute a restart to location 00 38 (hex).

The mode-2 interrupt is, perhaps, the most powerful of the Z80 interrupts. It allows an indirect call to any location in memory. The 8080A device and the Z80 operating in mode-0 permits only eight interrupt lines. But in mode-2, the Z80 can respond to as many as 128 different interrupt lines. Mode-2 interrupts are said to be vectored, because they can be made to jump to any location in the 65,536 bytes of memory.

INTERFACING THE Z80

The job of interfacing either I/O ports or memory with any microprocessor involves decoding the control signals and selected address. We discussed the Z80 control signals earlier in this chapter. Although further information will be given in the appendices, we will show how to generate system IN and OUT signals from the Z80 control signal.

Figure 2-10 shows a method of generating IN/OUT signals using a pair of three-input NOR gates. Recall the operation of any NOR gate:

    1. If any input is HIGH, then the output is LOW; and

    2. All inputs must be LOW for the output to be HIGH.

The control signals for the Z80 are active-LOW: $\overline{\text{WR}}$, $\overline{\text{RD}}$, and IORQ. These are paired as follows for input and output operations:

Input	Output
$\overline{\text{RD}} + \overline{\text{IORQ}}$	$\overline{\text{WR}} + \overline{\text{IORQ}}$

Thus for an input read operation, both $\overline{\text{RD}}$ and $\overline{\text{IORQ}}$ will drop LOW. In Fig. 2-10, a three-input NOR gate (G2) is connected to these signals and also to the $\overline{\text{SELECT}}$ signal. This latter signal will drop LOW if and only if the correct address for the I/O port or memory segment being served actually appears on the Z80 address bus. Thus, when all three signals ($\overline{\text{RD}}$, $\overline{\text{IORQ}}$ and $\overline{\text{SELECT}}$) are

Table 2-1. Decimal-BCD Equivalent Pin-outs for 7442.

Decimal	BCD	7442 Pin No.
0	0000	1
1	0001	2
2	0010	3
3	0011	4
4	0100	5
5	0101	6
6	0110	7
7	0111	9
8	1000	10
9	1001	11

active (i.e., LOW), then the selection criteria are satisfied, so the IN signal (i.e., the output of G2) goes HIGH. The $\overline{\text{OUT}}$ signal is generated in exactly the same manner, except that the $\overline{\text{WR}}$ signal is used in place of $\overline{\text{RD}}$. Also, G1 is used instead of G2.

Figure 2-11 shows a form of decoder circuit, in this case based on the 7442 TTL IC. The 7442 device is a *"Four-bit- BCD-to-1-of-10-decoder."* It was originally designed to drive a now obsolete form of digital display device. The 7442 examines a four-bit device. The 7442 examines a four-bit binary coded decimal (i.e., BCD) word and then issues an active-LOW output on the one of ten possible lines which represents the decimal equivalent of the applied BCD. Table 2-1 shows the BCD digits, their decimal equivalents, and the 7442 pinouts that represent those numbers.

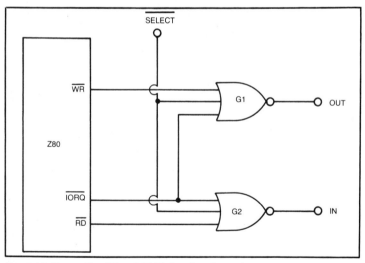

Fig. 2-10. Generating IN and OUT signals using gates.

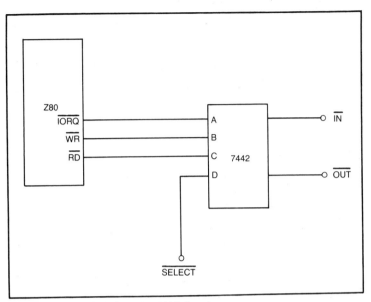

Fig. 2-11. IN and OUT from the 7442 decoder.

By examining Fig. 2-11, and noting which 7442 inputs are connected to Z80 control signals, we can determine which 7442 outputs are IN and OUT signals. The following information applies for Fig. 2-11. If, A=$\overline{\text{IORQ}}$, B=$\overline{\text{WR}}$, C=$\overline{\text{RD}}$, and D=$\overline{\text{SELECT}}$, then word DCBA for IN is 0010 and for OUT is 0100:

OP	Binary	Decimal	7442 Pin
IN	0010	2	3
OUT	0100	4	5

Thus, the "2" output (pin no. 3) of the 7442 is the active-LOW system IN signal, while the "4" output (pin no. 5) is the active-LOW system $\overline{\text{OUT}}$ signal. If greater drive capacity is needed (greater than provided by 7442 outputs), then noninverting high power bus drivers can be added to the circuit.

Our discussion of the Z80 has been in a little greater detail than will be offered for some other chips. The reason for this is that much of the material is redundant: techniques and definitions are much the same regardless of the chip involved.

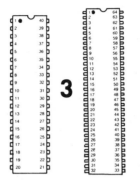

The 6502

Our next example of an eight-bit microprocessor chip is the 6502 device, which forms the basis for such computers as the ubiquitous *Apple-II, Franklin ACE, AIM-65, KIM-1, SYM-1*, and *Ohio Scientific's Superboard-II*. Because of its wide incorporation into popular microcomputers, the 6502 is about as popular as the Z80 device discussed in the previous chapter.

The 6502 device is designed to a different philosophy than the Z80. Where the Z80 is register-oriented, the 6502 is memory-oriented. Where the Z80 contains a large array of internal registers, the 6502 has but a few "standard" registers. Where the Z80 instruction set contains unique I/O instructions, the 6502 is *memory-mapped* i.e., I/O ports are addressed as if they are memory locations; hence, an *input* operation on 6502 is only a *memory read*, while an *output* operation is a *memory write*. Although it seems that the advantages are on the side of the Z80, a large number of designers selected the 6502. There are cases, incidentally, where a 2-MHz 6502 will execute a benchmark program faster than a 4 MHz Z80!

The 6502 microprocessor chip is available from the originator, *MOS Technology, Inc.,* and more than 15 secondary sources. Among the secondary sources are *Synertek* and *Rockwell International* who make the SYM-1 and AIM-65 microcomputer systems as well as in small-scale process controllers and other similar applications. Figure 3-1 shows the block diagram of the 6502 architecture, while Fig. 3-2 shows the pin-outs.

That there are certain similarities between the Z80 and 6502 devices testifies only to the fact that they are both microprocessor chips. The Z80 and 6502 devices are designed to different philosophies, which are reflected in their respective internal architectures. The Z80 allows separate input/output commands. The lower-order byte of the address bus will carry the port number (256 different ports numbered 000 to 255) address, while the high-order byte of the address bus carries the contents of the accumulator that is to be output. The I/O data is fed to and from the accumulator over the data bus. The 6502, on the other hand, uses a memory mapping technique in which each I/O port is designated as a separate location in memory. We can then read or write to that memory location, depending upon whether the operation is an input or an output. The 6502 also lacks the multiple internal registers of the Z80. But this feature, like the lack of discrete I/O ports, does not hinder most microcomputers designs. Very few microcomputers will need more than a total of a dozen or so I/O ports and/or registers. Also, very few microcomputers will need the entire 64K (i.e., 65,526 bytes) of available memory addresses. In fact, most systems have less than

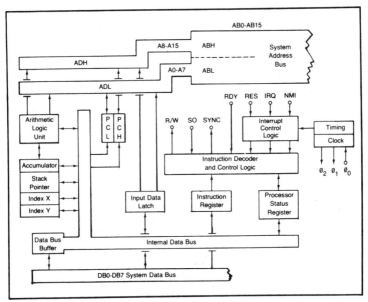

Fig. 3-1. 6502 architecture (courtesy of Mostek).

33

V_{SS}	1	40	$\overline{RES}$
RDY	2	39	ϕ_2 (OUT)
ϕ_1 (OUT)	3	38	S.O.
$\overline{IRQ}$	4	37	ϕ_0 (IN)
N.C.	5	36	N.C.
$\overline{NMI}$	6	35	N.C.
SYNC	7	34	R/W
V_{CC}	8	33	DB0
AB0	9	32	DB1
AB1	10	31	DB2
AB2	11	30	DB3
AB3	12	29	DB4
AB4	13	28	DB5
AB5	14	27	DB6
AB6	15	26	DB7
AB7	16	25	AB15
AB8	17	24	AB14
AB9	18	23	AB13
AB10	19	22	AB12
AB11	20	21	V_{SS}

Fig. 3-2. 6502 pinouts (courtesy of Mostek).

48K of memory. This allotment of memory would leave all locations above 48K for "firmware" (i.e., ROM) programs and I/O port or register selection.

Blocks in Fig. 3-1 that have names similar to blocks in the Z80 diagram perform roughly similar (sometimes exactly identical) jobs for the 6502 device. Note, however, that the *program counter* (PC) is divided into two eight-bit (1 byte) registers called PCL (for low-order byte) and PCH (for high-order byte of 16-bit address). Similarly, the address bus is divided into low (ADL) and high (ADH) order segments. Unlike the Z80, the 6502 uses a multiphase clock for timing of the operations. The 6502 pinouts shown in Fig. 3-2 are defined below. Some of them are similar to Z80 pinouts, while others are unique to the 6502.

6502 PINOUT DEFINITIONS

DB0-DB7. Eight-bit data bus.

AB0. Sixteen-bit address bus.

Φ_0. CPU clock.

Φ_1, Φ_2. System clocks.

R/W. Indicates a read operation when HIGH, and a write

operation when LOW. The normal inactive condition is read (i.e., HIGH). The CPU is writing data to the data bus (DB0-DB7) when this terminal is LOW.

$\overline{IRQ}$ **Interrupt Request.** This active-LOW input is used to interrupt the program being executed so that a subroutine can be executed instead. This interrupt line is maskable so it will respond only if the internal interrupt FF is enabled.

$\overline{NMI}$ **Nonmaskable Interrupt.** Similar to the interrupt request, except that this active-LOW input cannot be disabled by the programmer.

$\overline{RESET}$ **Active-LOW Rest.** Essentially a hardware jump to a location in page-F instruction. If this terminal is brought LOW, then the PC is loaded with the page-F address and program execution starts from there. Can be used for manual or power-on reset operations, and does not alter the contents of the accumulator.

RDY. The ready signal is an input that will insert a wait state into the normal cycle sequence. The RDY line must make a negative-going (i.e., HIGH-to-LOW) transition during the $_1$-HIGH clock cycle during any operation other than a write.

SO   Set Overflow Flag. This input will set the overflow flag if it makes a negative-going (i.e., HIGH-to-LOW transition during the trailing edge of the $_1$, clock cycle).

SYNC. Active-HIGH output that is used to indicate the instruction fetch machine cycle.

PROCESSOR STATUS REGISTER (6502)

Like the F- and F'-registers in the Z80, the 6502 device has a status register that can be used by the programmer in a number of important ways. The status register can be read by the program during certain operations, but is inaccessible to external hardware. The register has eight bits defined as follows:

Bit	Use
0	C-Carry. Indicates that a carry occurred from the accumulator on the last instruction executed. Active HIGH (logical-1)
1	Z-Zero. Indicates that the last operation performed resulted in a zero (if Z+HIGH) or nonzero (if Z=LOW).
2	(Unused)
3	D-Decimal Mode. When this bit is HIGH it causes a decimal add with a carry or subtract with borrow for BCD operations.

Bit	Use
4	B-Break. HIGH when an interrupt is executed.
5	(Blank)
6	O-Overflow
7	S-Sign. Indicates positive or negative results.

6502 TIMING AND CONTROL SIGNALS

The 6502 has relatively fewer control signals compared with the Z80 chip. There are complementary Phase-I and Phase-II clock signals (Fig. 3-3), which are derived from the 1 MHz signal generated at or input from the main CPU clock (Φ_0). The main difference in this respect between Z80 and 6502 is that 6502 has a single *read/write* signal labeled R/W. This signal is HIGH during the Phase-II period for *read* operations, and LOW during Phase-II for *write* operations. In both cases, we will examine the R/W line during the Phase-II period to generate the appropriate READ and WRITE system signals.

A *read* operation timing diagram is shown in Fig. 3-4. Note that the Phase-I period is a time of setup. During this period a valid address is stabilized on the address bus (A0-A15), and the R/W control signal goes HIGH. This operation commences a couple hundred nanoseconds into Phase-I and is completed by the onset of Phase-II. Thus, when the computer enters Phase-II, all is ready. When the Phase-II clock goes HIGH, the action will take place. A three-input NAND gate can be used to create a READ signal (or IN): one input looks at Phase-II, one looks at R/W and one at an active-HIGH SELECT signal. The confluence of these three active-HIGH signals determines the input and/or operation.

The timing diagram for a *write* operation (memory write or output) is shown in Fig. 3-5. It is essentially like the read operation,

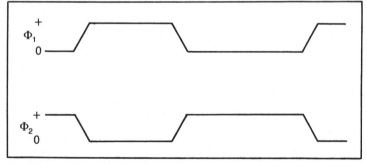

Fig. 3-3. Two-phase clock system.

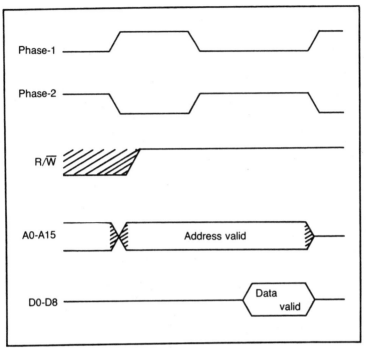

Fig. 3-4. Read cycle timing.

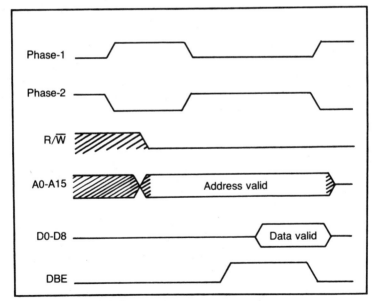

Fig. 3-5. Write cycle timing.

except that R/$\overline{\text{W}}$ goes LOW during Phase-I and remains LOW throughout Phase-II. During the last 300 nanoseconds of Phase-II the data is placed on the *data bus* (DB0-DB7); the data remains valid until after Phase-II goes LOW again.

In order to generate a device select signal (OUT), we can invert the R/$\overline{\text{W}}$ signal to form a $\overline{\text{R/W}}$ signal, and then use the same scheme as before (i.e., a three-input NAND gate). A further signal, DBE, goes HIGH coincident with Phase II during *write* operations.

All microprocessors include a *processor status register* (PSR) which contains information regarding the status of the registers immediately following instruction execution. The 6502 PSR contains eight bits, of which, seven are used and one is designated "for future expansion." Figure 3-6 shows the 6502 PSR. The functions are as follows:

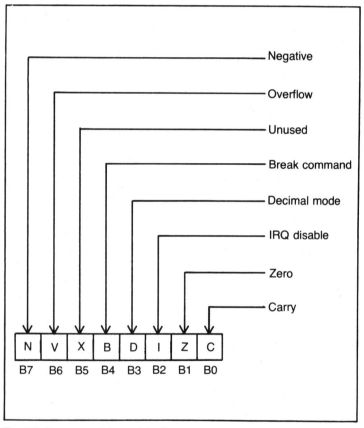

Fig. 3-6. Processor status register flags.

Bit	Flag	Use
0	C	*Carry Flag.* Will be HIGH (i.e., 1) if operation results in a carry, and LOW (i.e., 0) if the operation does *not* result in a carry.
1	Z	*Zero Flag.* This flag will be HIGH if an operation results in zero (00000000), and LOW (i.e.,0) if the result of an operation is anything *other* than zero.
2	I	*Interrupt Disable Flag.* The I-flag indicated whether or not the interrupt function is disabled. If the I-flag is HIGH (i.e., 1), then the interrupt function is disabled; if the I-flag is LOW (i.e., 0) then the 6502 will respond to interrupt requests on the $\overline{IRQ}$ line. The I-flag is *set* (made HIGH) by the reset command.
3	D	*Decimal Mode.* The D-flag will be HIGH (i.e., 1) if the 6502 is in the decimal mode (BCD), and LOW (i.e., 0) if in normal binary mode.
4	B	*Break Command.* A HIGH (i.e., 1) indicates that a *break* instruction was executed.
5	(X)	*Not Used.*
6	V	*Overflow Flag.* This flag is HIGH (i.e., 1) if the result of an arithmetic operation is greater than +127 or less than −127.
7	N	*Negative Flag.* The N-flag is HIGH (i.e., 1) if bit-7 of result is 1, and LOW (i.e., 0) if bit-7 is 0.

There are several instructions that examine the PST for specific bit conditions. For example, the BCC will branch (i.e., jump) when carry (C) is clear.

6502 INTERRUPT MODES

An interrupt line is an external control input that is used to grab control of the program. When the interrupt line goes active (LOW on most computers), the control goes to another portion of the program. There are three forms of interrupt used on 6502: *reset* ($\overline{RST}$), *interrupt request* ($\overline{IRQ}$), and *nonmaskable interrupt* (NMI). All three are active-LOW.

The *reset* line differs from that of the Z80 because it permits the programmer to select the reset "Jump-to" location (on the Z80 jump is to memory location 0000H). On the 6502 however, a LOW applied to $\overline{RST}$ will cause a jump to the memory location indicated by the contents of memory locations FFFCH and FFFDH. The low-order byte of the destination address is stored in FFCH, and the high-order byte is at FFFDH. For example, consider the following:

Location	Contents
FFFCH	08H
FFFDH	A0H

We have 08H stored at FFFCH, and A0H is at FFFDH. When $\overline{RST}$ is brought LOW, the control of the program jumps to the instruction stored at A008H. This is an example of a vectored reset.

The interrupt request ($\overline{IRQ}$) line is also vectored, with the "jump-to" location stored at locations FFFEH and FFFFH. There are two conditions on the interrupt request. The $\overline{IRQ}$ is an example of a *maskable* interrupt, that is, the 6502 will respond *only* if the I-flag in the processor status register is 0. This condition can only be created by deliberate programming step—the CLI instruction. The *reset* command (see above) forces the I-flag to 1, so disables the interrupt function of the 6502.

The second constraint on $\overline{IRQ}$ is that the $\overline{BRK}$ (i.e., break) instruction uses the same vector locations as $\overline{IRQ}$. If a "break" occurs, the B-flag of the PSR will be 1. The subroutine pointed to by the contents of FFFEH and FFFFH must contain a short routine to determine the status of the B-flag. Since the contents of the PSR are saved on the external stack, we can PULL the PSR contents back and test bit-4 for "1: (the AND instruction will do nicely).

The 6502 will want to resume operation at the point where it was interrupted. In order to do this trick, the 6502 stores the contents of both the PSR and the Program Counter (PC) on the external stack (Page-01H in memory).

The *nonmaskable interrupt* request ($\overline{NMI}$) does not depend upon the PSR I-flag. When the $\overline{NMI}$ line goes LOW, Program Control is transferred to the location vectored by the contents of locations FFFAH and FFFBH. Nothing can mask NMI. Like the case of IEQ, the contents of the PSR and PC are saved on the external stack.

The subroutines that service the $\overline{IRQ}$ and $\overline{NMI}$ requests must contain the *return from interrupt* (RTI) instruction. Furthermore, RTI must be the final instruction in the subroutine program. The function of RTI is to restore to the 6502 the PSR and PC contents saved at the time of the request. Thus, following execution of the interrupt subroutine, program control is restored to the original point in the program.

6502 ADDRESSING MODES

The 6502 microprocessor allows the following addressing modes: *accumulator, immediate, absolute, Zero-page, implied, indirect absolute, absolute indexed* X, *absolute indexed* Y, *indexed indirect, indirect indexed,* and *relative.* The modes are discussed below.

Accumulator Mode. This form of addressing is a kind of implied mode in which the operation will take place on the contents of the accumulator. There are only four instructions with accumulator mode addressing, and all are either *rotate* or *bit shift* instructions.

Immediate Mode. This mode will load the destination register (Accumulator, X or Y) with a number that forms the second byte of the instruction. The format is:

Byte No. 1	Op-Code
Byte No. 2	Data to be loaded

The LDA instruction has an immediate mode. An LDA #n" instruction will load the accumulator with the number "n." Consider the following example.

Byte No. 1	A9H	"LDA #n"	Op-Code
Byte No. 2	33H	"n"	

The above instruction will directly load the hexadecimal number 33H into the accumulator.

Absolute Mode. In the absolute mode the sixteen-bit address is specified by the two bytes following the op-code. The format is as follows:

Byte No. 1	Op-Code
Byte No. 2	Low-order byte of address
Byte No. 3	High-order byte of address

For example, consider the following

Byte No. 1	ADH	"LDA nnnn" op-code
Byte No. 2	45H	nn1
Byte No. 3	EFH	nn2

This sequence will load the accumulator with the contents of memory location EF45H.

Zero-Page Mode. This is a modified absolute mode in which the specified address will be within the 256 bytes of page-00 (i.e., 0000H to 00FFH). The advantage offered by zero-page addressing is that it is shorter (two bytes instead of three) and quicker.

Implied Mode. In this mode, the nature of the instruction determines the source of destination of an operation. The SEC (set carry flag) instruction is an example of implied addressing—the C-flag of the PSR is implied.

Indirect Absolute Mode. The address in an instruction that uses this mode is specified by the *contents* of the location given in the second and third bytes of the instruction. For example, consider the following:

Byte No. 1	6CH	Op-Code for JMP (nnnn)
Byte No. 2	00H	nn1
Byte No. 3	0FH	nn2
	.	
	.	
	.	
0F00H	08H	low-order byte of address
0F01H	A0H	high-order byte of address
	.	
	.	
	.	
A007H	_____	
A008H	(next instruction)	
A009H	_____	

The above code is an indirect absolute mode JUMP instruction. The code commands the 6502 with a "JMP (0F00H)" instruction. This means "transfer program control to the instruction whose address is stored at memory location 0F00H. The destination address is stored at location 0F00H and the next sequential location (i.e., 0F01H). In this example, 08H is found at 0F00H, and A0H is at 0F01H. Thus, the address of the next instruction is found at location A008H.

Absolute Indexed X & Y. These two addressing modes compute the effective address by adding the contents of either the X- or Y-register to the address given by the second and third bytes of the instruction. Figure 3-7 shows an example of a *absolute indexed*-X LDA operation (the absolute indexed Y is the same, except the Y-register is used). The operation is as follows:

☐ 1. At location 0200H and LDA 0400, X instruction is en-

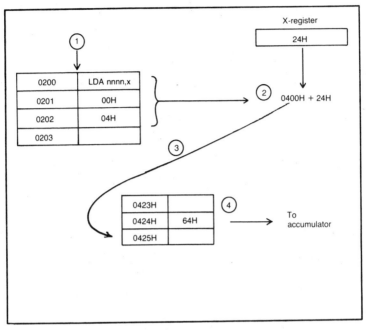

Fig. 3-7. Absolute index-X addressing.

countered, and 24H is in the X-register.

2. The effective address is 0420H + 24H, or 0424H.

3. The 6502 jumps to 0424H and fetches 64H.

4. The contents of 0424H (i.e., 64H) are stored in the accumulator.

Zero-Page Indexed-X & Y Modes. These modes are like the absolute indexed-X & Y modes, except that only page-zero addresses are allowed. The advantage is that only two bytes are needed, and execution is faster.

Indexed Indirect Mode. This mode combines indexed-X and indirect modes. The effective address is stored in a location in page-zero. An example of an LDA (nnnn,X) instruction is shown in Fig. 3-8. The operation is as follows:

1. At location 0200H an LDA (40,X) instruction is encountered.

2. The effective address is stored at a location in page computed by the operand at 0201H and the contents of the X-register.

3. The effective address is stored at location 0040H + 06H, or 0046H.

4. The 6502 finds EF30H stored at 0046H so transfers to that

43

location.

5. The number 60H is found at EF30H and this number is stuffed into the accumulator.

Indirect Indexed Mode. This mode also combines two other modes, but in a different way than the indexed-indirect mode. Figure 3-9 shows a typical indirect indexed LDA instruction. In this

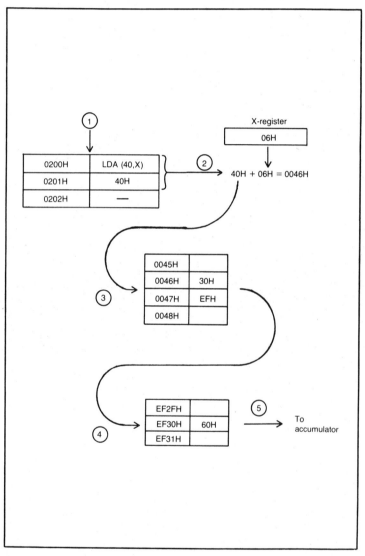

Fig. 3-8. Indexed-X indirect addressing.

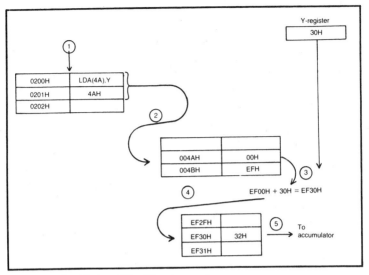

Fig. 3-9. Indirect indexed-Y addressing mode.

mode, the Y-register is used. Note in Fig. 3-9 that the computation of the effective address takes place *after*; an operand is fetched from a location in page-zero. The operation is as follows:

1. At location 0200H an "LDA (4A), Y" instruction is encountered.

2. The 6502 jumps to 004AH to pick up "EF00H."

3. The effective address is computed as EF00H + 30H (Y-register contents) or EF30H.

4. The 6502 jumps to EF30H to pick up data for the accumulator.

5. Data 32H is stored in the accumulator.

Relative Mode. This mode allows the control of a program to transfer forward or backward a specified distance. The second byte of the instruction gives the *distance* and *direction* of the branch. Positive hexadecimal numbers denote forward branches, and hexadecimal *two's complement* numbers denote backward branches. For example, 06H" denotes a branch six spaces forward, while FAH (2's complement for −06H) denotes a branch of six steps backward. Branches of $+127_{10}$ or -218_{10} bytes can be accommodated.

Figure 3-10 shows relative addressing used with the BCC instruction. Figure 3-10A is the forward case, and Fig. 3-10B is the backward case. Notice in each case the counting starts at the second byte from the BCC instruction.

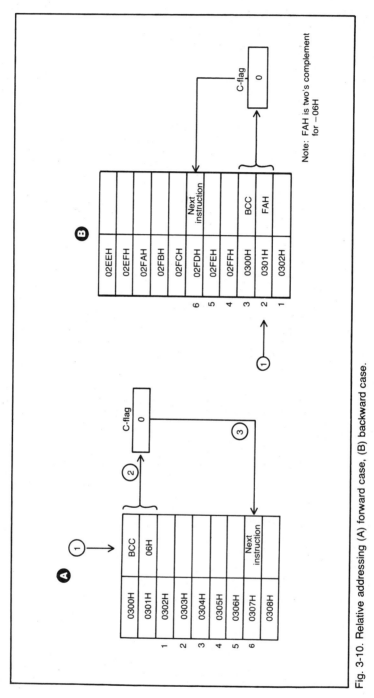

Fig. 3-10. Relative addressing (A) forward case, (B) backward case.

Note: FAH is two's complement for −06H

46

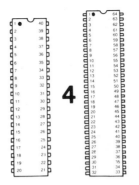

Intel 8080A Spec Sheets

- ■ **TTL Drive Capability**
- ■ **2 μs (− 1:1.3 μs, − 2:1.5 μs) Instruction Cycle**
- ■ **Powerful Problem Solving Instruction Set**
- ■ **6 General Purpose Registers and an Accumulator**
- ■ **16-Bit Program Counter for Directly Addressing up to 64K Bytes of Memory**
- ■ **16-Bit Stack Pointer and Stack Manipulation Instructions for Rapid Switching of the Program Environment**
- ■ **Decimal, Binary, and Double Precision Arithmetic**
- ■ **Ability to Provide Priority Vectored Interrupts**
- ■ **512 Directly Addressed I/O Ports**

The material in this chapter is reprinted by permission of Intel Corporation, copyright 1977.

The Intel® 8080A is a complete 8-bit parallel central processing unit (CPU). It is fabricated on a single LSI chip using Intel's n-channel silicon gate MOS process. This offers the user a high performance solution to control and processing applications.

The 8080A contains 6 8-bit general purpose working registers and an accumulator. The 6 general purpose registers may be addressed individually or in pairs providing both single and double precision operators. Arithmetic and logical instructions set or reset 4 testable flags. A fifth flag provides decimal arithmetic operation.

The 8080A has an external stack feature wherein any portion of memory may be used as a last in/first out stack to store/retrieve the contents of the accumulator, flags, program counter, and all of the 6 general purpose registers. The 16-bit stack pointer controls the addressing of this external stack. This stack gives the 8080A the ability to easily handle multiple level priority interrupts by rapidly storing and restoring processor status. It also provides almost unlimited subroutine nesting.

This microprocessor has been designed to simplify systems design. Separate 16-line address and 8-line bidirectional data busses are used to facilitate easy interface to memory and I/O. Signals to control the interface to memory and I/O are provided directly by the 8080A. Ultimate control of the address and data busses resides with the HOLD signal. It provides the ability to suspend processor operation and force the address and data busses into a high impedance state. This permits OR-tying these busses with other controlling devices for (DMA) direct memory access or multi-processor operation.

NOTE:
The 8080A is functionally and electrically compatible with the Intel® 8080.

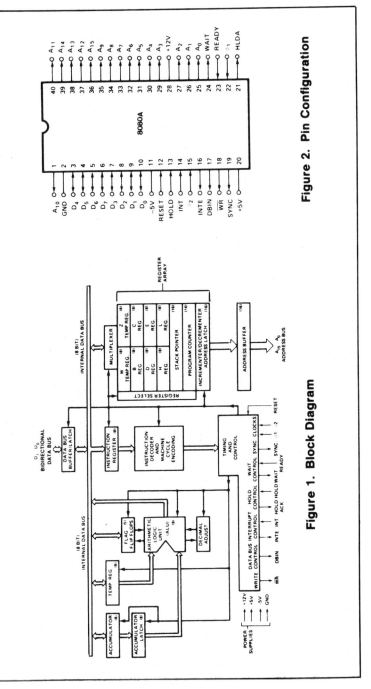

Figure 2. Pin Configuration

Figure 1. Block Diagram

49

Table 1. Pin Description

Symbol	Type	Name and Function
A_{15}-A_0	O	**Address Bus:** The address bus provides the address to memory (up to 64K 8-bit words) or denotes the I/O device number for up to 256 input and 256 output devices. A_0 is the least significant address bit.
D_7-D_0	I/O	**Data Bus:** The data bus provides bidirectional communication between the CPU, memory, and I/O devices for instructions and data transfers. Also, during the first clock cycle of each machine cycle, the 8080A outputs a status word on the data bus that describes the current machine cycle. D_0 is the least significant bit.
SYNC	O	**Synchronizing Signal:** The SYNC pin provides a signal to indicate the beginning of each machine cycle.
DBIN	O	**Data Bus In:** The DBIN signal indicates to external circuits that the data bus is in the input mode. This signal should be used to enable the gating of data onto the 8080A data bus from memory or I/O.
READY	I	**Ready:** The READY signal indicates to the 8080A that valid memory or input data is available on the 8080A data bus. This signal is used to synchronize the CPU with slower memory or I/O devices. If after sending an address out the 8080A does not receive a READY input, the 8080A will enter a WAIT state for as long as the READY line is low. READY can also be used to single step the CPU.
WAIT	O	**Wait:** The WAIT signal acknowledges that the CPU is in a WAIT state.
$\overline{WR}$	O	**Write:** The $\overline{WR}$ signal is used for memory WRITE or I/O output control. The data on the data bus is stable while the $\overline{WR}$ signal is active low ($\overline{WR}$ = 0).
HOLD	I	**Hold:** The HOLD signal requests the CPU to enter the HOLD state. The HOLD state allows an external device to gain control of the 8080A address and data bus as soon as the 8080A has completed its use of these busses for the current machine cycle. It is recognized under the following conditions: • the CPU is in the HALT state.

HLDA	O	• the CPU is in the T2 or TW state and the READY signal is active. As a result of entering the HOLD state the CPU ADDRESS BUS (A_{15}-A_0) and DATA BUS (D_7-D_0) will be in their high impedance state. The CPU acknowledges its state with the HOLD ACKNOWLEDGE (HLDA) pin. **Hold Acknowledge:** The HLDA signal appears in response to the HOLD signal and indicates that the data and address bus will go to the high impedance state. The HLDA signal begins at: • T3 for READ memory or input. • The Clock Period following T3 for WRITE memory or OUTPUT operation. In either case, the HLDA signal appears after the rising edge of ϕ_2.
INTE	O	**Interrupt Enable:** Indicates the content of the internal interrupt enable flip/flop. This flip/flop may be set or reset by the Enable and Disable Interrupt instructions and inhibits interrupts from being accepted by the CPU when it is reset. It is automatically reset (disabling further interrupts) at time T1 of the instruction fetch cycle (M1) when an interrupt is accepted and is also reset by the RESET signal.
INT	I	**Interrupt Request:** The CPU recognizes an interrupt request on this line at the end of the current instruction or while halted. If the CPU is in the HOLD state or if the Interrupt Enable flip/flop is reset it will not honor the request.
RESET[1]	I	**Reset:** While the RESET signal is activated, the content of the program counter is cleared. After RESET, the program will start at location 0 in memory. The INTE and HLDA flip/flops are also reset. Note that the flags, accumulator, stack pointer, and registers are not cleared.
V_{SS}		**Ground:** Reference.
V_{DD}		**Power:** +12 ±5% Volts.
V_{CC}		**Power:** +5 ±5% Volts.
V_{BB}		**Power:** −5 ±5% Volts.
ϕ_1, ϕ_2		**Clock Phases:** 2 externally supplied clock phases. (non TTL compatible)

ABSOLUTE MAXIMUM RATINGS*

Temperature Under Bias . . . .   0°C to +70° C
Storage Temperature . . . . -65°C to +150°C
All Input or Output Voltages
   With Respect to V_{BB} . . . .   -0.3V to +20V
V_{CC}, V_{DD} and V_{SS} With Respect to V_{BB} -0.3V to +20V
Power Dissipation 1.5W

D.C. CHARACTERISTICS (T_A = 0°C to 70°C, V_{DD} = +12V ±5%,
V_{CC} = +5V ±5%, V_{BB} = -5V ±5%, V_{SS} =0V; unless otherwise noted)

Symbol	Parameter	Min.	Typ.	Max.	Unit	Test Condition
V_{ILC}	Clock Input Low Voltage	V_{SS}−1		V_{SS}+0.8	V	
V_{IHC}	Clock Input High Voltage	9.0		V_{DD}+1	V	
V_{IL}	Input Low Voltage	V_{SS}−1		V_{SS}+0.8	V	
V_{IH}	Input High Voltage	3.3		V_{CC}+1	V	
V_{OL}	Output Low Voltage			0.45	V	I_{OL} = 1.9mA on all outputs, I_{OH} = −150μA.
V_{OH}	Output High Voltage	3.7			V	
$I_{DD (AV)}$	Avg. Power Supply Current (V_{DD})		40	70	mA	Operation T_{CY} = .48 μsec
$I_{CC (AV)}$	Avg. Power Supply Current (V_{CC})		60	80	mA	

Symbol	Parameter	Typ.	Max.	Unit	
$I_{BB\,(AV)}$	Avg. Power Supply Current (V_{BB})	.01	1	mA	
I_{IL}	Input Leakage		±10	µA	$V_{SS} \leq V_{IN} \leq V_{CC}$
I_{CL}	Clock Leakage		±10	µA	$V_{SS} \leq V_{CLOCK} \leq V_{DD}$
I_{DL} [2]	Data Bus Leakage in Input Mode		-100	µA	$V_{SS} \leq V_{IN} \leq V_{SS} + 0.8V$
			-2.0	mA	$V_{SS} + 0.8V \leq V_{IN} \leq V_{CC}$
I_{FL}	Address and Data Bus Leakage During HOLD		+10	µA	$V_{ADDR/DATA} = V_{CC}$
			-100		$V_{ADDR/DATA} = V_{SS} + 0.45V$

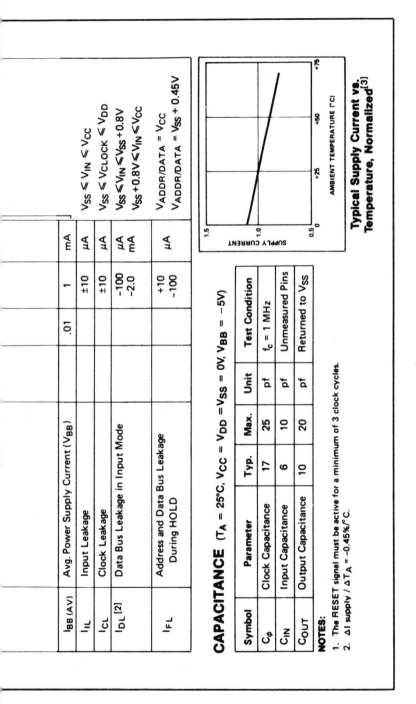

Typical Supply Current vs. Temperature, Normalized[3]

CAPACITANCE ($T_A = 25°C$, $V_{CC} = V_{DD} = V_{SS} = 0V$, $V_{BB} = -5V$)

Symbol	Parameter	Typ.	Max.	Unit	Test Condition
C_ϕ	Clock Capacitance	17	25	pf	$f_c = 1$ MHz
C_{IN}	Input Capacitance	6	10	pf	Unmeasured Pins
C_{OUT}	Output Capacitance	10	20	pf	Returned to V_{SS}

NOTES:

1. The RESET signal must be active for a minimum of 3 clock cycles.
2. ΔI supply / $\Delta T_A = -0.45\%/°C$.

A.C. CHARACTERISTICS (8080A)

($T_A = 0°C$ to $70°C$, $V_{DD} = +12V \pm 5\%$, $V_{CC} = +5V \pm 5\%$, $V_{BB} = -5V \pm 5\%$, $V_{SS} = 0V$; unless otherwise noted)

Symbol	Parameter	Min.	Max.	-1 Min.	-1 Max.	-2 Min.	-2 Max.	Unit	Test Condition
t_{CY}[3]	Clock Period	0.48	2.0	0.32	2.0	0.38	2.0	µsec	
t_r, t_f	Clock Rise and Fall Time	0	50	0	25	0	50	nsec	
$t_{ø1}$	ø1 Pulse Width	60		50		60		nsec	
$t_{ø2}$	ø2 Pulse Width	220		145		175		nsec	
t_{D1}	Delay ø1 to ø2	0		0		0		nsec	
t_{D2}	Delay ø2 to ø1	70		60		70		nsec	
t_{D3}	Delay ø1 to ø2 Leading Edges	80		60		70		nsec	
t_{DA}	Address Output Delay From ø2		200		150		175	nsec	$C_L = 100$ pF
t_{DD}	Data Output Delay From ø2		220		180		200	nsec	
t_{DC}	Signal Output Delay From ø2 or ø2 (SYNC, WR, WAIT, HLDA)		120		110		120	nsec	$C_L = 50$ pF
t_{DF}	DBIN Delay From ø2	25	140	25	130	25	140	nsec	
t_{DI}[1]	Delay for Input Bus to Enter Input Mode		t_{DF}		t_{DF}		t_{DF}	nsec	
t_{DS1}	Data Setup Time During ø1 and DBIN	30		10		20		nsec	
t_{DS2}	Data Setup Time to ø2 During DBIN	150		120		130		nsec	
t_{DH}[1]	Data Holt time From ø2 During DBIN	[1]		[1]		[1]		nsec	
t_{IE}	INTE Output Delay From ø2		200		200		200	nsec	$C_L = 50$ pF

Symbol	Parameter				Units
t_{RS}	READY Setup Time During $\varnothing_2$	120	90	90	nsec
t_{HS}	HOLD Setup Time to $\varnothing_2$	140	120	120	nsec
t_{IS}	INT Setup Time During $\varnothing_2$	120	100	100	nsec
t_H	Hold Time From $\varnothing_2$ (READY, INT, HOLD)	0	0	0	nsec
t_{FD}	Delay to Float During Hold (Address and Data Bus)	120	120	120	nsec
t_{AW}	Address Stable Prior to WR	[5]	[5]	[5]	nsec
t_{DW}	Output Data Stable Prior to WR	[6]	[6]	[6]	nsec
t_{WD}	Output Data Stable From WR	[7]	[7]	[7]	nsec
t_{WA}	Address Stable From WR	[7]	[7]	[7]	nsec
t_{HF}	HLDA to Float Delay	[8]	[8]	[8]	nsec
t_{WF}	WR to Float Delay	[9]	[9]	[9]	nsec
t_{AH}	Address Hold Time After DBIN During HLDA	-20	-20	-20	nsec

$C_L = 100$ pF:
Address, Data
$C_L = 50$ pF:
$\overline{WR}$, HLDA, DBIN

A.C. TESTING LOAD CIRCUIT

DEVICE UNDER TEST

$C_L = 100$ pF

C_L 100 pF
C_L INCLUDES JIG CAPACITANCE

WAVEFORMS

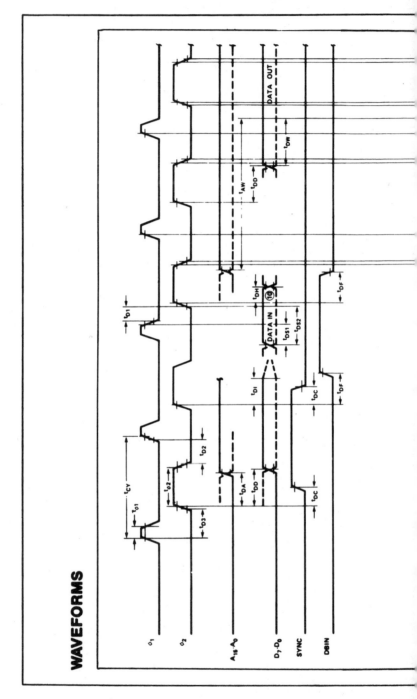

56

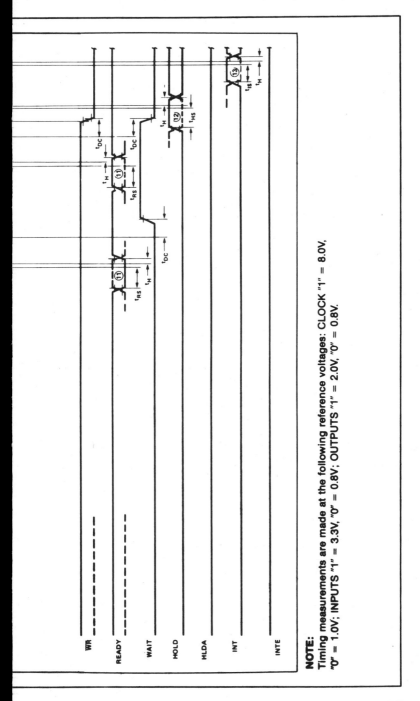

NOTE:
Timing measurements are made at the following reference voltages: CLOCK "1" = 8.0V, "0" = 1.0V; INPUTS "1" = 3.3V, "0" = 0.8V; OUTPUTS "1" = 2.0V, "0" = 0.8V.

57

WAVEFORMS (Continued)

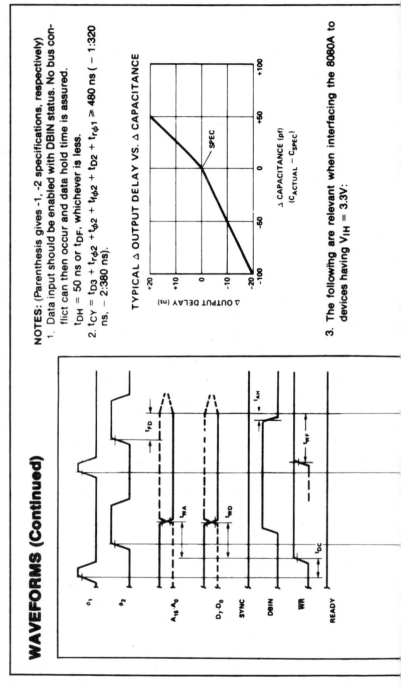

TYPICAL Δ OUTPUT DELAY VS. Δ CAPACITANCE

NOTES: (Parenthesis gives -1, -2 specifications, respectively)

1. Data input should be enabled with DBIN status. No bus conflict can then occur and data hold time is assured. t_{DH} = 50 ns or t_{DF}, whichever is less.

2. $t_{CY} = t_{D3} + t_{r\phi2} + t_{\phi2} + t_{r\phi2} + t_{D2} + t_{r\phi1} \geq 480$ ns (−1:320 ns, −2:380 ns).

3. The following are relevant when interfacing the 8080A to devices having V_{IH} = 3.3V:

58

a) Maximum output rise time from .8V to 3.3V = 100ns @ C_L = SPEC.

b) Output delay when measured to 3.0V = SPEC +60ns @ C_L = SPEC.

c) If C_L = SPEC, add .6ns/pF if $C_L > C_{SPEC}$, subtract .3ns/pF (from modified delay) if $C_L < C_{SPEC}$.

4. $t_{AW} = 2t_{CY} - t_{D3} - t_{r\phi2} - 140$ ns ($- 1$:110 ns, $- 2$:130 ns).

5. $t_{DW} = t_{CY} - t_{D3} - t_{r\phi2} - 170$ ns ($- 1$:150 ns, $- 2$:170 ns).

6. If not HLDA, $t_{WD} = t_{WA} = t_{D3} + t_{r\phi2} + 10$ ns. If HLDA, $t_{WD} = t_{WA} = t_{WF}$.

7. $t_{HF} = t_{D3} + t_{r\phi2} - 50$ ns).

8. $t_{WF} = t_{D3} + t_{r\phi2} - 10$ns.

9. Data in must be stable for this period during DBIN T_3. Both t_{DS1} and t_{DS2} must be satisfied.

10. Ready signal must be stable for this period during T_2 or T_W. (Must be externally synchronized.)

11. Hold signal must be stable for this period during T_2 or T_W when entering hold mode, and during T_3, T_4, T_5 and T_{WH} when in hold mode. (External synchronization is not required.)

12. Interrupt signal must be stable during this period of the last clock cycle of any instruction in order to be recognized on the following instruction. (External synchronization is not required.)

13. This timing diagram shows timing relationships only; it does not represent any specific machine cycle.

INSTRUCTION SET

The accumulator group instructions include arithmetic and logical operators with direct, indirect, and immediate addressing modes.

Move, load, and store instruction groups provide the ability to move either 8 or 16 bits of data between memory, the six working registers and the accumulator using direct, indirect, and immediate addressing modes.

The ability to branch to different portions of the program is provided with jump, jump conditional, and computed jumps. Also the ability to call to and return from subroutines is provided both conditionally and unconditionally. The RESTART (or single byte call instruction) is useful for interrupt vector operation.

Double precision operators such as stack manipulation and double add instructions extend both the arithmetic and interrupt handling capability of the 8080A. The ability to increment and decrement memory, the six general registers and the accumulator is provided as well as extended increment and decrement instructions to operate on the register pairs and stack pointer. Further capability is provided by the ability to rotate the accumulator left or right through or around the carry bit.

Input and output may be accomplished using memory addresses as I/O ports or the directly addressed I/O provided for in the 8080A instruction set.

The following special instruction group completes the 8080A instruction set: the NOP instruction, HALT to stop processor execution and the DAA instructions provide decimal arithmetic capability. STC allows the carry flag to be directly set, and the CMC instruction allows it to be complemented. CMA complements the contents of the accumulator and XCHG exchanges the contents of two 16-bit register pairs directly.

Data and Instruction Formats

Data in the 8080A is stored in the form of 8-bit binary integers. All data transfers to the system data bus will be in the same format.

D_7	D_6	D_5	D_4	D_3	D_2	D_1	D_0

DATA WORD

The program instructions may be one, two, or three bytes in length. Multiple byte instructions must be stored in successive words in program memory. The instruction formats then depend on the particular operation executed.

One Byte Instructions

D_7	D_6	D_5	D_4	D_3	D_2	D_1	D_0	OP CODE

TYPICAL INSTRUCTIONS

Register to register, memory reference, arithmetic or logical, rotate, return, push, pop, enable or disable interrupt instructions

Two Byte Instructions

D_7	D_6	D_5	D_4	D_3	D_2	D_1	D_0	OP CODE
D_7	D_6	D_5	D_4	D_3	D_2	D_1	D_0	OPERAND

Immediate mode or I/O instructions

Three Byte Instructions

D_7	D_6	D_5	D_4	D_3	D_2	D_1	D_0	OP CODE
D_7	D_6	D_5	D_4	D_3	D_2	D_1	D_0	LOW ADDRESS OR OPERAND 1
D_7	D_6	D_5	D_4	D_3	D_2	D_1	D_0	HIGH ADDRESS OR OPERAND 2

Jump, call or direct load and store instructions

For the 8080A a logic "1" is defined as a high level and a logic "0" is defined as a low level.

Table 2. Instruction Set Summary

Mnemonic	D7	D6	D5	D4	D3	D2	D1	D0	Operations Description	Clock Cycles [2]
MOVE, LOAD, AND STORE										
MOV r1,r2	0	1	D	D	D	S	S	S	Move register to register	5
MOV M,r	0	1	1	1	0	S	S	S	Move register to memory	7
MOV r,M	0	1	D	D	D	1	1	0	Move memory to register	7
MVI r	0	0	D	D	D	1	1	0	Move immediate register	7
MVI M	0	0	1	1	0	1	1	0	Move immediate memory	10
LXI B	0	0	0	0	0	0	0	1	Load immediate register Pair B & C	10
LXI D	0	0	0	1	0	0	0	1	Load immediate register Pair D & E	10
LXI H	0	0	1	0	0	0	0	1	Load immediate register Pair H & L	10
STAX B	0	0	0	0	0	0	1	0	Store A indirect	7
STAX D	0	0	0	1	0	0	1	0	Store A indirect	7
LDAX B	0	0	0	0	1	0	1	0	Load A indirect	7
LDAX D	0	0	0	1	1	0	1	0	Load A indirect	7
STA	0	0	1	1	0	0	1	0	Store A direct	13
LDA	0	0	1	1	1	0	1	0	Load A direct	13
SHLD	0	0	1	0	0	0	1	0	Store H & L direct	16
LHLD	0	0	1	0	1	0	1	0	Load H & L direct	16
XCHG	1	1	1	0	1	0	1	1	Exchange D & E, H & L Registers	4
STACK OPS										

Mnemonic	D7	D6	D5	D4	D3	D2	D1	D0	Operations Description	Clock Cycles [2]
JPO	1	1	1	0	0	0	1	0	Jump on parity odd	10
PCHL	1	1	1	0	1	0	0	1	H & L to program counter	5
CALL										
CALL	1	1	0	0	1	1	0	1	Call unconditional	17
CC	1	1	0	1	1	1	0	0	Call on carry	11/17
CNC	1	1	0	1	0	1	0	0	Call on no carry	11/17
CZ	1	1	0	0	1	1	0	0	Call on zero	11/17
CNZ	1	1	0	0	0	1	0	0	Call on no zero	11/17
CP	1	1	1	1	0	1	0	0	Call on positive	11/17
CM	1	1	1	1	1	1	0	0	Call on minus	11/17
CPE	1	1	1	0	1	1	0	0	Call on parity even	11/17
CPO	1	1	1	0	0	1	0	0	Call on parity odd	11/17
RETURN										
RET	1	1	0	0	1	0	0	1	Return	10
RC	1	1	0	1	1	0	0	0	Return on carry	5/11
RNC	1	1	0	1	0	0	0	0	Return on no carry	5/11
RZ	1	1	0	0	1	0	0	0	Return on zero	5/11
RNZ	1	1	0	0	0	0	0	0	Return on no zero	5/11
RP	1	1	1	1	0	0	0	0	Return on positive	5/11
RM	1	1	1	1	1	0	0	0	Return on minus	5/11
RPE	1	1	1	0	1	0	0	0	Return on parity even	5/11
RPO	1	1	1	0	0	0	0	0	Return on parity odd	5/11
RESTART										
RST	1	1	A	A	A	1	1	1	Restart	11
INCREMENT AND DECREMENT										
INR r	0	0	D	D	D	1	0	0	Increment register	5

Left table

Mnemonic	D7	D6	D5	D4	D3	D2	D1	D0	Description	Cycles
PUSH B	1	1	0	0	0	1	0	1	Push register Pair B & C on stack	11
PUSH D	1	1	0	1	0	1	0	1	Push register Pair D & E on stack	11
PUSH H	1	1	1	0	0	1	0	1	Push register Pair H & L on stack	11
PUSH PSW	1	1	1	1	0	1	0	1	Push A and Flags on stack	11
POP B	1	1	0	0	0	0	0	1	Pop register Pair B & C off stack	10
POP D	1	1	0	1	0	0	0	1	Pop register Pair D & E off stack	10
POP H	1	1	1	0	0	0	0	1	Pop register Pair H & L off stack	10
POP PSW	1	1	1	1	0	0	0	1	Pop A and Flags off stack	10
XTHL	1	1	1	0	0	0	1	1	Exchange top of stack, H & L	18
SPHL	1	1	1	1	1	0	0	1	H & L to stack pointer	5
LXI SP	0	0	1	1	0	0	0	1	Load immediate stack pointer	10
INX SP	0	0	1	1	0	0	1	1	Increment stack pointer	5
DCX SP	0	0	1	1	1	0	1	1	Decrement stack pointer	5
JUMP										
JMP	1	1	0	0	0	0	1	1	Jump unconditional	10
JC	1	1	0	1	1	0	1	0	Jump on carry	10
JNC	1	1	0	1	0	0	1	0	Jump on no carry	10
JZ	1	1	0	0	1	0	1	0	Jump on zero	10
JNZ	1	1	0	0	0	0	1	0	Jump on no zero	10
JP	1	1	1	1	0	0	1	0	Jump on positive	10
JM	1	1	1	1	1	0	1	0	Jump on minus	10
JPE	1	1	1	0	1	0	1	0	Jump on parity even	10

Right table

Mnemonic	D7	D6	D5	D4	D3	D2	D1	D0	Description	Cycles
DCR r	0	0	D	D	D	1	0	1	Decrement register	5
INR M	0	0	1	1	0	1	0	0	Increment memory	10
DCR M	0	0	1	1	0	1	0	1	Decrement memory	10
INX B	0	0	0	0	0	0	1	1	Increment B & C registers	5
INX D	0	0	0	1	0	0	1	1	Increment D & E registers	5
INX H	0	0	1	0	0	0	1	1	Increment H & L registers	5
DCX B	0	0	0	0	1	0	1	1	Decrement B & C	5
DCX D	0	0	0	1	1	0	1	1	Decrement D & E	5
DCX H	0	0	1	0	1	0	1	1	Decrement H & L	5
ADD										
ADD r	1	0	0	0	0	S	S	S	Add register to A	4
ADC r	1	0	0	0	1	S	S	S	Add register to A with carry	4
ADD M	1	0	0	0	0	1	1	0	Add memory to A	7
ADC M	1	0	0	0	1	1	1	0	Add memory to A with carry	7
ADI	1	1	0	0	0	1	1	0	Add immediate to A	7
ACI	1	1	0	0	1	1	1	0	Add immediate to A with carry	7
DAD B	0	0	0	0	1	0	0	1	Add B & C to H & L	10
DAD D	0	0	0	1	1	0	0	1	Add D & E to H & L	10
DAD H	0	0	1	0	1	0	0	1	Add H & L to H & L	10
DAD SP	0	0	1	1	1	0	0	1	Add stack pointer to H & L	10

Summary of Processor Instructions (Cont.)

Mnemonic	D7	D6	D5	D4	D3	D2	D1	D0	Operations Description	Clock Cycles [2]
SUBTRACT										
SUB r	1	0	0	1	0	S	S	S	Subtract register from A	4
SBB r	1	0	0	1	1	S	S	S	Subtract register from A with borrow	4
SUB M	1	0	0	1	0	1	1	0	Subtract memory from A	7
SBB M	1	0	0	1	1	1	1	0	Subtract memory from A with borrow	7
SUI	1	1	0	1	0	1	1	0	Subtract immediate from A	7
SBI	1	1	0	1	1	1	1	0	Subtract immediate from A with borrow	7
LOGICAL										
ANA r	1	0	1	0	0	S	S	S	And register with A	4
XRA r	1	0	1	0	1	S	S	S	Exclusive Or register with A	4

Mnemonic	D7	D6	D5	D4	D3	D2	D1	D0	Operations Description	Clock Cycles [2]
ROTATE										
RLC	0	0	0	0	0	1	1	1	Rotate A left	4
RRC	0	0	0	0	1	1	1	1	Rotate A right	4
RAL	0	0	0	1	0	1	1	1	Rotate A left through carry	4
RAR	0	0	0	1	1	1	1	1	Rotate A right through carry	4
SPECIALS										
CMA	0	0	1	0	1	1	1	1	Complement A	4
STC	0	0	1	1	0	1	1	1	Set carry	4
CMC	0	0	1	1	1	1	1	1	Complement carry	4
DAA	0	0	1	0	0	1	1	1	Decimal adjust A	4
INPUT/OUTPUT										
IN	1	1	0	1	1	0	1	1	Input	10
OUT	1	1	0	1	0	0	1	1	Output	10
CONTROL										
EI	1	1	1	1	1	0	1	1	Enable Interrupts	4

ORA r	1	0	1	1	0	S	S	S	Or register with A	4
CMP r	1	0	1	1	1	S	S	S	Compare register with A	4
ANA M	1	0	1	0	0	1	1	0	And memory with A	7
XRA M	1	0	1	0	1	1	1	0	Exclusive Or memory with A	7
ORA M	1	0	1	1	0	1	1	0	Or memory with A	7
CMP M	1	0	1	1	1	1	1	0	Compare memory with A	7
ANI	1	1	1	0	0	1	1	0	And immediate with A	7
XRI	1	1	1	0	1	1	1	0	Exclusive Or immediate with A	7
ORI	1	1	1	1	0	1	1	0	Or immediate with A	7
CPI	1	1	1	1	1	1	1	0	Compare immediate with A	7

DI	1	1	1	1	0	0	1	1	Disable Interrupt	4
NOP	0	0	0	0	0	0	0	0	No-operation	4
HLT	0	1	1	1	0	1	1	0	Halt	7

NOTES:

1. DDD or SSS: B=000, C=001, D=010, E=011, H=100, L=101, Memory=110, A=111.

2. Two possible cycle times (6/12) indicate instruction cycles dependent on condition flags.

*All mnemonics copyright ©Intel Corporation 1977

65

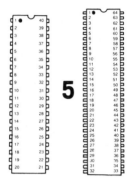

Motorola 6800 Spec Sheets

The MC6800 is a monolithic 8-bit microprocessor forming the central control function for Motorola's M6800 family. Compatible with TTL, the MC6800, as with all M6800 system parts, requires only one + 5.0-volt power supply, and no external TTL devices for bus interface.

The MC6800 is capable of addressing 64K bytes of memory with its 16-bit address lines. The 8-bit data bus is bidirectional as well as three-state, making direct memory addressing and multiprocessing applications realizable.

- 8-Bit Parallel Processing
- Bidirectional Data Bus
- 16-Bit Address Bus — 64K Bytes of Addressing
- 72 Instructions — Variable Length
- Seven Addressing Modes — Direct, Relative, Immediate, Indexed, Extended, Implied and Accumulator
- Variable Length Stack
- Vectored Restart
- Maskable Interrupt Vector
- Separate Non-Maskable Interrupt — Internal Registers Saved in Stack
- Six Internal Registers — Two Accumulators, Index Register, Program Counter, Stack Pointer and Condition Code Register
- Direct Memory Addressing (DMA) and Multiple Processor Capability
- Simplified Clocking Characteristics
- Clock Rates as High as 2.0 MHz
- Simple Bus Interface Without TTL
- Halt and Single Instruction Execution Capability

The material in this chapter is reprinted by courtesy of Motorola, Inc.

MAXIMUM RATINGS

Rating	Symbol	Value	Unit
Supply Voltage	V_{CC}	− 0.3 to + 7.0	V
Input Voltage	V_{in}	− 0.3 to + 7.0	V
Operating Temperature Range MC6800, MC68A00, MC68B00 MC6800C, MC68A00C	T_A	T_L to T_H 0 to + 70 − 40 to + 85	°C
Storage Temperature Range	T_{stg}	− 55 to + 150	°C

THERMAL RESISTANCE

Rating	Symbol	Value	Unit
Plastic Package Cerdip Package Ceramic Package	θ_{JA}	100 60 50	°C/W

This device contains circuitry to protect the inputs against damage due to high static voltages or electrical fields; however, it is advised that normal precautions be taken to avoid application of any voltage higher than maximum-rated voltages to this high-impedance circuit. Reliability of operation is enhanced if unused inputs are tied to an appropriate logic voltage (e.g., either V_{SS} or V_{CC}).

PIN ASSIGNMENT

V_{SS}	1 ●	40	$\overline{RESET}$
$\overline{HALT}$	2	39	TSC
$\phi 1$	3	38	N.C.
$\overline{IRQ}$	4	37	$\phi 2$
VMA	5	36	DBE
$\overline{NMI}$	6	35	N.C.
BA	7	34	$R/\overline{W}$
V_{CC}	8	33	D0
A0	9	32	D1
A1	10	31	D2
A2	11	30	D3
A3	12	29	D4
A4	13	28	D5
A5	14	27	D6
A6	15	26	D7
A7	16	25	A15
A8	17	24	A14
A9	18	23	A13
A10	19	22	A12
A11	20	21	V_{SS}

POWER CONSIDERATIONS

The average chip-junction temperature, T_J, in °C can be obtained from:

$$T_J = T_A + (P_D \cdot \theta_{JA}) \tag{1}$$

Where:

T_A = Ambient Temperature, °C

θ_{JA} = Package Thermal Resistance, Junction-to-Ambient, °C/W

P_D = $P_{INT} + P_{PORT}$

P_{INT} = $I_{CC} \times V_{CC}$, Watts — Chip Internal Power

P_{PORT} = Port Power Dissipation, Watts — User Determined

For most applications $P_{PORT} \ll P_{INT}$ and can be neglected. P_{PORT} may become significant if the device is configured to drive Darlington bases or sink LED loads.

An approximate relationship between P_D and T_J (if P_{PORT} is neglected) is:

$$P_D = K + (T_J + 273°C) \tag{2}$$

Solving equations 1 and 2 for K gives:

$$K = P_D \cdot (T_A + 273°C) + \theta_{JA} \cdot P_D{}^2 \tag{3}$$

Where K is a constant pertaining to the particular part. K can be determined from equation 3 by measuring P_D (at equilibrium) for a known T_A. Using this value of K the values of P_D and T_J can be obtained by solving equations (1) and (2) iteratively for any value of T_A.

DC ELECTRICAL CHARACTERISTICS (V_{CC} = 5.0 Vdc, ±5%, V_{SS} = 0, $T_A = T_L$ to T_H unless otherwise noted)

Characteristic		Symbol	Min	Typ	Max	Unit
Input High Voltage	Logic	V_{IH}	$V_{SS}+2.0$	—	V_{CC}	V
	$\phi1, \phi2$	V_{IHC}	$V_{CC}-0.6$	—	$V_{CC}+0.3$	
Input Low Voltage	Logic	V_{IL}	$V_{SS}-0.3$	—	$V_{SS}+0.8$	V
	$\phi1, \phi2$	V_{ILC}	$V_{SS}-0.3$	—	$V_{SS}+0.4$	
Input Leakage Current ($V_{in}=0$ to 5.25 V, $V_{CC}=$ Max) ($V_{in}=0$ to 5.25 V, $V_{CC}=0$ V to 5.25 V)	Logic $\phi1, \phi2$	I_{in}	—	1.0 —	2.5 100	μA
Three-State Input Leakage Current ($V_{in}=0.4$ to 2.4 V, $V_{CC}=$ Max)	D0-D7 A0-A15, R/$\overline{W}$	I_{IZ}	—	2.0 —	10 100	μA
Output High Voltage ($I_{Load}=-205\,\mu$A, $V_{CC}=$ Min) ($I_{Load}=-145\,\mu$A, $V_{CC}=$ Min) ($I_{Load}=-100\,\mu$A, $V_{CC}=$ Min)	D0-D7 A0-A15, R/$\overline{W}$, VMA BA	V_{OH}	$V_{SS}+2.4$ $V_{SS}+2.4$ $V_{SS}+2.4$	— — —	— — —	V
Output Low Voltage ($I_{Load}=1.6$ mA, $V_{CC}=$ Min)		V_{OL}	—	—	$V_{SS}+0.4$	V
Internal Power Dissipation (Measured at $T_A=T_L$)		P_{INT}	—	0.5	1.0	W
Capacitance ($V_{in}=0$, $T_A=25°C$, f=1.0 MHz)	$\phi1$ $\phi2$ D0-D7 Logic Inputs	C_{in}	— — — —	25 45 10 6.5	35 70 12.5 10	pF
	A0-A15, R/$\overline{W}$, VMA	C_{out}	—	—	12	pF

CLOCK TIMING ($V_{CC}=5.0$ V, $\pm 5\%$, $V_{SS}=0$, $T_A=T_L$ to T_H unless otherwise noted)

Characteristic		Symbol	Min	Typ	Max	Unit
Frequency of Operation	MC6800	f	0.1	—	1.0	MHz
	MC68A00		0.1	—	1.5	
	MC68B00		0.1	—	2.0	
Cycle Time (Figure 1)	MC6800	t_{cyc}	1.000	—	10	µs
	MC68A00		0.666	—	10	
	MC68B00		0.500	—	10	
Clock Pulse Width	$\phi 1, \phi 2$ — MC6800	$PW_{\phi H}$	400	—	9500	ns
(Measured at $V_{CC}-0.6$ V)	$\phi 1, \phi 2$ — MC68A00		230	—	9500	
	$\phi 1, \phi 2$ — MC68B00		180	—	9500	
Total $\phi 1$ and $\phi 2$ Up Time	MC6800	t_{ut}	900	—	—	ns
	MC68A00		600	—	—	
	MC68B00		440	—	—	
Rise and Fall Time (Measured between $V_{SS}+0.4$ and $V_{CC}-0.6$)		t_r, t_f	—	—	100	ns
Delay Time or Clock Separation (Figure 1)		t_d				ns
(Measured at $V_{OV}=V_{SS}+0.6$ V@$t_r=t_f \leq 100$ ns)			0	—	9100	
(Measured at $V_{OV}=V_{SS}+1.0$ V@$t_r=t_f \leq 35$ ns)			0	—	9100	

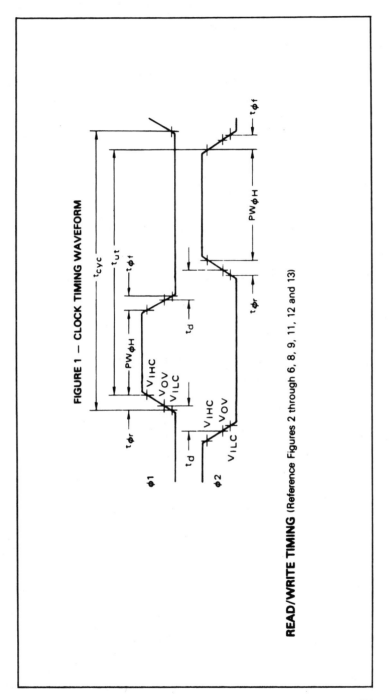

FIGURE 1 — CLOCK TIMING WAVEFORM

READ/WRITE TIMING (Reference Figures 2 through 6, 8, 9, 11, 12 and 13)

71

Characteristic	Symbol	MC6800			MC68A00			MC68B00			Unit
		Min	Typ	Max	Min	Typ	Max	Min	Typ	Max	
Address Delay	tAD										ns
C = 90 pF		—	—	270	—	—	180	—	—	150	
C = 30 pF		—	—	250	—	—	165	—	—	135	
Peripheral Read Access Time tacc = tut − (tAD + tDSR)	tacc	605	—	—	400	—	—	290	—	—	ns
Data Setup Time (Read)	tDSR	100	—	—	60	—	—	40	—	—	ns
Input Data Hold Time	tH	10	—	—	10	—	—	10	—	—	ns
Output Data Hold Time	tH	10	25	—	10	25	—	10	25	—	ns
Address Hold Time (Address, R/W̄, VMA)	tAH	30	50	—	30	50	—	30	50	—	ns
Enable High Time for DBE Input	tEH	450	—	—	280	—	—	220	—	—	ns
Data Delay Time (Write)	tDDW	—	—	225	—	—	200	—	—	160	ns
Processor Controls											
Processor Control Setup Time	tPCS	200	—	—	140	—	—	110	—	—	ns
Processor Control Rise and Fall Time	tPCr, tPCf	—	—	100	—	—	100	—	—	100	
Bus Available Delay	tBA	—	—	250	—	—	165	—	—	135	
Three-State Enable	tTSE	—	—	40	—	—	40	—	—	40	
Three-State Delay	tTSD	—	—	270	—	—	270	—	—	220	
Data Bus Enable Down Time During φ1 Up Time	tDBE	150	—	—	120	—	—	75	—	—	
Data Bus Enable Rise and Fall Times	tDBEr, tDBEf	—	—	25	—	—	25	—	—	25	

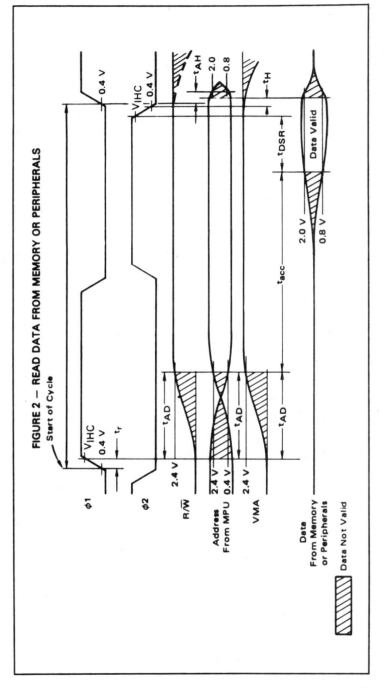

FIGURE 2 — READ DATA FROM MEMORY OR PERIPHERALS

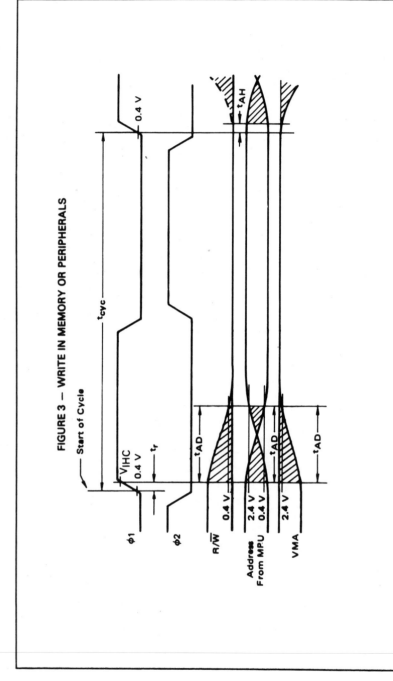

FIGURE 3 — WRITE IN MEMORY OR PERIPHERALS

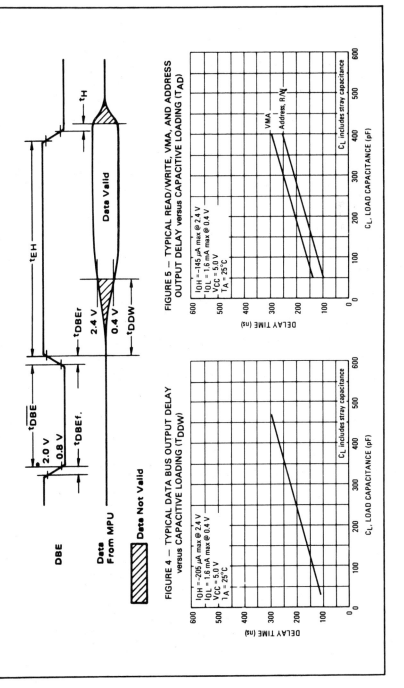

DBE

Data
From MPU

$t_{\overline{DBE}}$

$t_{\overline{DBE}f.}$

t_{EH}

t_{DBEr}

t_H

2.0 V
0.8 V

2.4 V
0.4 V

t_{DDW}

Data Valid

Data Not Valid

FIGURE 4 — TYPICAL DATA BUS OUTPUT DELAY
versus CAPACITIVE LOADING (T_{DDW})

$I_{OH} = -205\ \mu A$ max @ 2.4 V
$I_{OL} = 1.6$ mA max @ 0.4 V
$V_{CC} = 5.0$ V
$T_A = 25°C$

C_L includes stray capacitance

DELAY TIME (ns)

C_L, LOAD CAPACITANCE (pF)

FIGURE 5 — TYPICAL READ/WRITE, VMA, AND ADDRESS
OUTPUT DELAY versus CAPACITIVE LOADING (T_{AD})

$I_{OH} = -145\ \mu A$ max @ 2.4 V
$I_{OL} = 1.6$ mA max @ 0.4 V
$V_{CC} = 5.0$ V
$T_A = 25°C$

VMA

Address, R/W

C_L includes stray capacitance

DELAY TIME (ns)

C_L, LOAD CAPACITANCE (pF)

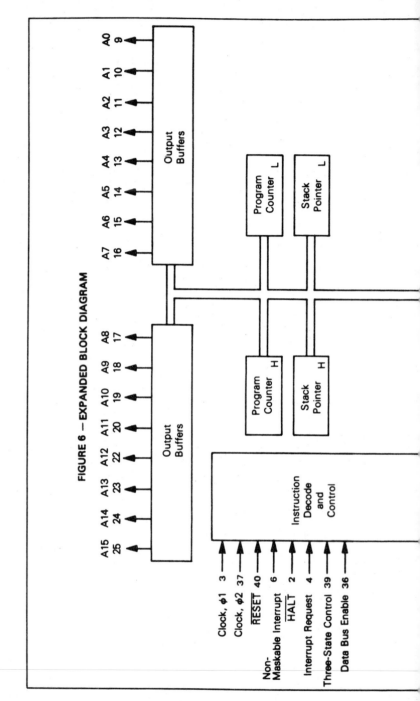

FIGURE 6 — EXPANDED BLOCK DIAGRAM

76

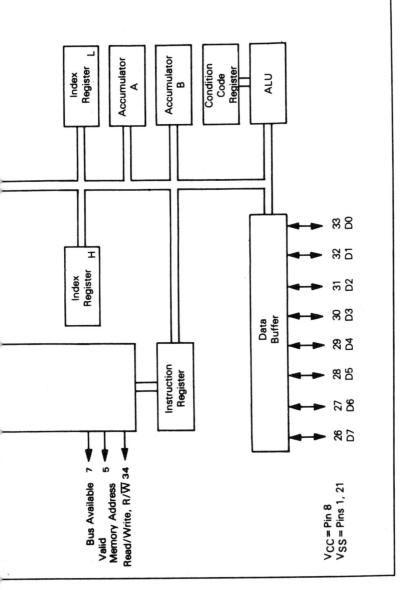

Index Register L

Accumulator A

Accumulator B

Condition Code Register

ALU

Index Register H

Instruction Register

Data Buffer

26 27 28 29 30 31 32 33
D7 D6 D5 D4 D3 D2 D1 D0

Bus Available 7
Valid Memory Address 5
Read/Write, R/$\overline{W}$ 34

V_{CC} = Pin 8
V_{SS} = Pins 1, 21

77

FIGURE 7 — BUS TIMING TEST LOADS

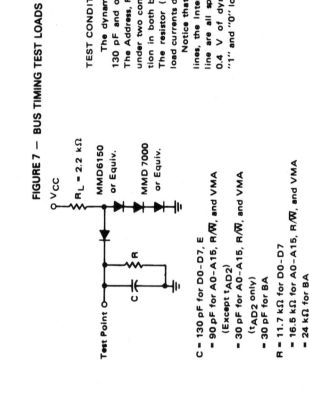

C = 130 pF for D0–D7, E
  = 90 pF for A0–A15, R/$\overline{W}$, and VMA
    (Except t_{AD2})
  = 30 pF for A0–A15, R/$\overline{W}$, and VMA
    (t_{AD2} only)
  = 30 pF for BA

R = 11.7 kΩ for D0–D7
  = 16.5 kΩ for A0–A15, R/$\overline{W}$, and VMA
  = 24 kΩ for BA

TEST CONDITIONS

The dynamic test load for the Data Bus is 130 pF and one standard TTL load as shown. The Address, R/$\overline{W}$, and VMA outputs are tested under two conditions to allow optimum operation in both buffered and unbuffered systems. The resistor (R) is chosen to insure specified load currents during V_{OH} measurement.

Notice that the Data Bus lines, the Address lines, the Interrupt Request line, and the DBE line are all specified and tested to guarantee 0.4 V of dynamic noise immunity at both "1" and "0" logic levels.

MPU SIGNAL DESCRIPTION

Proper operation of the MPU requires that certain control and timing signals be provided to accomplish specific functions and that other signal lines be monitored to determine the state of the processor.

Clocks Phase One and Phase Two ($\phi1$, $\phi2$) — Two pins are used for a two-phase non-overlapping clock that runs at the V_{CC} voltage level.

Figure 1 shows the microprocessor clocks. The high level is specified at V_{IHC} and the low level is specified at V_{ILC}. The allowable clock frequency is specified by f (frequency). The minimum $\phi1$ and $\phi2$ high level pulse widths are specified by $PW_{\phi H}$ (pulse width high time). To guarantee the required access time for the peripherals, the clock up time, t_{ut}, is specified. Clock separation, t_d, is measured at a maximum voltage of V_{OV} (overlap voltage). This allows for a multitude of clock variations at the system frequency rate.

Address Bus (A0-A15) — Sixteen pins are used for the address bus. The outputs are three-state bus drivers capable of driving one standard TTL load and 90 pF. When the output is turned off, it is essentially an open circuit. This permits the

MPU to be used in DMA applications. Putting TSC in its high state forces the Address bus to go into the three-state mode.

Data Bus (D0-D7) — Eight pins are used for the data bus. It is bidirectional, transferring data to and from the memory and peripheral devices. It also has three-state output buffers capable of driving one standard TTL load and 130 pF. Data Bus is placed in the three-state mode when DBE is low.

Data Bus Enable (DBE) — This level sensitive input is the three-state control signal for the MPU data bus and will enable the bus drivers when in the high state. This input is TTL compatible; however in normal operation, it would be driven by the phase two clock. During an MPU read cycle, the data bus drivers will be disabled internally. When it is desired that another device control the data bus, such as in Direct Memory Access (DMA) applications, DBE should be held low.

If additional data setup or hold time is required on an MPU write, the DBE down time can be decreased, as shown in Figure 3 (DBE≠$\phi2$). The minimum down time for DBE is t_{DBE} as shown. By skewing DBE with respect to E, data setup or hold time can be increased.

Bus Available (BA) — The Bus Available signal will normally be in the low state; when activated, it will go to the high state indicating that the microprocessor has stopped and that the address bus is available. This will occur if the HALT line is in the low state or the processor is in the WAIT state as a result of the execution of a WAIT instruction. At such time, all three-state output drivers will go to their off state and other outputs to their normally inactive level. The processor is removed from the WAIT state by the occurrence of a maskable (mask bit I = 0) or nonmaskable interrupt. This output is capable of driving one standard TTL load and 30 pF. If TSC is in the high state, Bus Available will be low.

Read/Write (R/$\overline{W}$) — This TTL compatible output signals the peripherals and memory devices wether the MPU is in a Read (high) or Write (low) state. The normal standby state of this signal is Read (high). Three-State Control going high will turn Read/Write to the off (high impedance) state. Also, when the processor is halted, it will be in the off state. This output is capable of driving one standard TTL load and 90 pF.

$\overline{RESET}$ — The $\overline{RESET}$ input is used to reset and start the MPU from a power down condition resulting from a power failure or initial start-up of the processor. This level sensitive input can also be used to reinitialize the machine at any time after start-up.

If a high level is detected in this input, this will signal the MPU to begin the reset sequence. During the reset sequence, the contents of the last two locations (FFFE, FFFF) in memory will be loaded into the Program Counter to point to the beginning of the reset routine. During the reset routine, the interrupt mask bit is set and must be cleared under program control before the MPU can be interrupted by IRQ. While $\overline{RESET}$ is low (assuming a minimum of 8 clock cycles have occurred) the MPU output signals will be in the following states: VMA = low, BA = low, Data Bus = high impedance, R/$\overline{W}$ = high (read state), and the Address Bus will contain the reset address FFFE. Figure 8 illustrates a power up sequence using the $\overline{RESET}$ control line. After the power supply reaches 4.75 V, a minimum of eight clock cycles are required for the processor to stabilize in preparation for restarting. During these eight cycles, VMA will be in an indeterminate state so any devices that are enabled by VMA which could accept a false write during this time (such as battery-backed RAM) must be disabled until VMA is forced low after eight cycles. $\overline{\text{RESET}}$ can go high asynchronously with the system clock any time after the eighth cycle.

$\overline{\text{RESET}}$ timing is shown in Figure 8. The maximum rise and fall transition times are specified by t_{PCr} and t_{PCf}. If $\overline{\text{RESET}}$ is high at t_{PCS} (processor control setup time), as shown in Figure 8, in any given cycle then the restart sequence will begin on the next cycle as shown. The $\overline{\text{RESET}}$ control line may also be used to reinitialize the MPU system at any time during its operation. This is accomplished by pulsing RESET low for the duration of a minimum of three complete $\phi2$ cycles. The $\overline{\text{RESET}}$ pulse can be completely asynchronous with the MPU system clock and will be recognized during $\phi2$ if setup time t_{PCS} is met.

Interrupt Request ($\overline{\text{IRQ}}$) — This level sensitive input requests that an interrupt sequence be generated within the machine. The processor will wait until it completes the current instruction that is being executed before it recognizes the request. At that time, if the interrupt mask bit in the Condition Code Register is not set, the machine will begin an interrupt sequence. The Index Register, Program Counter, Accumulators, and Condition Code Register are stored away on the stack. Next, the MPU will respond to the interrupt request by setting the interrupt mask bit high so that no further interrupts may occur. At the end of the cycle, a 16-bit address will be loaded that points to a vectoring address which is located in memory locations FFF8 and FFF9. An address loaded at these locations causes the MPU to branch to an interrupt routine in memory. Interrupt timing is shown in Figure 9.

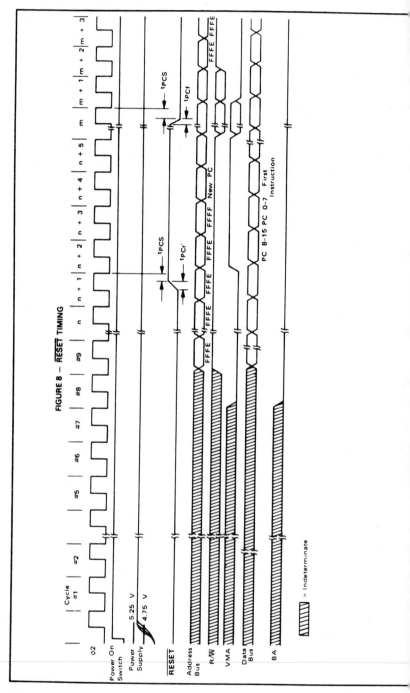

FIGURE 8 — RESET TIMING

= Indeterminate

82

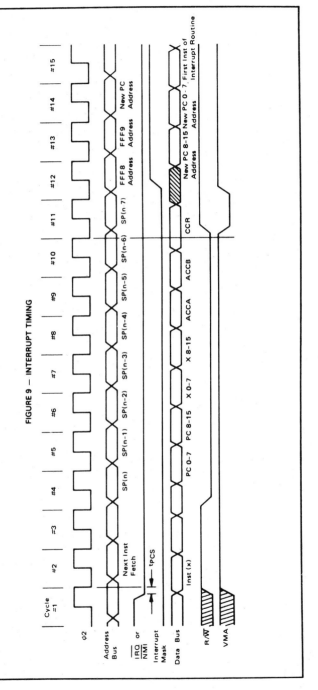

FIGURE 9 — INTERRUPT TIMING

83

The HALT line must be in the high state for interrupts to be serviced. Interrupts will be latched internally while HALT is low.

The IRQ has a high-impedance pullup device internal to the chip; however, a 3 kΩ external resistor to VCC should be used for wire-OR and optimum control of interrupts.

Non-Maskable Interrupt (NMI) and Wait for Interrupt (WAI) — The MC6800 is capable of handling two types of interrupts: maskable (IRQ) as described earlier, and nonmaskable (NMI) which is an edge sensitive input. IRQ is maskable by the interrupt mask in the condition code register while NMI is not maskable. The handling of these interrupts by the MPU is the same except that each has its own vector address. The behavior of the MPU when interrupted is shown in Figure 9 which details the MPU response to an interrupt while the MPU is executing the control program. The interrupt shown could be either IRQ or NMI and can be asynchronous with respect to $\phi2$. The interrupt is shown going low at time tPCS in cycle #1 which precedes the first cycle of an instruction (OP code fetch). This instruction is not executed but instead the Program Counter (PC), Index Register (IX), Accumulators (ACCX), and the Condition Code Register (CCR) are pushed onto the stack.

The Interrupt Mask bit is set to prevent further interrupts. The address of the interrupt service routine is then fetched from FFFC, FFFD for an NMI interrupt and from FFF8, FFF9 for an IRQ interrupt. Upon completion of the interrupt service routine, the execution of RTI will pull the PC, IX, ACCX, and CCR off the stack; the Interrupt Mask bit is restored to its condition prior to Interrupts (see Figure 10).

Figure 11 is a similar interrupt sequence, except in this

time $PW_{\phi H}$ without destroying data within the MPU. TSC then can be used in a short Direct Memory Access (DMA) application.

Figure 12 shows the effect of TSC on the MPU. TSC must have its transitions at tTSE (three-state enable) while holding $\phi1$ high and $\phi2$ low as shown. The Address Bus and R/W line will reach the high-impedance state at tTSD (three-state delay), with VMA being forced low. In this example, the Data Bus is also in the high-impedance state while $\phi2$ is being held low since DBE = $\phi2$. At this point in time, a DMA transfer could occur on cycles #3 and #4. When TSC is returned low, the MPU Address and R/W lines return to the bus. Because it is too late in cycle #5 to access memory, this cycle is dead and used for synchronization. Program execution resumes in cycle #6.

Valid Memory Address (VMA) — This output indicates to peripheral devices that there is a valid address on the address bus. In normal operation, this signal should be utilized for enabling peripheral interfaces such as the PIA and ACIA. This signal is not three-state. One standard TTL load and 90 pF may be directly driven by this active high signal.

HALT — When this level sensitive input is in the low state, all activity in the machine will be halted. This input is level sensitive.

The HALT line provides an input to the MPU to allow control of program execution by an outside source. If HALT is high, the MPU will execute the instructions; if it is low, the MPU will go to a halted or idle mode. A response signal, Bus Available (BA) provides an indication of the current MPU status. When BA is low, the MPU is in the process of ex-case, a WAIT instruction has been executed in preparation for the interrupt. This technique speeds up the MPU's response to the interrupt because the stacking of the PC, IX, ACCX, and the CCR is already done. While the MPU is waiting for the interrupt, Bus Available will go high indicating the following states of the control lines: VMA is low, and the Address Bus, R/W̄ and Data Bus are all in the high impedance state. After the interrupt occurs, it is serviced as previously described.

A 3-10 kΩ external resistor to VCC should be used for wire-OR and optimum control of interrupts.

MEMORY MAP FOR INTERRUPT VECTORS

Vector		Description
MS	LS	
FFFE	FFFF	Reset
FFFC	FFFD	Non-Maskable Interrupt
FFFA	FFFB	Software Interrupt
FFF8	FFF9	Interrupt Request

Refer to Figure 10 for program flow for Interrupts

Three-State Control (TSC) — When the level sensitive Three-State Control (TSC) line is a logic "1", the Address Bus and the R/W̄ line are placed in a high-impedance state. VMA and BA are forced low when TSC = "1" to prevent false reads or writes on any device enabled by VMA. It is necessary to delay program execution while TSC is held high. This is done by insuring that no transitions of φ1 (or φ2) occur during this period. (Logic levels of the clocks are irrelevant so long as they do not change). Since the MPU is a dynamic device, the φ1 clock can be stopped for a maximum

executing the control program; if BA is high, the MPU has halted and all internal activity has stopped.

When BA is high, the Address Bus, Data Bus, and R/W̄ line will be in a high-impedance state, effectively removing the MPU from the system bus. VMA is forced low so that the floating system bus will not activate any device on the bus that is enabled by VMA.

While the MPU is halted, all program activity is stopped, and if either an NMI or IRQ interrupt occurs, it will be latched into the MPU and acted on as soon as the MPU is taken out of the halted mode. If a RESET command occurs while the MPU is halted, the following states occur: VMA = low, BA = low, Data Bus = high impedance, R/W̄ = high (read state), and the Address Bus will contain address FFFE as long as RESET is low. As soon as the RESET line goes high, the MPU will go to locations FFFE and FFFF for the address of the reset routine.

Figure 13 shows the timing relationships involved when halting the MPU. The instruction illustrated is a one byte, 2 cycle instruction such as CLRA. When HALT goes low, the MPU will halt after completing execution of the current instruction. The transition of HALT must occur tPCS before the trailing edge of φ1 of the last cycle of an instruction (point A of Figure 13). HALT must not go low any time later than the minmum tPCS specified.

The fetch of the OP code by the MPU is the first cycle of the instruction. If HALT had not been low at Point A but went low during φ2 of that cycle, the MPU would have halted after completion of the following instruction. BA will go high by time tBA (bus available delay time) after the last instruction cycle. At this point in time, VMA is low and R/W̄, Address Bus, and the Data Bus are in the high-impedance state.

To debug programs it is advantageous to step through programs instruction by instruction. To do this, HALT must be brought high for one MPU cycle and then returned low as shown at point B of Figure 13. Again, the transitions of HALT must occur tPCS before the trailing edge of φ1. BA will go low at tBA after the leading edge of the next φ1, indicating that the Address Bus, Data Bus, VMA and R/W lines are back on the bus. A single byte, 2 cycle instruction such as LSR is used for this example also. During the first cycle, the instruction Y is fetched from address M + 1. BA returns high at tBA on the last cycle of the instruction indicating the MPU is off the bus. If instruction Y had been three cycles, the width of the BA low time would have been increased by one cycle.

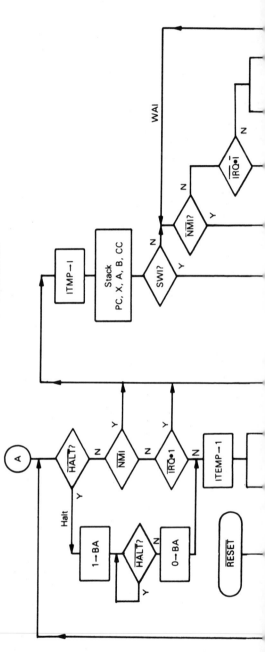

FIGURE 10 — MPU FLOWCHART

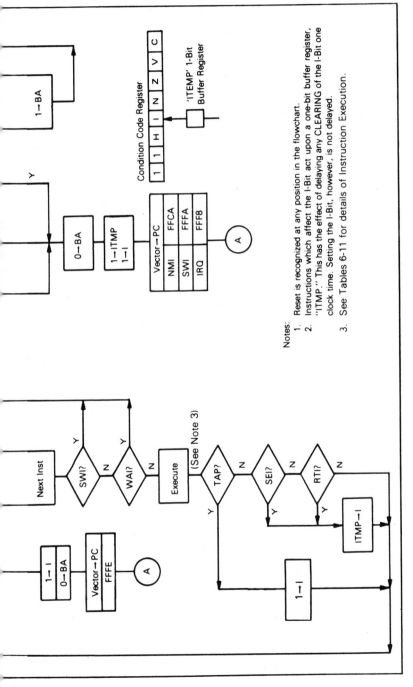

Condition Code Register

1	1	H	I	N	Z	V	C

'ITEMP' 1-Bit Buffer Register

Vector→PC

NMI	FFCA
SWI	FFFA
IRQ	FFF8

Ⓐ

Notes:
1. Reset is recognized at any position in the flowchart.
2. Instructions which affect the I-Bit act upon a one-bit buffer register, "ITMP." This has the effect of delaying any CLEARING of the I-Bit one clock time. Setting the I-Bit, however, is not delayed.
3. See Tables 6-11 for details of Instruction Execution.

Next Inst

SWI? — Y
SWI? — N

WAI? — Y
WAI? — N

Execute

(See Note 3)

TAP? — Y
TAP? — N

SEI? — Y
SEI? — N

RTI? — Y
RTI? — N

ITMP→I

1→I
0→BA

Vector→PC
FFFE

Ⓐ

1→I

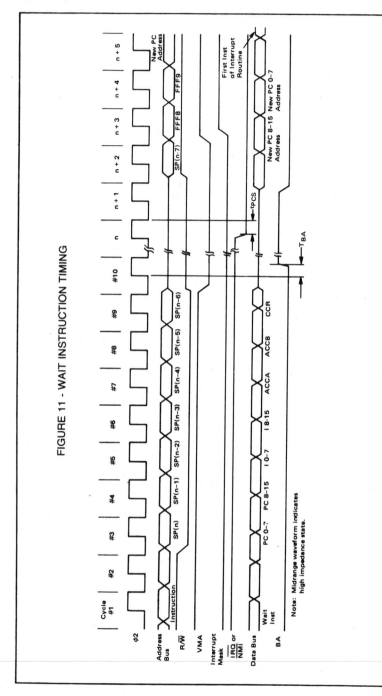

FIGURE 11 - WAIT INSTRUCTION TIMING

Note: Midrange waveform indicates high impedance state.

88

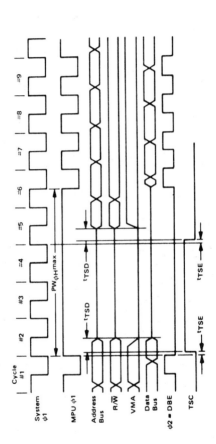

FIGURE 12 - THREE-STATE CONTROL TIMING

Motorola 6809 Spec Sheets

The MC6809 is a revolutionary high-performance 8-bit microprocessor which supports modern programming techniques such as position independence, reentrancy, and modular programming.

This third-generation addition to the M6800 Family has major architectural improvements which include additional registers, instructions, and addressing modes.

The basic instructions of any computer are greatly enhanced by the presence of powerful addressing modes. The MC6809 has the most complete set of addressing modes available on any 8-bit microprocessor today.

The MC6809 has hardware and software features which make it an ideal processor for higher level language execution or standard controller applications.

MC6800 COMPATIBLE
- Hardware — Interfaces with All M6800 Peripherals
- Software — Upward Source Code Compatible Instruction Set and Addressing Modes

ARCHITECTURAL FEATURES
- Two 16-Bit Index Registers
- Two 16-Bit Indexable Stack Pointers
- Two 8-Bit Accumulators can be Concatenated to Form One 16-Bit Accumulator
- Direct Page Register Allows Direct Addressing Throughout Memory

HARDWARE FEATURES
- On-Chip Oscillator (Crystal Frequency = 4 × E)
- $\overline{\text{DMA}}/\overline{\text{BREQ}}$ Allows DMA Operation on Memory Refresh
- Fast Interrupt Request Input Stacks Only Condition Code Register and Program Counter
- MRDY Input Extends Data Access Times for Use with Slow Memory
- Interrupt Acknowledge Output Allows Vectoring by Devices
- Sync Acknowledge Output Allows for Synchronization to External Event
- Single Bus-Cycle $\overline{\text{RESET}}$
- Single 5-Volt Supply Operation
- $\overline{\text{NMI}}$ Inhibited After $\overline{\text{RESET}}$ Until After First Load of Stack Pointer
- Early Address Valid Allows Use with Slower Memories
- Early Write Data for Dynamic Memories

SOFTWARE FEATURES

- 10 Addressing Modes
  - 6800 Upward Compatible Addressing Modes
  - Direct Addressing Anywhere in Memory Map
  - Long Relative Branches
  - Program Counter Relative
  - True Indirect Addressing
  - Expanded Indexed Addressing:
    - 0-, 5-, 8-, or 16-Bit Constant Offsets
    - 8- or 16-Bit Accumulator Offsets
    - Auto Increment/Decrement by 1 or 2
- Improved Stack Manipulation
- 1464 Instructions with Unique Addressing Modes
- 8 × 8 Unsigned Multiply
- 16-Bit Arithmetic
- Transfer/Exchange All Registers
- Push/Pull Any Registers or Any Set of Registers
- Load Effective Address

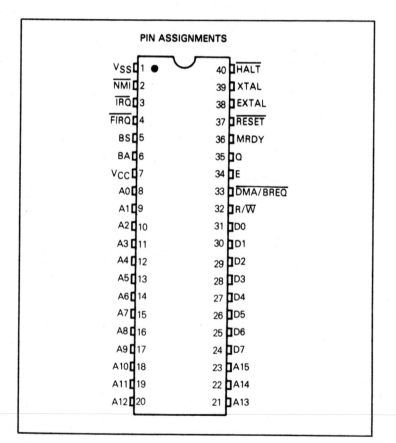

PIN ASSIGNMENTS

V_{SS}	1	40	$\overline{HALT}$
$\overline{NMI}$	2	39	XTAL
$\overline{IRQ}$	3	38	EXTAL
$\overline{FIRQ}$	4	37	$\overline{RESET}$
BS	5	36	MRDY
BA	6	35	Q
V_{CC}	7	34	E
A0	8	33	$\overline{DMA/BREQ}$
A1	9	32	$R/\overline{W}$
A2	10	31	D0
A3	11	30	D1
A4	12	29	D2
A5	13	28	D3
A6	14	27	D4
A7	15	26	D5
A8	16	25	D6
A9	17	24	D7
A10	18	23	A15
A11	19	22	A14
A12	20	21	A13

MAXIMUM RATINGS

Rating	Symbol	Value	Unit
Supply Voltage	V_{CC}	-0.3 to $+7.0$	V
Input Voltage	V_{in}	-0.3 to $+7.0$	V
Operating Temperature Range MC6809, MC68A09, MC68B09 MC6809C, MC68A09C, MC68B09C	T_A	T_L to T_H 0 to $+70$ -40 to $+85$	°C
Storage Temperature Range	T_{stg}	-55 to $+150$	°C

This device contains circuitry to protect the inputs against damage due to high static voltages or electric fields; however, it is advised that normal precautions be taken to avoid application of any voltage higher than maximum rated voltages to this high impedance circuit. Reliability of operation is enhanced if unused inputs are tied to an appropriate logic voltage levels (e.g., either V_{SS} or V_{CC}).

THERMAL CHARACTERISTICS

Characteristic	Symbol	Value	Unit
Thermal Resistance Ceramic Cerdip Plastic	θ_{JA}	50 60 100	°C/W

POWER CONSIDERATIONS

The average chip-junction temperature, T_J, in °C can be obtained from:

$$T_J = T_A + (P_D \bullet \theta_{JA}) \tag{1}$$

Where:

T_A = Ambient Temperature, °C

θ_{JA} = Package Thermal Resistance, Junction-to-Ambient, °C/W

P_D = P_{INT} + P_{PORT}

P_{INT} = $I_{CC} \times V_{CC}$, Watts — Chip Internal Power

P_{PORT} = Port Power Dissipation, Watts — User Determined

For most applications $P_{PORT} \ll P_{INT}$ and can be neglected. P_{PORT} may become significant if the device is configured to drive Darlington bases or sink LED loads.

An approximate relationship between P_D and T_J (if P_{PORT} is neglected) is:

$$P_D = K + (T_J + 273°C) \tag{2}$$

Solving equations 1 and 2 for K gives:

$$K = P_D \bullet (T_A + 273°C) + \theta_{JA} \bullet P_D{}^2 \tag{3}$$

Where K is a constant pertaining to the particular part. K can be determined from equation 3 by measuring P_D (at equilibrium) for a known T_A. Using this value of K the values of P_D and T_J can be obtained by solving equations (1) and (2) iteratively for any value of T_A.

ELECTRICAL CHARACTERISTICS (V_{CC} = 5.0 V ±5%, V_{SS} = 0, $T_A = T_L$ to T_H unless otherwise noted)

Characteristic		Symbol	Min	Typ	Max	Unit
Input High Voltage	Logic, EXTAL RESET	V_{IH} V_{IHR}	$V_{SS}+2.0$ $V_{SS}+4.0$	— —	V_{CC} V_{CC}	V
Input Low Voltage	Logic, EXTAL, RESET	V_{IL}	$V_{SS}-0.3$	—	$V_{SS}+0.8$	V
Input Leakage Current ($V_{in}=0$ to 5.25 V, $V_{CC}=$ max)	Logic	I_{in}	—	—	2.5	µA
dc Output High Voltage ($I_{Load}=-205$ µA, $V_{CC}=$ min) ($I_{Load}=-145$ µA, $V_{CC}=$ min) ($I_{Load}=-100$ µA, $V_{CC}=$ min)	D0-D7 A0-A15, R/$\overline{\text{W}}$, Q, E BA, BS	V_{OH}	$V_{SS}+2.4$ $V_{SS}+2.4$ $V_{SS}+2.4$	— — —	— — —	V
dc Output Low Voltage ($I_{Load}=2.0$ mA, $V_{CC}=$ min)		V_{OL}	—	—	$V_{SS}+0.5$	V
Internal Power Dissipation (Measured at $T_A=T_L$ in Steady State Operation)		P_{INT}	—	—	1.0	W
Capacitance * ($V_{in}=0$, $T_A=25°C$, f=1.0 MHz)	D0-D7, RESET Logic Inputs, EXTAL, XTAL A0-A15, R/$\overline{\text{W}}$, BA, BS	C_{in} C_{out}	— — —	10 10 —	15 15 15	pF pF
Frequency of Operation (Crystal or External Input)	MC6809 MC68A09 MC68B09	f_{XTAL}	0.4 0.4 0.4	— — —	4 6 8	MHz
Hi-Z (Off State) Input Current ($V_{in}=0.4$ to 2.4 V, $V_{CC}=$ max)	D0-D7 A0-A15, R/$\overline{\text{W}}$	I_{TSI}	— —	2.0 —	10 100	µA

* Capacitances are periodically tested rather than 100% tested.

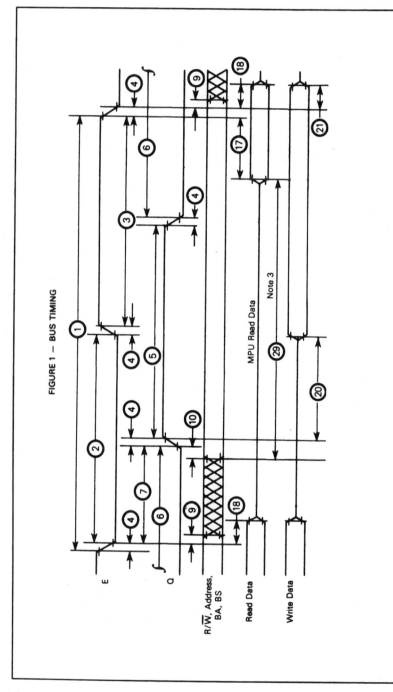

FIGURE 1 — BUS TIMING

BUS TIMING CHARACTERISTICS (See Notes 1 and 2)

Ident. Number	Characteristics	Symbol	MC6809 Min	MC6809 Max	MC68A09 Min	MC68A09 Max	MC68B09 Min	MC68B09 Max	Unit
1	Cycle Time (See Note 5)	t_{cyc}	1.0	10	0.667	10	0.5	10	µs
2	Pulse Width, E Low	PW_{EL}	430	5000	280	5000	210	5000	ns
3	Pulse Width, E High	PW_{EH}	450	15500	280	15700	220	15700	ns
4	Clock Rise and Fall Time	t_r, t_f	–	25	–	25	–	20	ns
5	Pulse Width, Q High	PW_{QH}	430	5000	280	5000	210	5000	ns
6	Pulse Width, Q Low	PW_{QL}	450	15500	280	15700	220	15700	ns
7	Delay Time, E to Q Rise	t_{AVS}	200	250	130	165	80	125	ns
9	Address Hold Time* (See Note 4)	t_{AH}	20	–	20	–	20	–	ns
10	BA, BS, R/W, and Address Valid Time to Q Rise	t_{AQ}	50	–	25	–	15	–	ns
17	Read Data Setup Time	t_{DSR}	80	–	60	–	40	–	ns
18	Read Data Hold Time*	t_{DHR}	10	–	10	–	10	–	ns
20	Data Delay Time from Q	t_{DDQ}	–	200	–	140	–	110	ns
21	Write Data Hold Time*	t_{DHW}	30	–	30	–	30	–	ns
29	Usable Access Time (See Note 3)	t_{ACC}	695	–	440	–	330	–	ns
	Processor Control Setup Time (MRDY, Interrupts, DMA/BREQ, HALT, RESET) (Figures 6, 8, 9, 10, 12, and 13)	t_{PCS}	200	–	140	–	110	–	ns
	Crystal Oscillator Start Time (Figures 6 and 7)	t_{RC}	–	100	–	100	–	100	ms
	Processor Control Rise and Fall Time (Figures 6 and 8)	t_{PCr}, t_{PCf}	–	100	–	100	–	100	ns

* Address and data hold times are periodically tested rather than 100% tested.

NOTES:
1. Voltage levels shown are $V_L \leq 0.4$ V, $V_H \geq 2.4$ V, unless otherwise specified.
2. Measurement points shown are 0.8 V and 2.0 V, unless otherwise specified.
3. Usable access time is computed by: $1 - 4 - 7$ max $+ 10 - 17$.
4. Hold time ((9)) for BA and BS is not specified.
5. Maximum t_{cyc} during MRDY or DMA/BREQ is 16 µs.

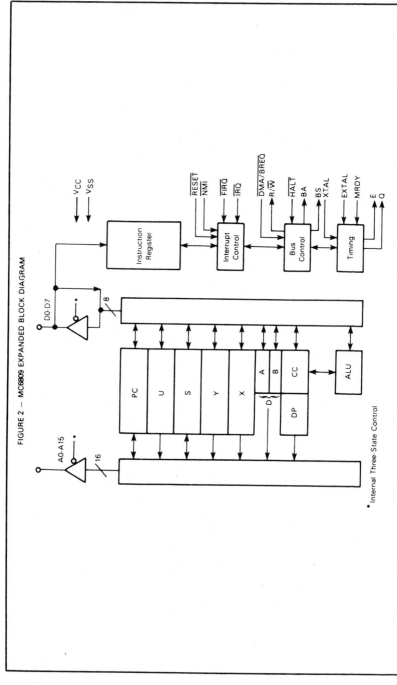

FIGURE 2 — MC6809 EXPANDED BLOCK DIAGRAM

* Internal Three-State Control

PROGRAMMING MODEL

As shown in Figure 4, the MC6809 adds three registers to the set available in the MC6800. The added registers include a direct page register, the user stack pointer, and a second index register.

ACCUMULATORS (A, B, D)

The A and B registers are general purpose accumulators which are used for arithmetic calculations and manipulation of data.

Certain instructions concatenate the A and B registers to form a single 16-bit accumulator. This is referred to as the D register, and is formed with the A register as the most significant byte.

DIRECT PAGE REGISTER (DP)

The direct page register of the MC6809 serves to enhance the direct addressing mode. The content of this register appears at the higher address outputs (A8-A15) during direct addressing instruction execution. This allows the direct mode to be used at any place in memory, under program control. To ensure M6800 compatibility, all bits of this register are cleared during processor reset.

FIGURE 3 — BUS TIMING TEST LOAD

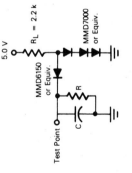

$R_L = 2.2$ k

5.0 V

MMD6150 or Equiv.

MMD7000 or Equiv.

Test Point

C ⊥ R

$R = 11.7$ kΩ for D0-D7
16.5 kΩ for A0-A15, E, Q, R/$\overline{W}$
24 kΩ for BA, BS

$C = 30$ pF for BA, BS
130 pF for D0-D7, E, Q
90 pF for A0-A15, R/$\overline{W}$

99

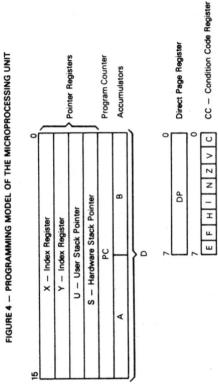

FIGURE 4 — PROGRAMMING MODEL OF THE MICROPROCESSING UNIT

INDEX REGISTERS (X, Y)

The index registers are used in indexed mode of addressing. The 16-bit address in this register takes part in the calculation of effective addresses. This address may be used to point to data directly or may be modified by an optional constant or register offset. During some indexed modes, the contents of the index register are incremented or decremented to point to the next item of tabular type data. All four pointer registers (X, Y, U, S) may be used as index registers.

STACK POINTER (U,S)

The hardware stack pointer (S) is used automatically by the processor during subroutine calls and interrupts. The stack pointers of the MC6809 point to the top of the stack, in contrast to the MC6800 stack pointer, which pointed to the next free location on the stack. The user stack pointer (U) is controlled exclusively by the programmer. This allows arguments to be passed to and from subroutines with ease. Both stack pointers have the same indexed mode addressing capabilities as the X and Y registers, but also support **Push** and **Pull** instructions. This allows the MC6809 to be used efficiently as a stack processor, greatly enhancing its ability to support higher level languages and modular programming.

PROGRAM COUNTER

The program counter is used by the processor to point to the address of the next instruction to be executed by the processor. Relative addressing is provided allowing the program counter to be used like an index register in some situations.

CONDITION CODE REGISTER

The condition code register defines the state of the processor at any given time. See Figure 5.

FIGURE 5 — CONDITION CODE REGISTER FORMAT

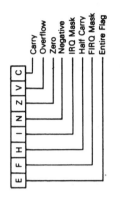

| E | F | H | I | N | Z | V | C |

- Carry
- Overflow
- Zero
- Negative
- IRQ Mask
- Half Carry
- FIRQ Mask
- Entire Flag

CONDITION CODE REGISTER DESCRIPTION

BIT 0 (C)

Bit 0 is the carry flag, and is usually the carry from the binary ALU. C is also used to represent a 'borrow' from subtract-like instructions (CMP, NEG, SUB, SBC) and is the complement of the carry from the binary ALU.

BIT 1 (V)

Bit 1 is the overflow flag, and is set to a one by an operation which causes a signed twos complement arithmetic overflow. This overflow is detected in an operation in which the carry from the MSB in the ALU does not match the carry from the MSB-1.

BIT 2 (Z)

Bit 2 is the zero flag, and is set to a one if the result of the previous operation was identically zero.

BIT 3 (N)

Bit 3 is the negative flag, which contains exactly the value of the MSB of the result of the preceding operation. Thus, a negative twos-complement result will leave N set to a one.

BIT 4 (I)

Bit 4 is the $\overline{\text{IRQ}}$ mask bit. The processor will not recognize interrupts from the $\overline{\text{IRQ}}$ line if this bit is set to a one. $\overline{\text{NMI}}$, $\overline{\text{FIRQ}}$, $\overline{\text{IRQ}}$, $\overline{\text{RESET}}$, and SWI all set I to a one. SWI2 and SWI3 do not affect I.

BIT 5 (H)

Bit 5 is the half-carry bit, and is used to indicate a carry from bit 3 in the ALU as a result of an 8-bit addition only (ADC or ADD). This bit is used by the DAA instruction to perform a BCD decimal add adjust operation. The state of this flag is undefined in all subtract-like instructions.

BIT 6 (F)

Bit 6 is the $\overline{\text{FIRQ}}$ mask bit. The processor will not recognize interrupts from the $\overline{\text{FIRQ}}$ line if this bit is a one. $\overline{\text{NMI}}$, $\overline{\text{FIRQ}}$, SWI, and $\overline{\text{RESET}}$ all set F to a one. $\overline{\text{IRQ}}$, SWI2, and SWI3 do not affect F.

BIT 7 (E)

Bit 7 is the entire flag, and when set to a one indicates that the complete machine state (all the registers) was stacked, as opposed to the subset state (PC and CC). The E bit of the stacked CC is used on a return from interrupt (RTI) to determine the extent of the unstacking. Therefore, the current E left in the condition code register represents past action.

PIN DESCRIPTIONS

POWER (V$_{SS}$, V$_{CC}$)

Two pins are used to supply power to the part: V$_{SS}$ is ground or 0 volts, while V$_{CC}$ is +5.0 V ±5%.

ADDRESS BUS (A0-A15)

Sixteen pins are used to output address information from the MPU onto the address bus. When the processor does not require the bus for a data transfer, it will output address FFFF$_{16}$, R/$\overline{\text{W}}$ = 1, and BS = 0; this is a "dummy access" or $\overline{\text{VMA}}$ cycle. Addresses are valid on the rising edge of Q. All address bus drivers are made high impedance when output bus available (BA) is high. Each pin will drive one Schottky TTL load or four LSTTL loads, and 90 pF.

DATA BUS (D0-D7)

These eight pins provide communication with the system bidirectional data bus. Each pin will drive one Schottky TTL load or four LSTTL loads, and 130 pF.

READ/WRITE (R/$\overline{\text{W}}$)

This signal indicates the direction of data transfer on the data bus. A low indicates that the MPU is writing data onto the data bus. R/$\overline{\text{W}}$ is made high impedance when BA is high. R/$\overline{\text{W}}$ is valid on the rising edge of Q.

$\overline{\text{RESET}}$

A low level on this Schmitt-trigger input for greater than one bus cycle will reset the MPU, as shown in Figure 6. The reset vectors are fetched from locations $FFFE_{16}$ and $FFFF_{16}$ (Table 1) when interrupt acknowledge is true, ($\overline{\text{BA}} \bullet \text{BS} = 1$). During initial power on, the $\overline{\text{RESET}}$ line should be held low until the clock oscillator is fully operational. See Figure 7.

Because the MC6809 $\overline{\text{RESET}}$ pin has a Schmitt-trigger input with a threshold voltage higher than that of standard peripherals, a simple R/C network may be used to reset the entire system. This higher threshold voltage ensures that all peripherals are out of the reset state before the processor.

$\overline{\text{HALT}}$

A low level on this input pin will cause the MPU to stop running at the end of the present instruction and remain halted indefinitely without loss of data. When halted, the BA output is driven high indicating the buses are high impedance. BS is also high which indicates the processor is in the halt or bus grant state. While halted, the MPU will not respond to external real-time requests ($\overline{\text{FIRQ}}$, $\overline{\text{IRQ}}$) although $\overline{\text{DMA}}/\overline{\text{BREQ}}$ will always be accepted, and $\overline{\text{NMI}}$ or $\overline{\text{RESET}}$ will be latched for later response. During the halt state, Q and E continue to run normally. If the MPU is not running ($\overline{\text{RESET}}$, $\overline{\text{DMA}}/\overline{\text{BREQ}}$), a halted state ($\text{BA} \bullet \text{BS} = 1$) can be achieved by pulling $\overline{\text{HALT}}$ low while $\overline{\text{RESET}}$ is still low. If $\overline{\text{DMA}}/\overline{\text{BREQ}}$ and $\overline{\text{HALT}}$ are both pulled low, the processor will reach the last cycle of the instruction (by reverse cycle stealing) where the machine will the become halted. See Figure 8.

BUS AVAILABLE, BUS STATUS (BA, BS)

The bus available output is an indication of an internal control signal which makes the MOS buses of the MPU high impedance. This signal does not imply that the bus will be available for more than one cycle. When BA goes low, a dead cycle will elapse before the MPU acquires the bus.

The bus status output signal, when decoded with BA, represents the MPU state (valid with leading edge of Q).

MPU State		MPU State Definition
BA	BS	
0	0	Normal (Running)
0	1	Interrupt or Reset Acknowledge
1	0	Sync Acknowledge
1	1	Halt or Bus Grant Acknowledge

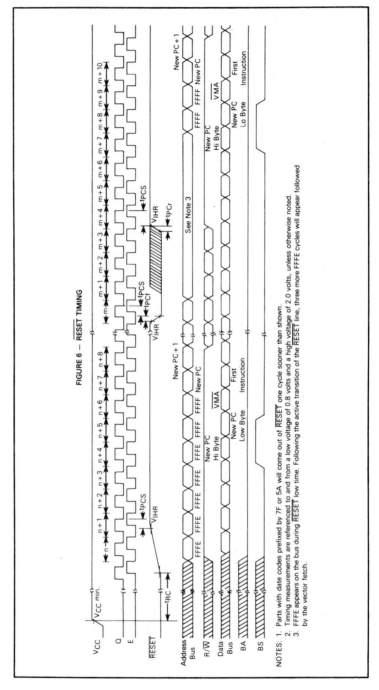

FIGURE 6 – RESET TIMING

NOTES: 1. Parts with date codes prefixed by 7F or 5A will come out of RESET one cycle sooner than shown.
2. Timing measurements are referenced to and from a low voltage of 0.8 volts and a high voltage of 2.0 volts, unless otherwise noted.
3. FFFE appears on the bus during RESET low time. Following the active transition of the RESET line, three more FFFE cycles will appear followed by the vector fetch.

104

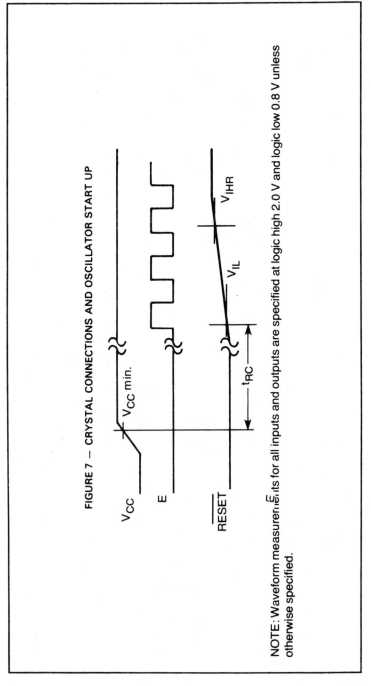

FIGURE 7 — CRYSTAL CONNECTIONS AND OSCILLATOR START UP

NOTE: Waveform measurements for all inputs and outputs are specified at logic high 2.0 V and logic low 0.8 V unless otherwise specified.

105

MC6809

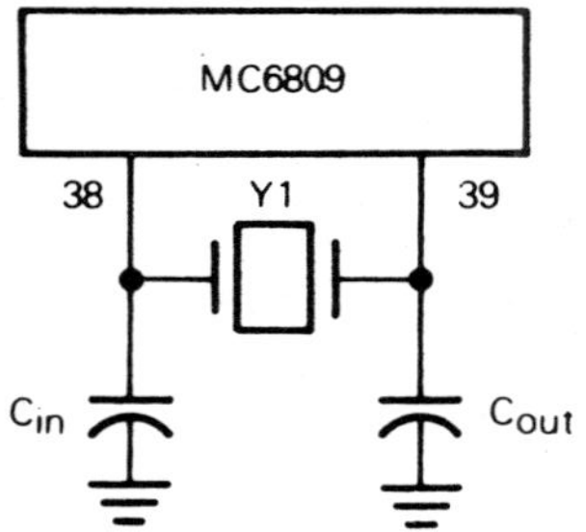

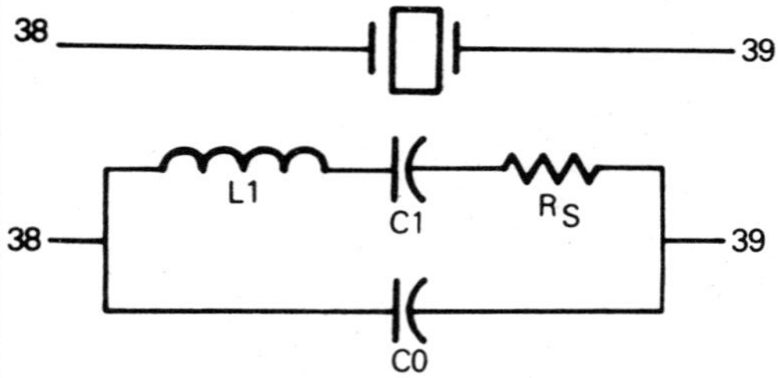

Nominal Crystal Parameters

	3.58 MHz	4.00 MHz	6.0 MHz	8.0 MHz
R_S	60 Ω	50 Ω	30-50 Ω	20-40 Ω
$C0$	3.5 pF	6.5 pF	4-6 pF	4-6 pF
$C1$	0.015 pF	0.025 pF	0.01-0.02 pF	0.01-0.02 pF
Q	>40 k	>30 k	>20 k	>20 k

All parameters are 10%

NOTE: These are representative AT-cut crystal parameters only. Crystals of other types of cut may also be used.

Y1	C_{in}	C_{out}
8 MHz	18 pF	18 pF
6 MHz	20 pF	20 pF
4 MHz	24 pF	24 pF

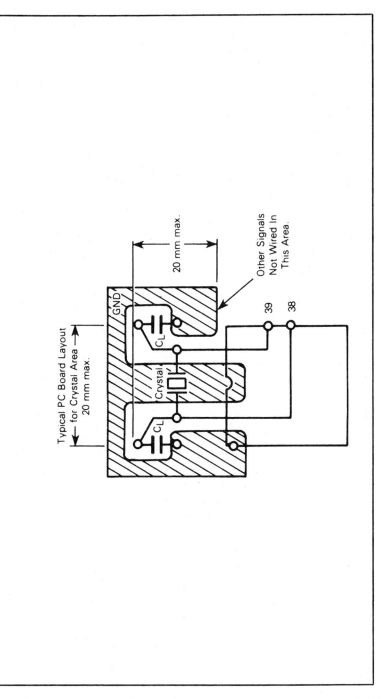

Typical PC Board Layout for Crystal Area — 20 mm max.

20 mm max.

GND

C_L

Crystal

C_L

39

38

Other Signals Not Wired In This Area.

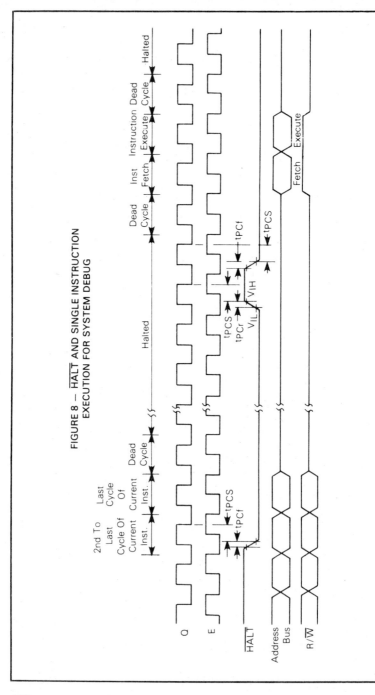

FIGURE 8 — HALT AND SINGLE INSTRUCTION
EXECUTION FOR SYSTEM DEBUG

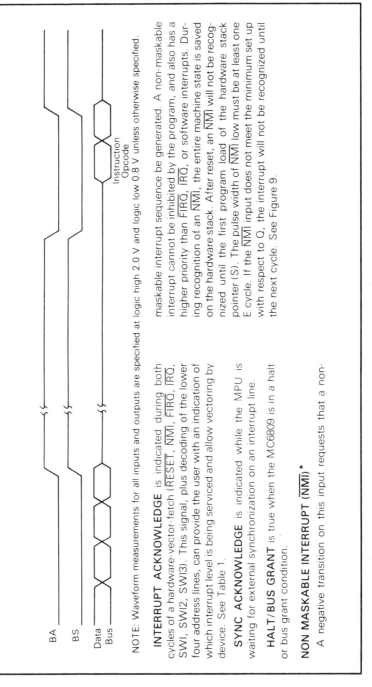

BA

BS

Data
Bus

Instruction
Opcode

NOTE: Waveform measurements for all inputs and outputs are specified at logic high 2.0 V and logic low 0.8 V unless otherwise specified.

INTERRUPT ACKNOWLEDGE is indicated during both cycles of a hardware-vector-fetch (RESET, NMI, FIRQ, IRQ, SWI, SWI2, SWI3). This signal, plus decoding of the lower four address lines, can provide the user with an indication of which interrupt level is being serviced and allow vectoring by device. See Table 1.

SYNC ACKNOWLEDGE is indicated while the MPU is waiting for external synchronization on an interrupt line.

HALT/BUS GRANT is true when the MC6809 is in a halt or bus grant condition.

NON MASKABLE INTERRUPT (NMI)*

A negative transition on this input requests that a non-maskable interrupt sequence be generated. A non-maskable interrupt cannot be inhibited by the program, and also has a higher priority than FIRQ, IRQ, or software interrupts. During recognition of an NMI, the entire machine state is saved on the hardware stack. After reset, an NMI will not be recognized until the first program load of the hardware stack pointer (S). The pulse width of NMI low must be at least one E cycle. If the NMI input does not meet the minimum set up with respect to Q, the interrupt will not be recognized until the next cycle. See Figure 9.

109

FAST-INTERRUPT REQUEST (FIRQ)*

A low level on this input pin will initiate a fast interrupt sequence, provided its mask bit (F) in the CC is clear. This sequence has priority over the standard interrupt request (IRQ), and is fast in the sense that it stacks only the contents of the condition code register and the program counter. The interrupt service routine should clear the source of the interrupt before doing an RTI. See Figure 10.

INTERRUPT REQUEST (IRQ)*

A low level input on this pin will initiate an interrupt request sequence provided the mask bit (I) in the CC is clear. Since IRQ stacks the entire machine state it provides a slower response to interrupts than FIRQ. IRQ also has a lower priority than FIRQ. Again, the interrupt service routine should clear the source of the interrupt before doing an RTI. See Figure 9.

TABLE 1 — MEMORY MAP FOR INTERRUPT VECTORS

Memory Map For Vector Locations		Interrupt Vector Description
MS	LS	
FFFE	FFFF	RESET
FFFC	FFFD	NMI
FFFA	FFFB	SWI
FFF8	FFF9	IRQ
FFF6	FFF7	FIRQ
FFF4	FFF5	SWI2
FFF2	FFF3	SWI3
FFF0	FFF1	Reserved

*NMI, FIRQ, and IRQ requests are sampled on the falling edge of Q. One cycle is required for synchronization before these interrupts are recognized. The pending interrupt(s) will not be serviced until completion of the current instruction unless a SYNC or CWAI condition is present. If IRQ and FIRQ do not remain low for one cycle. No interrupts are recognized or latched between the falling edge of RESET and the rising edge of BS indicating RESET acknowledge.

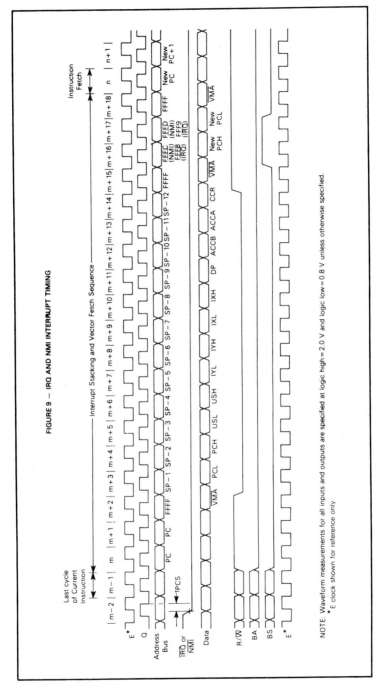

FIGURE 9 — IRQ AND NMI INTERRUPT TIMING

NOTE: Waveform measurements for all inputs and outputs are specified at logic high = 2.0 V and logic low = 0.8 V unless otherwise specified.

* E clock shown for reference only.

FIGURE 10 — FIRQ INTERRUPT TIMING

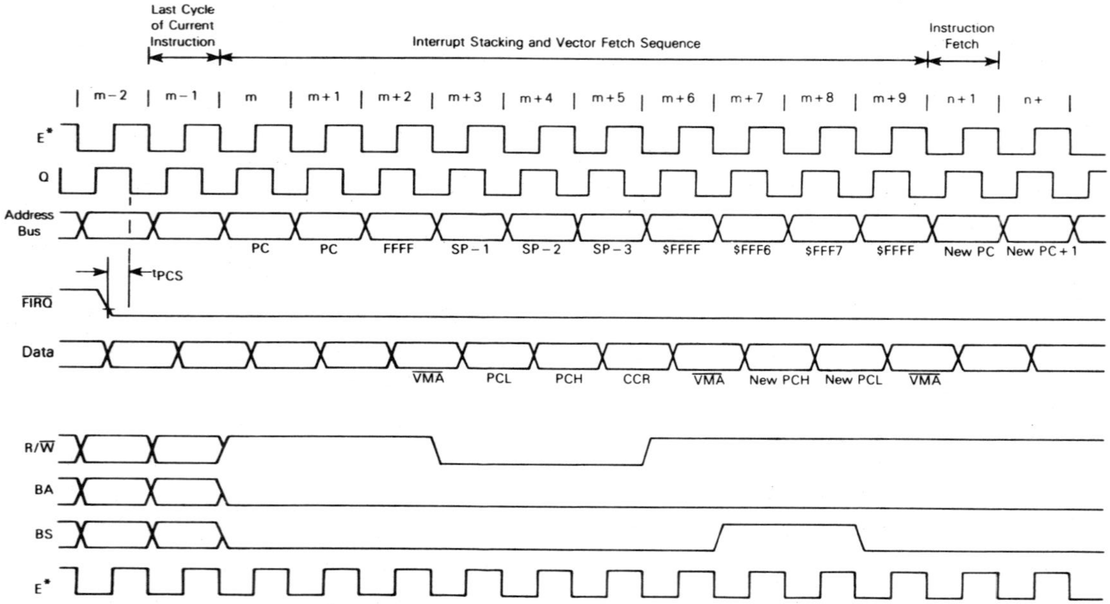

NOTE: Waveform measurements for all inputs and outputs are specified at logic high = 2.0 V and logic low = 0.8 V unless otherwise specified.
* E clock shown for reference only.

112

XTAL, EXTAL

These inputs are used to connect the on-chip oscillator to an external parallel-resonant crystal. Alternately, the pin EXTAL may be used as a TTL level input for external timing by grounding XTAL. The crystal or external frequency is four times the bus frequency. Proper RF layout techniques should be observed in the layout of printed circuit boards.

E, Q

E is similar to the MC6800 bus timing signal phase 2; Q is a quadrature clock signal which leads E. Q has no parallel on the MC6800. Addresses from the MPU will be valid with the leading edge of Q. Data is latched on the falling edge of E. Timing for E and Q is shown in Figure 11.

MRDY*

This input control signal allows stretching of E and Q to extend data-access time. E and Q operate normally while MRDY is high. When MRDY is low, E and Q may be stretched in integral multiples of quarter (¼) bus cycles, thus allowing interface to slow memories, as shown in Figure 12(a). During non-valid memory access ($\overline{VMA}$ cycles), MRDY has no effect on stretching E and Q; this inhibits slowing the pro-

cessor during "don't care" bus accesses. MRDY may also be used to stretch clocks (for slow memory) when bus control has been transferred to an external device (through the use of $\overline{HALT}$ and $\overline{DMA}/\overline{BREQ}$).

NOTE

Four of the early production mask sets (G7F, T5A, P6F, T6M) require synchronization of the MRDY input with the 4f clock. The synchronization necessitates an external oscillator as shown in Figure 12(b). The negative transition of the MRDY signal, normally derived from the chip select decoding, must meet the tPCS timing. With these four mask sets, MRDY's positive transition must occur with the rising edge of 4f.

In addition, on these same mask sets, MRDY will not stretch the E and Q signals if the machine is executing either a TFR or EXG instruction during the $\overline{HALT}$ high-to-low transition. If the MPU executes a CWAI instruction, the machine pushes the internal registers onto the stack and then awaits an interrupt. During this waiting period, it is possible to place the MPU into a halt mode to three-state the machine, but MRDY will not stretch the clocks.

The mask set for a particular part may be determined by examining the markings on top of the part. Below the part number is a string of characters. The first two characters are the last two characters of the mask set code. If there are only four digits the part is the G7F mask set. The last four digits, the date code, show when the part was manufactured. These four digits represent year and week. For example a ceramic part marked:

is a T5A mask set made the twelfth week of 1980.

DMA/BREQ *

The DMA/BREQ input provides a method of suspending execution and acquiring the MPU bus for another use, as shown in Figure 13. Typical uses include DMA and dynamic memory refresh.

A low level on this pin will stop instruction execution at the end of the current cycle unless pre-empted by self-refresh. The MPU will acknowledge $\overline{DMA}/\overline{BREQ}$ by setting BA and BS to a one. The requesting device will now have up to 15 bus cycles before the MPU retrieves the bus for self-refresh. Self-refresh requires one bus cycle with a leading and trailing dead cycle. See Figure 14. The self-refresh counter is only cleared if $\overline{DMA}/\overline{BREQ}$ is inactive for two or more MPU cycles.

Typically, the DMA controller will request to use the bus by asserting $\overline{DMA}/\overline{BREQ}$ pin low on the leading edge of E. When the MPU replies by setting BA and BS to a one, that cycle will be a dead cycle used to transfer bus mastership to the DMA controller.

False memory accesses may be prevented during any dead cycles by developing a system $\overline{DMAVMA}$ signal which is LOW in any cycle when BA has changed.

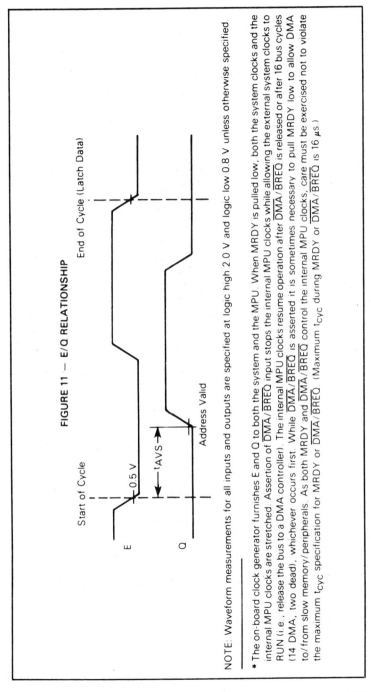

FIGURE 11 — E/Q RELATIONSHIP

NOTE: Waveform measurements for all inputs and outputs are specified at logic high 2.0 V and logic low 0.8 V unless otherwise specified.

* The on-board clock generator furnishes E and Q to both the system and the MPU. When MRDY is pulled low, both the system clocks and the internal MPU clocks are stretched. Assertion of $\overline{DMA}/\overline{BREQ}$ input stops the internal MPU clocks while allowing the external system clocks to RUN (i.e., release the bus to a DMA controller). The internal MPU clocks resume operation after $\overline{DMA}/\overline{BREQ}$ is released or after 16 bus cycles (14 DMA, two dead), whichever occurs first. While $\overline{DMA}/\overline{BREQ}$ is asserted it is sometimes necessary to pull MRDY low to allow DMA to/from slow memory/peripherals. As both MRDY and $\overline{DMA}/\overline{BREQ}$ control the internal MPU clocks, care must be exercised not to violate the maximum t_{cyc} specification for MRDY or $\overline{DMA}/\overline{BREQ}$ (Maximum t_{cyc} during MRDY or $\overline{DMA}/\overline{BREQ}$ is 16 μs.)

When BA goes low (either as a result of $\overline{\text{DMA}/\text{BREQ}}$ = HIGH or MPU self-refresh), the DMA device should be taken off the bus. Another dead cycle will elapse before the MPU accesses memory to allow transfer of bus mastership without contention.

MPU OPERATION

During normal operation, the MPU fetches an instruction from memory and then executes the requested function. This sequence begins after $\overline{\text{RESET}}$ and is repeated indefinitely unless altered by a special instruction or hardware occurrence. Software instructions that alter normal MPU operation are: SWI, SWI2, SWI3, CWAI, RTI, and SYNC. An interrupt, $\overline{\text{HALT}}$, or $\overline{\text{DMA}/\text{BREQ}}$ can also alter the normal execution of instructions. Figure 15 illustrates the flowchart for the MC6809.

FIGURE 12 — MRDY TIMING AND SYNCHRONIZATION
(a) Timing

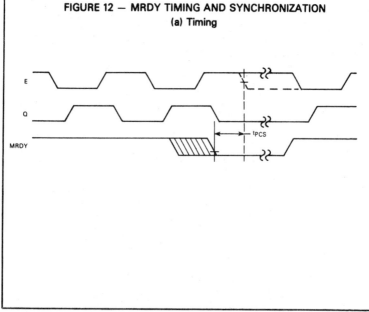

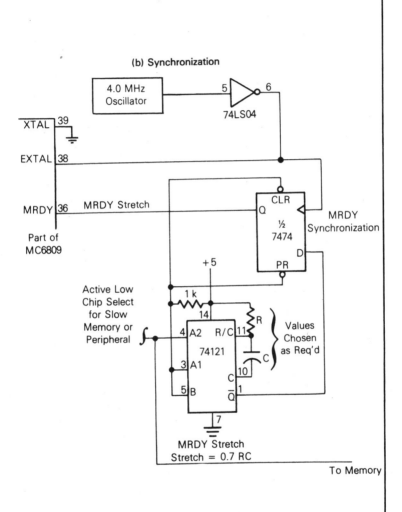

(b) Synchronization

117

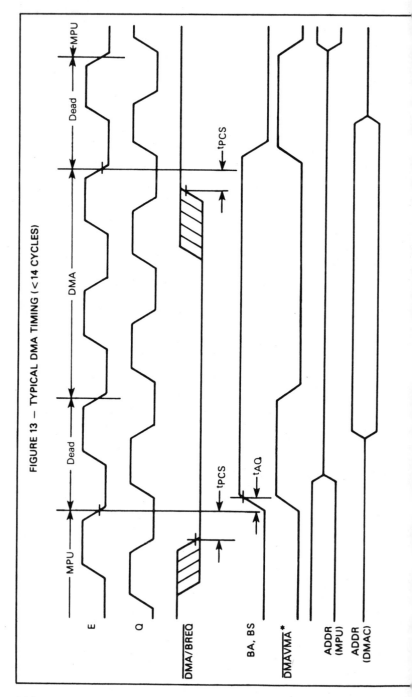

FIGURE 13 — TYPICAL DMA TIMING (<14 CYCLES)

E

Q

$\overline{DMA}/\overline{BREQ}$

BA, BS

$\overline{DMAVMA}^{*}$

ADDR (MPU)

ADDR (DMAC)

MPU · Dead · DMA · Dead · MPU

t_{PCS}

t_{AQ}

t_{PCS}

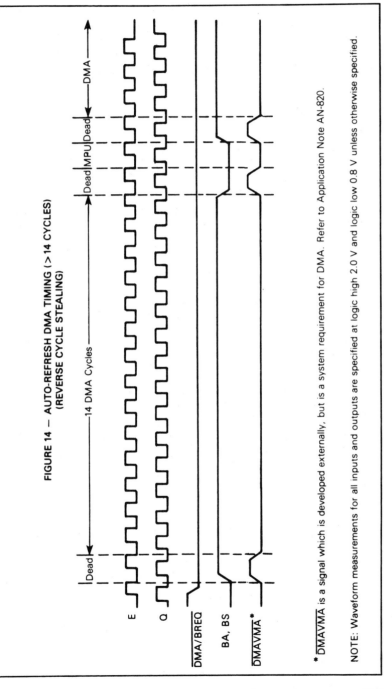

FIGURE 14 — AUTO-REFRESH DMA TIMING (>14 CYCLES)
(REVERSE CYCLE STEALING)

* DMAVMA is a signal which is developed externally, but is a system requirement for DMA. Refer to Application Note AN-820.

NOTE: Waveform measurements for all inputs and outputs are specified at logic high 2.0 V and logic low 0.8 V unless otherwise specified.

FIGURE 15 — FLOWCHART FOR MC6809 INSTRUCTIONS

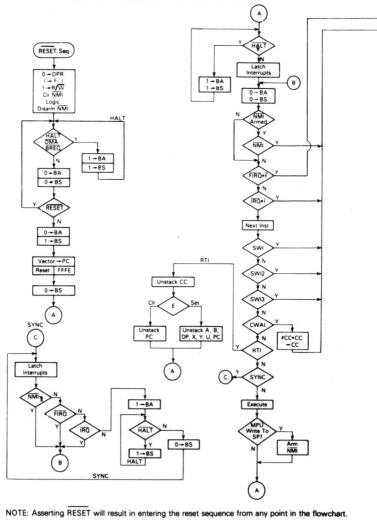

NOTE: Asserting $\overline{\text{RESET}}$ will result in entering the reset sequence from any point in the flowchart.

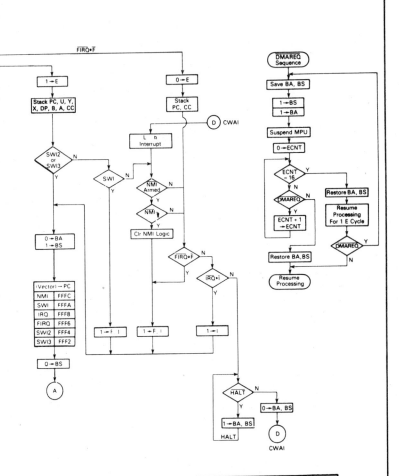

Bus State	BA	BS
Normal (Running)	0	0
Interrupt or Reset Acknowledge	0	1
Sync Acknowledge	1	0
Halt or Bus Grant Acknowledge	1	1

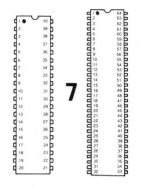

7

Intel 8085 Spec Sheets

- ■ Single +5V Power Supply
- ■ 100% Software Compatible with 8080A
- ■ 1.3 μs Instruction Cycle
- ■ On-Chip Clock Generator (with External Crystal or RC Network)
- ■ On-Chip System Controller
- ■ Four Vectored Interrupts (One is non-Maskable)
- ■ Serial In/Serial Out Port
- ■ Decimal, Binary and Double Precision Arithmetic
- ■ Direct Addressing Capability to 64K Bytes of Memory

The Intel® is a new generation, complete 8 bit parallel central processing unit (CPU). Its instruction set is 100% software compatible with the 8080A microprocessor, and it is designed to improve the present 8080's performance by higher system speed. Its high level of system integration allows a minimum system of three IC's: 8085 (CPU), 8156 (RAM) and 8355/8755 (ROM/PROM).

The 8085 incorporates all of the features that the 8224 (clock generator) and 8228 (system controller) provided for the 8080, thereby offering a high level of system integration.

The 8085 uses a multiplexed Data Bus. The address is split between the 8 bit address bus and the 8 bit data bus. The on-chip address latches of 8155/8355/8755 memory products allows a direct interface with 8085.

Material in this chapter is reprinted by courtesy of Intel Corporation, copyright 1977.

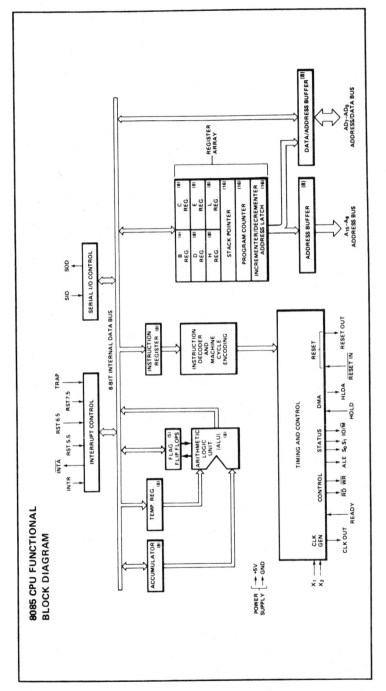

8085 CPU FUNCTIONAL BLOCK DIAGRAM

8085 FUNCTIONAL PIN DEFINITION

The following describes the function of each pin:

A$_8$-A$_{15}$ (Output 3-State)

Address Bus; The most significant 8-bits of the memory address or the 8-bits of the I/O address, 3-stated during Hold and Halt modes.

AD$_{0-7}$ (Input/Output 3-state)

Multiplexed Address/Data Bus; Lower 8-bits of the memory address (or I/O address) appear on the bus during the first clock cycle of a machine state. It then becomes the data bus during the second and third clock cycles.

3-stated during Hold and Halt modes.

ALE (Output 3-state)

Address Latch Enable: It occurs during the first clock cycle of a machine state and enables the address to get latched into the on-chip latch of peripherals. The falling edge of ALE is set to guarantee setup and hold times for the address information. ALE can also be used to strobe the status information. 3-stated during Hold and Halt modes.

S0, S1 (Output)

Data Bus Status. Encoded status of the bus cycle:

S$_1$	S$_0$	
0	0	HALT
0	1	WRITE
1	0	READ
1	1	FETCH

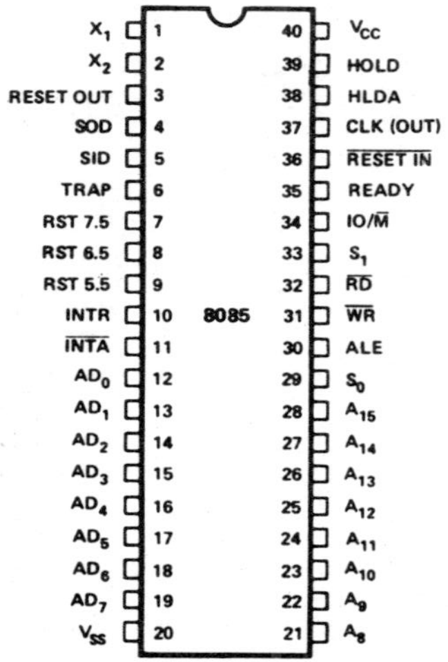

Figure 1. 8085 PINOUT DIAGRAM

buses in the next clock cycle. HLDA goes low after the Hold request is removed. The CPU takes the buses one half clock cycle after HLDA goes low.

S_1 can be used as an advanced R/$\overline{W}$ status.

$\overline{RD}$ (Output 3-state)

READ: indicates the selected memory or I/O device is to be read and that the Data Bus is available for the data transfer. Tri-stated during Hold and Halt.

$\overline{WR}$ (Output 3-state)

WRITE: indicates the data on the Data Bus is to be written into the selected memory or I/O location. Data is set up at the trailing edge of $\overline{WR}$. Tri-stated during Hold and Halt modes.

READY (Input)

If Ready is high during a read or write cycle, it indicates that the memory or peripheral is ready to send or receive data. If Ready is low, the CPU will wait for Ready to go high before completing the read or write cycle.

HOLD (Input)

HOLD: indicates that another Master is requesting the use of the Address and Data Buses. The CPU, upon receiving the Hold request, will relinquish the use of buses as soon as the completion of the current machine cycle. Internal processing can continue. The processor can regain the buses only after the Hold is removed. When the Hold is acknowledged, the Address, Data, $\overline{RD}$, $\overline{WR}$, IO/$\overline{M}$, and ALE lines are tri-stated.

HLDA (Output)

HOLD ACKNOWLEDGE: indicates that the CPU has received the Hold request and that it will relinquish the buses in the next clock cycle. HLDA goes low after the Hold request is removed. The CPU takes the buses one half clock cycle after HLDA goes low.

INTR (Input)

INTERRUPT REQUEST: is used as a general purpose interrupt. It is sampled only during the last clock cycle of the instruction. If it is active, the Program Counter (PC) will be inhibited from incrementing and an $\overline{INTA}$ will be issued. During this cycle a RESTART or CALL instruction can be inserted to jump to the interrupt service routine. The INTR is enabled and disabled by software. It is disabled by Reset and immediately after an interrupt is accepted.

$\overline{INTA}$ (Output)

INTERRUPT ACKNOWLEDGE: is used instead of (and has the same timing as) $\overline{RD}$ during the Instruction cycle after an INTR is accepted. It can be used to activate the 8259 Interrupt chip or some other interrupt port.

$$\left. \begin{array}{l} \text{RST 5.5} \\ \text{RST 6.5} \\ \text{RST 7.5} \end{array} \right\} \text{(Inputs)}$$

RESTART INTERRUPTS: These three inputs have the same timing as INTR except they cause an internal RESTART to be automatically inserted.

RST 7.5 → Highest Priority
RST 6.5
RST 5.5 → Lowest Priority

The priority of these interrupts is ordered as shown above. These interrupts have a higher priority than the INTR.

TRAP (Input)

Trap interrupt is a nonmaskable restart interrupt. It is recognized at the same time as INTR. It is unaffected by any mask or Interrupt Enable. It has the highest priority of any interrupt.

$\overline{\text{RESET IN}}$ (Input)

Reset sets the Program Counter to zero and resets the Interrupt Enable and HLDA flip-flops. None of the other flags or registers (except the instruction register) are affected. The CPU is held in the reset condition as long as Reset is applied.

RESET OUT (Output)

Indicates CPU is being reset. Can be used as a system RESET. The signal is synchronized to the processor clock.

X_1, X_2 (Input)

Crystal or R/C network connections to set the internal clock generator. X1 can also be an external clock input instead of a crystal.

CLK (Output)

Clock Output for use as a system clock when a crystal or R/C network is used as an input to the CPU.

IO/$\overline{\text{M}}$ (Output)

IO/$\overline{\text{M}}$ indicates whether the Read/Write is to memory or I/O. Tri-stated during Hold and Halt modes.

The 8085 provides $\overline{\text{RD}}$, $\overline{\text{WR}}$, and IO/Memory signals for bus control. An Interrupt Acknowledge signal ($\overline{\text{INTA}}$) is also provided. Hold, Ready, and all Interrupts are synchronized. The 8085 also provides serial input data (SID) and serial output data (SOD) lines for simple serial interface.

In addition to these features, the 8085 has three maskable, restart interrupts and one nonmaskable trap interrupt.

8085 vs. 8080

The 8085 includes the following features on-chip in addition to all of the 8080 functions.

a. Internal clock generator
b. Clock output
c. Fully synchronized Ready
d. Schmitt action on $\overline{\text{RESET IN}}$
e. $\overline{\text{RESET OUT}}$ pin
f. $\overline{\text{RD}}$, $\overline{\text{WR}}$, and IO/$\overline{\text{M}}$ Bus Control Signals
g. Encoded Status information
h. Multiplexed Address and Data
i. Direct Restarts and nonmaskable Interrupt
j. Serial Input/Output lines.

The internal clock generator requires an external crystal or R-C network. It will oscillate at twice the basic CPU operating frequency. A 50% duty cycle, two phase, nonoverlapping clock is generated from this oscillator internally and one phase of the clock ($\phi2$) is available as an external clock. The 8085 directly provides the external

SID (Input)

Serial input data line. The data on this line is loaded into accumulator bit 7 whenever a RIM instruction is executed.

SOD (output)

Serial output data line. The output SOD is set or reset as specified by the SIM instruction.

V_{cc}

+5 volt supply.

V_{ss}

Ground Reference.

FUNCTIONAL DESCRIPTION

The 8085 is a complete 8 bit parallel central processor. It is designed with N-channel depletion loads and requires a single +5 volt supply. Its basic clock speed is 3 MHz thus improving on the present 8080's performance with higher system speed. Also it is designed to fit into a minimum system of three IC's: The CPU, a RAM/IO, and a ROM or PROM/IO chip.

The 8085 uses a multiplexed Data Bus. The address is split between the higher 8-bit Address Bus and the lower 8-bit Address/Data Bus. During the first cycle the address is sent out. The lower 8-bits are latched into the peripherals by the Address Latch Enable (ALE). During the rest of the machine cycle the Data Bus is used for memory or I/O data.

RDY synchronization previously provided by the 8224. The RESET IN input is provided with a Schmitt action input so that power-on reset only requires a resistor and capacitor. RESET OUT is provided for System RESET.

The 8085 provides $\overline{RD}$, $\overline{WR}$ and IO/$\overline{M}$ signals for Bus control. An $\overline{INTA}$ which was previously provided by the 8228 in 8080 system is also included in 8085.

STATUS INFORMATION

Status information is directly available from the 8085. ALE serves as a status strobe. The status is partially encoded, and provides the user with advanced timing of the type of bus transfer being done. IO/$\overline{M}$ cycle status signal is provided directly also. Decoded S_0, S_1 carries the following status information:

	S_1	S_0
HALT	0	0
WRITE	0	1
READ	1	0
FETCH	1	1

S_1 can be interpreted as R/$\overline{W}$ in all bus transfers.

In the 8085 the 8 LSB of address are multiplexed with the data instead of status. The ALE line is used as a strobe to enter the lower half of the address into the memory or peripheral address latch. This also frees extra pins for expanded interrupt capability.

INTERRUPT AND SERIAL I/O

The 8085 has 5 interrupt inputs: INTR, RST 5.5, RST 6.5, RST 7.5, and TRAP. INTR is identical in function to the 8080 INT. Each of three RESTART inputs, 5.5, 6.5, 7.5, has a programmable mask. TRAP is also a RESTART interrupt except it is non-maskable.

The three RESTART interrupts cause the internal execution of RST (saving the program counter in the stack and branching to the RESTART address) if the interrupts are enabled and if the interrupt mask is not set. The nonmaskable TRAP causes the internal execution of a RST independent of the state of the interrupt enable or masks.

Name	RESTART Address (Hex)
TRAP	24_{16}
RST 5.5	$2C_{16}$
RST 6.5	34_{16}
RST 7.5	$3C_{16}$

There are two different types of inputs in the restart interrupts. RST 5.5 and RST 6.5 are high level-sensitive like INTR (and INT on the 8080) and are recognized with the same timing as INTR. RST 7.5 is rising edge-sensitive.

For RST 7.5, only a pulse is required to set an internal flip flop which generates the internal interrupt request. The RST 7.5 request flip flop remains set until the request is serviced. Then it is reset automatically. This flip flop may also be reset by using the SIM instruction or by issuing a RESET IN to the 8085. The RST 7.5 internal flip flop will be set by a pulse on the RST 7.5 pin even when the RST 7.5 interrupt is masked out.

The status of the three RST interrupt masks can only be affected by the SIM instruction and RESET IN.

The interrupts are arranged in a fixed priority that determines which interrupt is to be recognized if more than one is pending as follows: TRAP - highest priority, RST 7.5, RST 6.5, RST 5.5, INTR - lowest priority. This priority scheme does not take into account the priority of a routine that was started by a higher priority interrupt. RST 5.5 can interrupt a RST 7.5 routine if the interrupts were re-enabled before the end of the RST 7.5 routine.

The TRAP interrupt is useful for catastrophic errors such as power failure or bus error. The TRAP input is recognized just as any other interrupt but has the highest priority. It is not affected by any flag or mask. The TRAP input is both edge and level sensitive. The TRAP input must go high and remain high to be acknowledged, but will not be recognized again until it goes low, then high again. This avoids any false triggering due to noise or logic glitches.

The following diagram illustrates the TRAP interrupt request circuitry within the 8085.

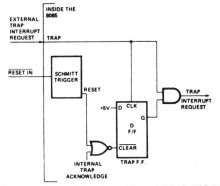

Note that the servicing of any interrupt (TRAP, RST 7.5, RST 6.5, RST 5.5, INTR) disables all future interrupts (except TRAPs) until an EI instruction is executed.

Since a TRAP interrupt can occur and disable the other interrupts whether they were previously enabled or not, it is not possible to restore the previous interrupt enable status following a TRAP.

The serial I/O system is also controlled by the RIM and SIM instructions. SID is read by RIM, and SIM sets the SOD data.

BASIC SYSTEM TIMING

The 8085 has a multiplexed Data Bus. ALE is used as a strobe to sample the lower 8-bits of address on the Data Bus. Figure 2 shows an instruction fetch, memory read and I/O write cycle (OUT). Note that during the I/O write and read cycle that the I/O port address is copied on both the upper and lower half of the address.

As in the 8080, the READY line is used to extend the read and write pulse lengths so that the 8085 can be used with slow memory. Hold causes the CPU to relinquish the bus when it is through with it by floating the Address and Data Buses.

SYSTEM INTERFACE

8085 family includes memory components, which are directly compatible to the 8085 CPU. For example, a system consisting of the three chips, 8085, 8156, and 8355 will have the following features:

- 2K Bytes ROM
- 256 Bytes RAM
- 1 Timer/Counter
- 4 8-bit I/O Ports
- 1 6-bit I/O Port
- 4 Interrupt Levels
- Serial In/Serial Out Ports

This minimum system, using the standard I/O technique is as shown in Figure 3.

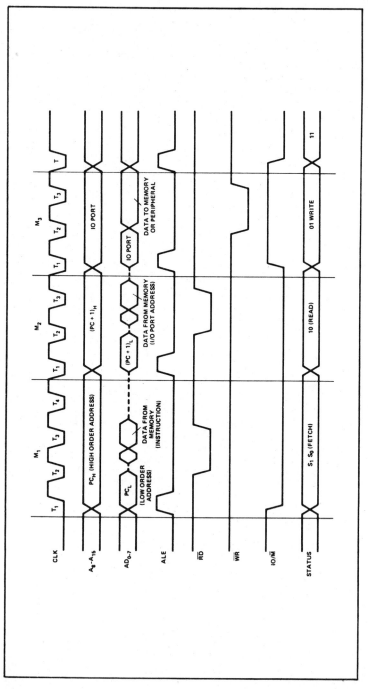

In addition to standard I/O, the memory mapped I/O offers an efficient I/O addressing technique. With this technique, an area of memory address space is assigned for I/O address, thereby, using the memory address for I/O manipulation. Figure 4 shows the system configuration of Memory Mapped I/O using 8085.

The 8085 CPU can also interface with the standard memory that does *not* have the multiplexed address/data bus. It will require a simple 8212 (8-bit latch) as shown in Figure 5.

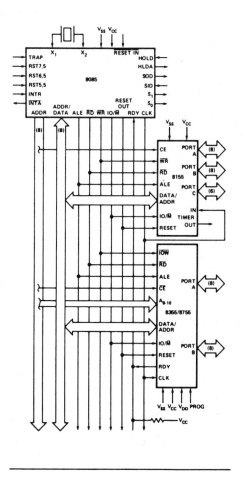

FIGURE 3. 8085 MINIMUM SYSTEM (STANDARD I/O TECHNIQUE)

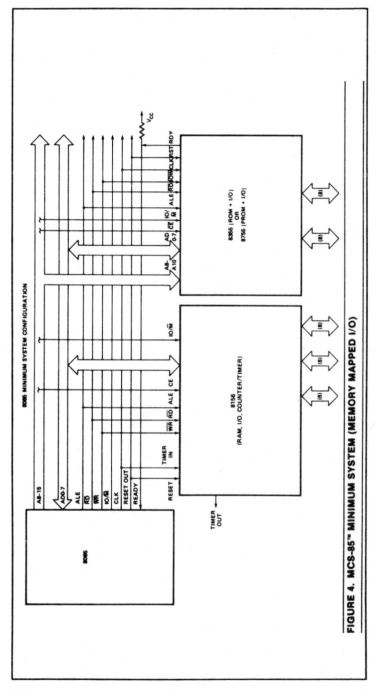

FIGURE 4. MCS-85™ MINIMUM SYSTEM (MEMORY MAPPED I/O)

132

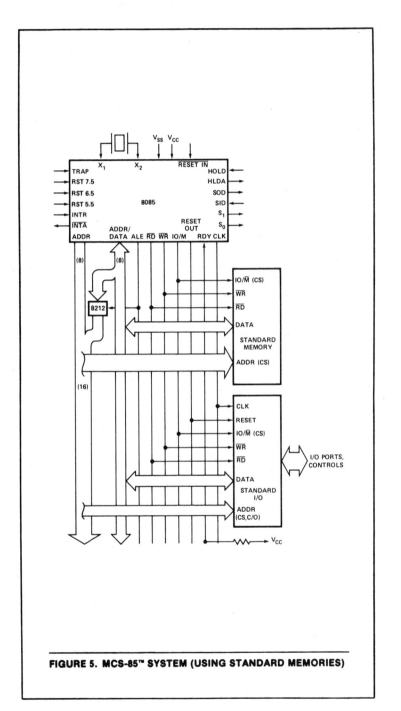

FIGURE 5. MCS-85™ SYSTEM (USING STANDARD MEMORIES)

133

DRIVING THE X1 AND X2 INPUTS

The user may drive the X_1 and X_2 inputs of the 8085 with a crystal, an external clock source or an RC network as shown below:

PARALLEL RESONANT CRYSTAL (30pf LOADING)

1-6 MHz
INPUT FREQUENCY

1-6 MHz
INPUT FREQUENCY

(DUTY CYCLE AT 6MHz: 25 ~ 50%)
*WITH AN EXTERNAL CLOCK SOURCE X_2 SHOULD BE LEFT FLOATING.

134

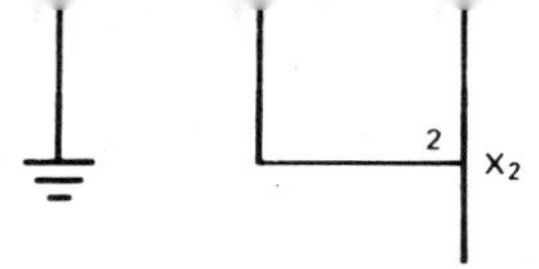

≈ 3 MHz
INPUT FREQUENCY

RC Mode causes a large drift in clock frequency because of the variation in on-chip timing generation parameters. Use of RC Mode should be limited to an application, which can tolerate a wide frequency variation.

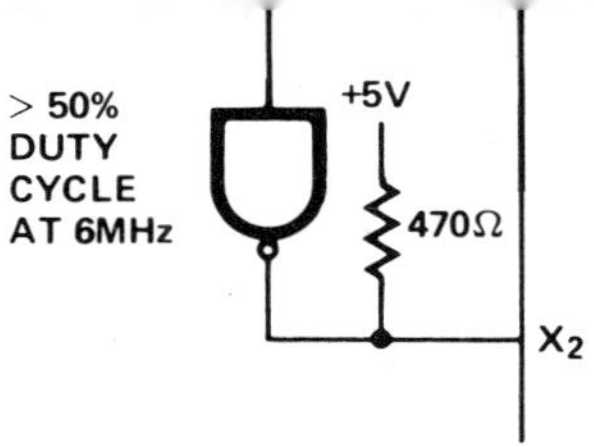

FIGURE 6. DRIVING THE CLOCK INPUTS (X1 AND X2) OF 8085

> 50%
DUTY
CYCLE
AT 6MHz

~6 MHz
INPUT FREQUENCY

This circuit may be used when the clock input has > 50% duty cycle at 6MHz.

GENERATING 8085 WAIT STATE

The following circuit may be used to insert one WAIT state in each 8085 machine cycle.

The D flip flops should be chosen such that
- CLK is rising edge triggered
- CLEAR is low-level active.

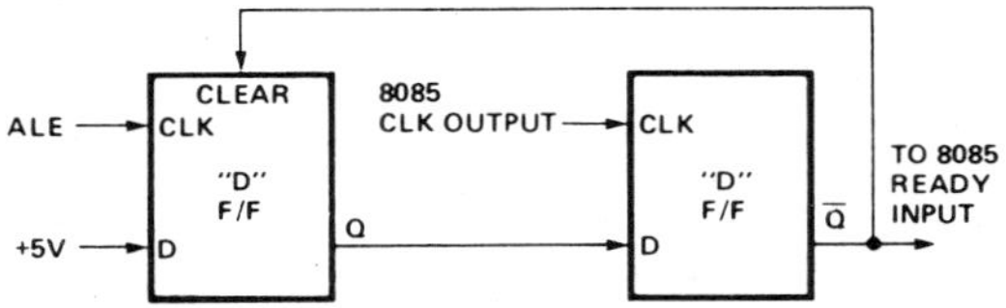

FIGURE 7. GENERATION OF A WAIT STATE FOR 8085 CPU

135

ABSOLUTE MAXIMUM RATINGS*

Ambient Temperature Under Bias. . . . . 0°C to 70°C
Storage Temperature . . . . −65°C to +150°C
Voltage on Any Pin
With Respect to Ground. . . . . −0.3 to +7V
Power Dissipation . . . . 1.5 Watt

*COMMENT: Stresses above those listed under "Absolute Maximum Ratings" may cause permanent damage to the device. This is a stress rating only and functional operation of the device at these or any other conditions above those indicated in the operational sections of this specification is not implied. Exposure to absolute maximum rating conditions for extended periods may affect device reliability.

D.C. CHARACTERISTICS

(T$_A$ = 0°C to 70°C; V$_{CC}$ = 5V ±5%; V$_{SS}$ = 0V; unless otherwise specified)

Symbol	Parameter	Min.	Max.	Units	Test Conditions
V$_{IL}$	Input Low Voltage	−0.5	+0.8	V	
V$_{IH}$	Input High Voltage	2.0	V$_{CC}$ +0.5	V	
V$_{OL}$	Output Low Voltage		0.45	V	I$_{OL}$ = 2mA
V$_{OH}$	Output High Voltage	2.4		V	I$_{OH}$ = −400µA
I$_{CC}$	Power Supply Current		170	mA	
I$_{IL}$	Input Leakage		±10	µA	V$_{in}$ = V$_{CC}$
I$_{LO}$	Output Leakage		±10	µA	0.45V ≤ V$_{out}$ ≤ V$_{CC}$
V$_{ILR}$	Input Low Level, RESET	−0.5	+0.8	V	
V$_{IHR}$	Input High Level, RESET	2.4	V$_{CC}$ +0.5	V	
V$_{HY}$	Hysteresis, RESET	0.25		V	

Bus Timing Specification as a T_{CYC} Dependent

t_{AL}	—	$(1/2)\,T - 50$	MIN
t_{LA}	—	$(1/2)\,T - 60$	MIN
t_{LL}	—	$(1/2)\,T - 40$	MIN
t_{LCK}	—	$(1/2)\,T - 60$	MIN
t_{LC}	—	$(1/2)\,T - 30$	MIN
t_{AD}	—	$(5/2 + N)\,T - 225$	MAX
t_{RD}	—	$(3/2 + N)\,T - 200$	MAX
t_{RAE}	—	$(1/2)\,T - 60$	MIN
t_{CA}	—	$(1/2)\,T - 40$	MIN
t_{DW}	—	$(3/2 + N)\,T - 60$	MIN
t_{WD}	—	$(1/2)\,T - 80$	MIN
t_{CC}	—	$(3/2 + N)\,T - 80$	MIN
t_{CL}	—	$(1/2)\,T - 110$	MIN
t_{ARY}	—	$(3/2)\,T - 260$	MAX
t_{HACK}	—	$(1/2)\,T - 50$	MIN
t_{HABF}	—	$(1/2)\,T + 30$	MAX
t_{HABE}	—	$(1/2)\,T + 30$	MAX
t_{AC}	—	$(2/2)\,T - 50$	MIN
t_1	—	$(1/2)\,T - 80$	MIN
t_2	—	$(1/2)\,T - 40$	MIN
t_{RV}	—	$(3/2)\,T - 80$	MIN
t_{INS}	—	$(1/2)\,T + 200$	MIN

NOTE: N is equal to the total WAIT states.

$T = t_{CYC}$.

A.C. CHARACTERISTICS ($T_A = 0°C$ to $70°C$; $V_{CC} = 5V \pm 5\%$; $V_{SS} = 0V$)

Symbol	Parameter	Min.	Max.	Units	Test Conditions
T_{CYC}	CLK Cycle Period	320	2000	ns	See notes 1, 2, 3, 4, 5
t_1	CLK Low Time	80		ns	
t_2	CLK High Time	120		ns	
t_r, t_f	CLK Rise and Fall Time		30	ns	
t_{AL}	Address Valid Before Trailing Edge of ALE	110		ns	
t_{LA}	Address Hold Time After ALE	100		ns	
t_{LL}	ALE Width	120		ns	
t_{LCK}	ALE Low During CLK High	100		ns	
t_{LC}	Trailing Edge of ALE to Leading Edge of Control	130		ns	
t_{AFR}	Address Float After Leading Edge of READ ($\overline{\text{INTA}}$)		0	ns	
t_{AD}	Valid Address to Valid Data In		575	ns	
t_{RD}	$\overline{\text{READ}}$ (or $\overline{\text{INTA}}$) to Valid Data		280	ns	
t_{RDH}	Data Hold Time After $\overline{\text{READ}}$ ($\overline{\text{INTA}}$)	0		ns	
t_{RAE}	Trailing Edge of $\overline{\text{READ}}$ to Re-Enabling of Address	120		ns	$T_{CYC} = 320ns;$ $C_L = 150$ pF
t_{CA}	Address (A8–A15) Valid After Control	120		ns	
t_{DW}	Data Valid to Trailing Edge of $\overline{\text{WRITE}}$	420		ns	

Symbol	Description			Units
t_{WD}	Data Valid After Trailing Edge of $\overline{\text{WRITE}}$	80		ns
t_{CC}	Width of Control Low ($\overline{\text{RD}}$, $\overline{\text{WR}}$, $\overline{\text{INTA}}$)	400		ns
t_{CL}	Trailing Edge of Control to Leading Edge of ALE	50		ns
t_{ARY}	READY Valid From Address Valid		220	ns
t_{RYS}	READY Setup Time to Leading Edge of CLK	110		ns
t_{RYH}	READY Hold Time	0		ns
t_{HACK}	HLDA Valid to Trailing Edge of CLK	110		ns
t_{HABF}	Bus Float After HLDA		190	ns
t_{RV}	Control Trailing Edge to Leading Edge of Next Control	400		ns
t_{AC}	Address Valid to Leading Edge of Control	270		ns
t_{HDS}	HOLD Setup Time to Trailing Edge of CLK	170		ns
t_{HDH}	HOLD Hold Time	0		ns
t_{INS}	INTR Setup Time to Leading Edge of CLK (M1, T1 only). Also RST and TRAP	360		ns
t_{INH}	INTR Hold Time	0		ns

NOTES:
1. A8-15 Address Specs apply to IO/$\overline{\text{M}}$, S0 and S1.
2. For all output timing where $C_L \neq 150\text{pf}$ use the following correction factors:

   $25\text{pf} \leqslant C_L < 150\text{pf}$: $-.10$ ns/pf
   $150\text{pf} < C_L \leqslant 300\text{pf}$: $+.30$ ns/pf

3. Output timings are measured with purely capacitive load.
4. All timings are measured at output voltage $V_L = .8V$, $V_H = 2.0V$, and $1.5V$ with 20ns rise and fall time on inputs.
5. To calculate timing specifications at other values of T_{CYC} use the table in Table 2.
6. L.E. = Leading Edge   T.E. = Trailing Edge

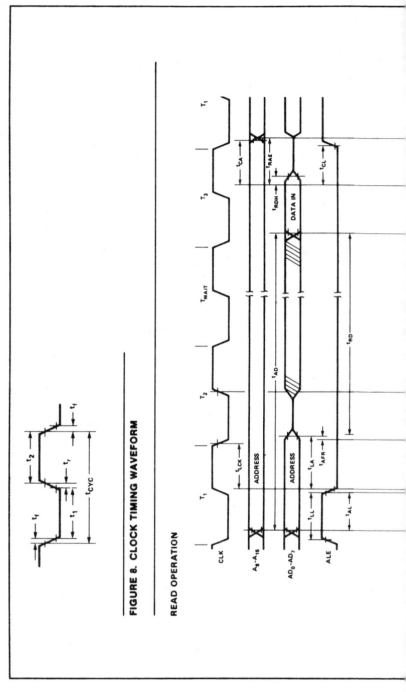

FIGURE 8. CLOCK TIMING WAVEFORM

READ OPERATION

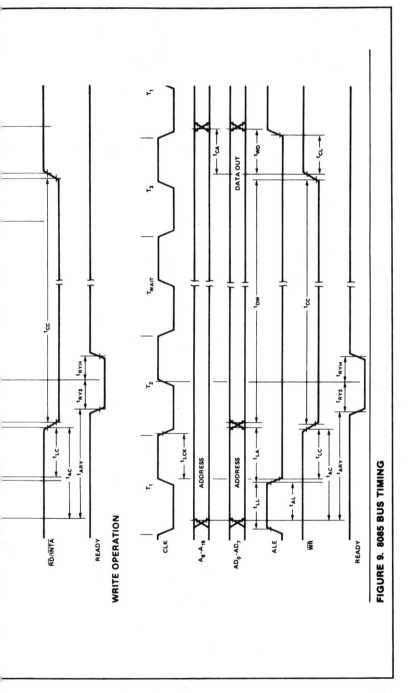

WRITE OPERATION

FIGURE 9. 8085 BUS TIMING

141

HOLD OPERATION

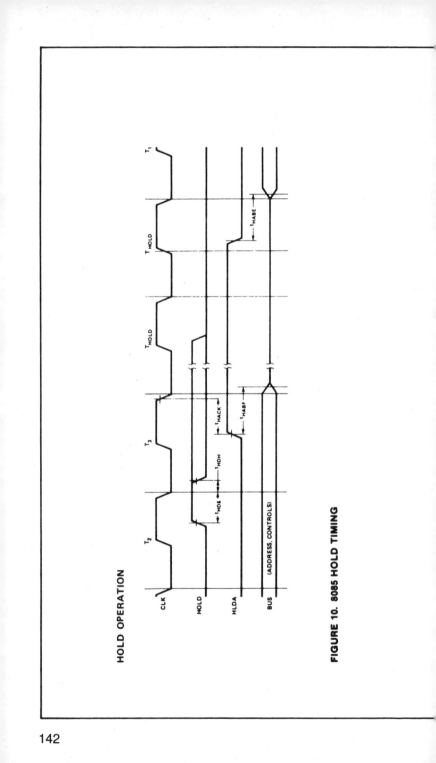

FIGURE 10. 8085 HOLD TIMING

142

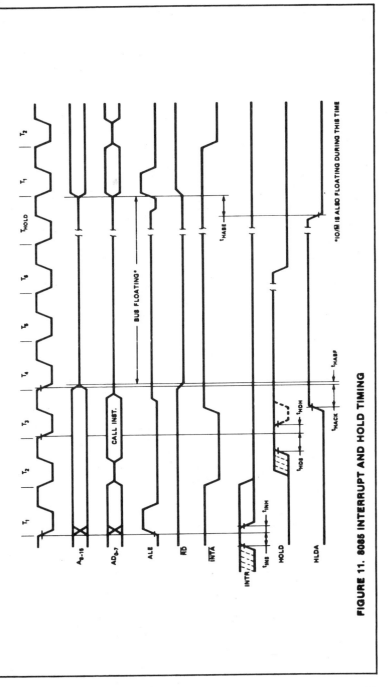

FIGURE 11. 8085 INTERRUPT AND HOLD TIMING

143

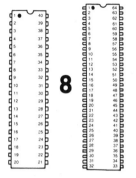

Intel 8086 Spec Sheets

- **Direct Addressing Capability to 1 MByte of Memory**

- **Architecture Designed for Powerful Assembly Language and Efficient High Level Languages.**

- **14 Word, by 16-Bit Register Set with Symmetrical Operations**

- **24 Operand Addressing Modes**

- **Bit, Byte, Word, and Block Operations**

- **8 and 16-Bit Signed and Unsigned Arithmetic in Binary or Decimal Including Multiply and Divide**

- **Range of Clock Rates:**
  5 MHz for 8086,
  8 MHz for 8086-2,
  10 MHz for 8086-1

- **MULTIBUS™ System Compatible Interface**

The Intel iAPX 86/10 high performance 16-bit CPU is available in three clock rates: 5, 8 nd 10 MHz. The CPU is implemented in N-Channel, depletion load, silicon gate technology (HMOS), and packaged in a 40-pin CerDIP package. The iAPX 86/10 operates in both single processor and multiple processor configurations to achieve high performance levels.

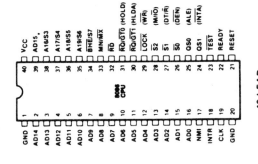

Figure 2. IAPX 86/10 Pin Configuration

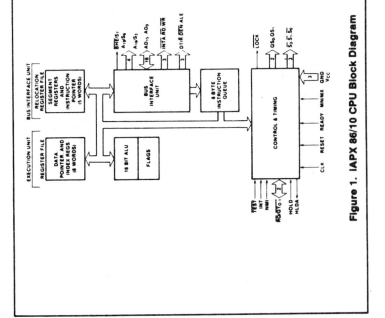

Figure 1. IAPX 86/10 CPU Block Diagram

Table 1. Pin Description

The following pin function descriptions are for iAPX 86 systems in either minimum or maximum mode. The "Local Bus" in these descriptions is the direct multiplexed bus interface connection to the 8086 (without regard to additional bus buffers).

Symbol	Pin No.	Type	Name and Function
AD_{15}-AD_0	2-16, 39	I/O	**Address Data Bus:** These lines constitute the time multiplexed memory/IO address (T_1) and data (T_2, T_3, T_W, T_4) bus. A_0 is analogous to $\overline{BHE}$ for the lower byte of the data bus, pins D_7-D_0. It is LOW during T_1 when a byte is to be transferred on the lower portion of the bus in memory or I/O operations. Eight-bit oriented devices tied to the lower half would normally use A_0 to condition chip select functions. (See $\overline{BHE}$.) These lines are active HIGH and float to 3-state OFF during interrupt acknowledge and local bus "hold acknowledge."
A_{19}/S_6, A_{18}/S_5, A_{17}/S_4, A_{16}/S_3	35-38	O	**Address/Status:** During T_1 these are the four most significant address lines for memory operations. During I/O operations these lines are LOW. During memory and I/O operations, status information is available on these' lines during T_2, T_3, T_W, and T_4. The status of the interrupt enable FLAG bit (S_5) is updated at the beginning of each CLK cycle. A_{17}/S_4 and A_{16}/S_3 are encoded as shown. This information indicates which relocation register is presently being used for data accessing. These lines float to 3-state OFF during local bus "hold acknowledge." | $A_{17}S_4$	$A_{16}S_3$	Characteristics
---	---	---
0 (LOW)	0	Alternate Data
0	1	Stack
1 (HIGH)	0	Code or None
1	1	Data
S_6 is 0 (LOW)			
$\overline{BHE}$/S_7	34	O	**Bus High Enable/Status:** During T_1 the bus high enable signal ($\overline{BHE}$) should be used to enable data onto the

146

BHE	A0	Characteristics
0	0	Whole word
0	1	Upper byte from/to odd address
1	0	Lower byte from/to even address
1	1	None

most significant half of the data bus, pins D_{15}-D_8. Eight-bit oriented devices tied to the upper half of the bus would normally use BHE to condition chip select functions. BHE is LOW during T_1 for read, write, and interrupt acknowledge cycles when a byte is to be transferred on the high portion of the bus. The S_7 status information is available during T_2, T_3, and T_4. The signal is active LOW, and floats to 3-state OFF in "hold." It is LOW during T_1 for the first interrupt acknowledge cycle.

RD — 32 — O

Read: Read strobe indicates that the processor is performing a memory of I/O read cycle, depending on the state of the S_2 pin. This signal is used to read devices which reside on the 8086 local bus. RD is active LOW during T_2, T_3 and T_w of any read cycle, and is guaranteed to remain HIGH in T_2 until the 8086 local bus has floated.

This signal floats to 3-state OFF in "hold acknowledge."

READY — 22 — I

READY: is the acknowledgement from the addressed memory or I/O device that it will complete the data transfer. The READY signal from memory/IO is synchronized by the 8284A Clock Generator to form READY. This signal is active HIGH. The 8086 READY input is not synchronized. Correct operation is not guaranteed if the setup and hold times are not met.

INTR — 18 — I

Interrupt Request: is a level triggered input which is sampled during the last clock cycle of each instruction to determine if the processor should enter into an interrupt acknowledge operation. A subroutine is vectored to via an interrupt vector lookup table located in system memory. It can be internally masked by software resetting the interrupt enable bit. INTR is internally synchronized. This signal is active HIGH.

TEST — 23 — I

TEST: input is examined by the "Wait" instruction. If the TEST input is LOW execution continues, otherwise the processor waits in an "Idle" state. This input is synchronized internally during each clock cycle on the leading edge of CLK.

Table 1. Pin Description (Continued)

Symbol	Pin No.	Type	Name and Function
NMI	17	I	**Non-maskable Interrupt:** an edge triggered input which causes a type 2 interrupt. A subroutine is vectored to via an interrupt vector lookup table located in system memory. NMI is not maskable internally by software. A transition from a LOW to HIGH initiates the interrupt at the end of the current instruction. This input is internally synchronized.
RESET	21	I	**Reset:** causes the processor to immediately terminate its present activity. The signal must be active HIGH for at least four clock cycles. It restarts execution, as described in the Instruction Set description, when RESET returns LOW. RESET is internally synchronized.
CLK	19	I	**Clock:** provides the basic timing for the processor and bus controller. It is asymmetric with a 33% duty cycle to provide optimized internal timing.
V_{CC}	40		V_{CC}: + 5V power supply pin.
GND	1, 20		**Ground**
$MN/\overline{MX}$	33	I	**Minimum/Maximum:** indicates what mode the processor is to operate in. The two modes are discussed in the following sections.

The following pin function descriptions are for the 8086/8288 system in maximum mode (i.e., $MN/\overline{MX} = V_{SS}$). Only the pin functions which are unique to maximum mode are described; all other pin functions are as described above.

Symbol	Pin No.	Type	Name and Function			
$\overline{S_2}, \overline{S_1}, \overline{S_0}$	26-28	O	**Status:** active during T_4, T_1, and T_2 and is returned to the passive state (1,1,1) during T_3 or during T_W when READY is HIGH. This status is used by the 8288 Bus Controller to generate all memory and I/O access control signals. Any change by $\overline{S_2}$, $\overline{S_1}$, or $\overline{S_0}$ during T_4 is used to indicate the beginning of a bus cycle, and the return to the passive state in T_3 or T_W is used to indicate the end of a bus cycle.	$\overline{S_2}$	$\overline{S_1}$	$\overline{S_0}$	Characteristics

$\overline{S_2}$	$\overline{S_1}$	$\overline{S_0}$	Characteristics
0 (LOW)	0	0	Interrupt Acknowledge
0	0	1	Read I/O Port
0	1	0	Write I/O Port
0	1	1	Halt
1 (HIGH)	0	0	Code Access
1	0	1	Read Memory
1	1	0	Write Memory

					1		1	1	Passive

These signals float to 3-state OFF in "hold acknowledge." These status lines are encoded as shown.

$\overline{RQ}/\overline{GT}_0$, $\overline{RQ}/\overline{GT}_1$	30, 31	I/O	**Request/Grant:** pins are used by other local bus masters to force the processor to release the local bus at the end of the processor's current bus cycle. Each pin is bidirectional with $\overline{RQ}/\overline{GT}_0$ having higher priority than $\overline{RQ}/\overline{GT}_1$. $\overline{RQ}/\overline{GT}$ has an internal pull-up resistor so may be left unconnected. The request/grant sequence is as follows (see Figure 9):

1. A pulse of 1 CLK wide from another local bus master indicates a local bus request ("hold") to the 8086 (pulse 1).

2. During a T_4 or T_1 clock cycle, a pulse 1 CLK wide from the 8086 to the requesting master (pulse 2), indicates that the 8086 has allowed the local bus to float and that it will enter the "hold acknowledge" state at the next CLK. The CPU's bus interface unit is disconnected logically from the local bus during "hold acknowledge."

3. A pulse 1 CLK wide from the requesting master indicates to the 8086 (pulse 3) that the "hold" request is about to end and and that the 8086 can reclaim the local bus at the next CLK.

Each master-master exchange of the local bus is a sequence of 3 pulses. There must be one dead CLK cycle after each bus exchange. Pulses are active LOW.

If the request is made while the CPU is performing a memory cycle, it will release the local bus during T_4 of the cycle when all the following conditions are met:

1. Request occurs on or before T_2.
2. Current cycle is not the low byte of a word (on an odd address).
3. Current cycle is not the first acknowledge of an interrupt acknowledge sequence.
4. A locked instruction is not currently executing.

149

Table 1. Pin Description (Continued)

Symbol	Pin No.	Type	Name and Function
			If the local bus is idle when the request is made the two possible events will follow: 1. Local bus will be released during the next clock. 2. A memory cycle will start within 3 clocks. Now the four rules for a currently active memory cycle apply with condition number 1 already satisfied.
$\overline{LOCK}$	29	O	$\overline{LOCK}$: output indicates that other system bus masters are not to gain control of the system bus while $\overline{LOCK}$ is active LOW. The $\overline{LOCK}$ signal is activated by the "$\overline{LOCK}$" prefix instruction and remains active until the completion of the next instruction. This signal is active LOW, and floats to 3-state OFF in "hold acknowledge."
QS_1, QS_0	24, 25	O	Queue Status: The queue status is valid during the CLK cycle after which the queue operation is performed. QS_1 and QS_0 provide status to allow external tracking of the internal 8086 instruction queue.

The following pin function descriptions are for the 8086 in minimum mode (i.e., $MN/\overline{MX} = V_{CC}$). Only the pin functions which are unique to minimum mode are described; all other pin functions are as described above.

Symbol	Pin No.	Type	Name and Function
$M/\overline{IO}$	28	O	Status line: logically equivalent to S_2 in the maximum mode. It is used to distinguish a memory access from an I/O access. $M/\overline{IO}$ becomes valid in the T_4 preceding a bus cycle and remains valid until the final T_4 of the cycle (M = HIGH, IO = LOW). $M/\overline{IO}$ floats to 3-state OFF in local bus "hold acknowledge."
$\overline{WR}$	29	O	Write: indicates that the processor is performing a write memory or write I/O cycle, depending on the state of the $M/\overline{IO}$ signal. $\overline{WR}$ is active for T_2, T_3 and T_W of any write cycle. It is active LOW, and floats to 3-state OFF in local bus "hold acknowledge."

INTA	24	O	INTA is used as a read strobe for interrupt acknowledge cycles. It is active LOW during T_2, T_3 and T_W of each interrupt acknowledge cycle.
ALE	25	O	Address Latch Enable: provided by the processor to latch the address into the 8282/8283 address latch. It is a HIGH pulse active during T_1 of any bus cycle. Note that ALE is never floated.
DT/R̄	27	O	Data Transmit/Receive: needed in minimum system that desires to use an 8286/8287 data bus transceiver. It is used to control the direction of data flow through the transceiver. Logically DT/R̄ is equivalent to S̄$_1$ in the maximum mode, and its timing is the same as for M/IŌ. (T = HIGH, R = LOW.) This signal floats to 3-state OFF in local bus "hold acknowledge."
DĒN	26	O	Data Enable: provided as an output enable for the 8286/8287 in a minimum system which uses the transceiver. DĒN is active LOW during each memory and I/O access and for INTA cycles. For a read or INTA cycle it is active from the middle of T_2 until the middle of T_4, while for a write cycle it is active from the beginning of T_2 until the middle of T_4. DĒN floats to 3-state OFF in local bus "hold acknowledge."
HOLD, HLDA	31, 30	I/O	HOLD: indicates that another master is requesting a local bus "hold." To be acknowledged, HOLD must be active HIGH. The processor receiving the "hold" request will issue HLDA (HIGH) as an acknowledgement in the middle of a T_4 or T_1 clock cycle. Simultaneous with the issuance of HLDA the processor will float the local bus and control lines. After HOLD is detected as being LOW, the processor will LOWer HLDA, and when the processor needs to run another cycle, it will again drive the local bus and control lines. The same rules as for RQ̄/GT̄ apply regarding when the local bus will be released. HOLD is not an asynchronous input. External synchronization should be provided if the system cannot otherwise guarantee the setup time.

FUNCTIONAL DESCRIPTION

GENERAL OPERATION

The internal functions of the iAPX 86/10 processor are partitioned logically into two processing units. The first is the Bus Interface Unit (BIU) and the second is the Execution Unit (EU) as shown in the block diagram of Figure 1.

These units can interact directly but for the most part perform as separate asynchronous operational processors. The bus interface unit provides the functions related to instruction fetching and queuing, operand fetch and store, and address relocation. This unit also provides the basic bus control. The overlap of instruction pre-fetching provided by this unit serves to increase processor performance through improved bus bandwidth utilization. Up to 6 bytes of the instruction stream can be queued while waiting for decoding and execution.

The instruction stream queuing mechanism allows the BIU to keep the memory utilized very efficiently. Whenever there is space for at least 2 bytes in the queue, the BIU will attempt a word fetch memory cycle. This greatly reduces "dead time" on the memory bus. The queue

MEMORY ORGANIZATION

The processor provides a 20-bit address to memory which locates the byte being referenced. The memory is organized as a linear array of up to 1 million bytes, addressed as 00000(H) to FFFFF(H). The memory is logically divided into code, data, extra data, and stack segments of up to 64K bytes each, with each segment falling on 16-byte boundaries. (See Figure 3a.)

All memory references are made relative to base addresses contained in high speed segment registers. The segment types were chosen based on the addressing needs of programs. The segment register to be selected is automatically chosen according to the rules of the following table. All information in one segment type share the same logical attributes (e.g. code or data). By structuring memory into relocatable areas of similar characteristics and by automatically selecting segment registers, programs are shorter, faster, and more structured.

Word (16-bit) operands can be located on even or odd address boundaries and are thus not constrained to even boundaries as is the case in many 16-bit computers. For address and data operands, the least significant byte of the word is stored in the lower valued address location and the most significant byte in the next higher address location. The BIU automatically performs the proper number of memory accesses, one if

acts as a First-In-First-Out (FIFO) buffer, from which the EU extracts instruction bytes as required. If the queue is empty (following a branch instruction, for example), the first byte into the queue immediately becomes available to the EU.

The execution unit receives pre-fetched instructions from the BIU queue and provides un-relocated operand addresses to the BIU. Memory operands are passed through the BIU for processing by the EU, which passes results to the BIU for storage. See the Instruction Set description for further register set and architectural descriptions.

the word operand is on an even byte boundary and two if it is on an odd byte boundary. Except for the performance penalty, this double access is transparent to the software. This performance penalty does not occur for instruction fetches, only word operands.

Physically, the memory is organized as a high bank (D_{15}-D_8) and a low bank (D_7-D_0) of 512K 8-bit bytes addressed in parallel by the processor's address lines A_{19} - A_1. Byte data with even addresses is transferred on the D_7-D_0 bus lines while odd addressed byte data (A_0 HIGH) is transferred on the D_{15}-D_8 bus lines. The processor provides two enable signals, BHE and A_0, to selectively allow reading from or writing into either an odd byte location, even byte location, or both. The instruction stream is fetched from memory as words and is addressed internally by the processor to the byte level as necessary.

Memory Reference Need	Segment Register Used	Segment Selection Rule
Instructions	CODE (CS)	Automatic with all instruction prefetch.
Stack	STACK (SS)	All stack pushes and pops. Memory references relative to BP base register except data references.
Local Data	DATA (DS)	Data references when: relative to stack, destination of string operation, or explicitly overridden.
External (Global) Data	EXTRA (ES)	Destination of string operations: Explicitly selected using a segment override.

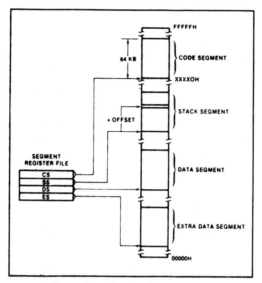

Figure 3a. Memory Organization

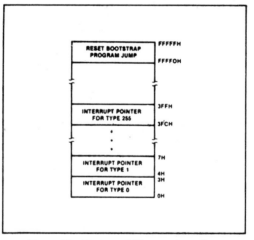

Figure 3b. Reserved Memory Locations

154

In referencing word data the BIU requires one or two memory cycles depending on whether or not the starting byte of the word is on an even or odd address, respectively. Consequently, in referencing word operands performance can be optimized by locating data on even address boundaries. This is an especially useful technique for using the stack, since odd address references to the stack may adversely affect the context switching time for interrupt processing or task multiplexing.

Certain locations in memory are reserved for specific CPU operations (see Figure 3b.) Locations from address FFFF0H through FFFFFH are reserved for operations including a jump to the initial program loading routine. Following RESET, the CPU will always begin execution at location FFFF0H where the jump must be. Locations 00000H through 003FFH are reserved for interrupt operations. Each of the 256 possible interrupt types has its service routine pointed to by a 4-byte pointer element consisting of a 16-bit segment address and a 16-bit offset address. The pointer elements are assumed to have been stored at the respective places in reserved memory prior to occurrence of interrupts.

MINIMUM AND MAXIMUM MODES

The requirements for supporting minimum and maximum iAPX 86/10 systems are sufficiently different that they cannot be done efficiently with 40 uniquely defined pins. Consequently, the 8086 is equipped with a strap pin (MN/$\overline{\text{MX}}$) which defines the system configuration. The definition of a certain subset of the pins changes dependent on the condition of the strap pin. When MN/$\overline{\text{MX}}$ pin is strapped to GND, the 8086 treats pins 24 through 31 in maximum mode. An 8288 bus controller interprets status information coded into $\overline{S}_0, \overline{S}_1, \overline{S}_2$ to generate bus timing and control signals compatible with the MULTIBUS™ architecture. When the MN/$\overline{\text{MX}}$ pin is strapped to V_{CC}, the 8086 generates bus control signals itself on pins 24 through 31, as shown in parentheses in Figure 2. Examples of minimum mode and maximum mode systems are shown in Figure 4.

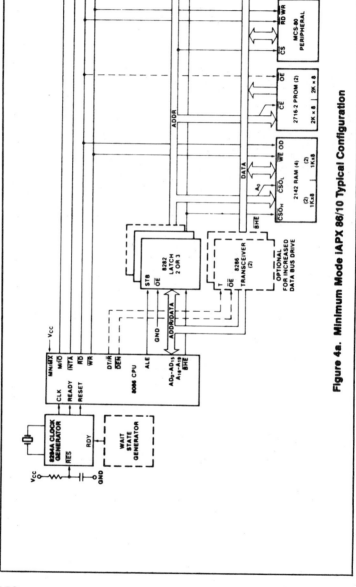

Figure 4a. Minimum Mode iAPX 86/10 Typical Configuration

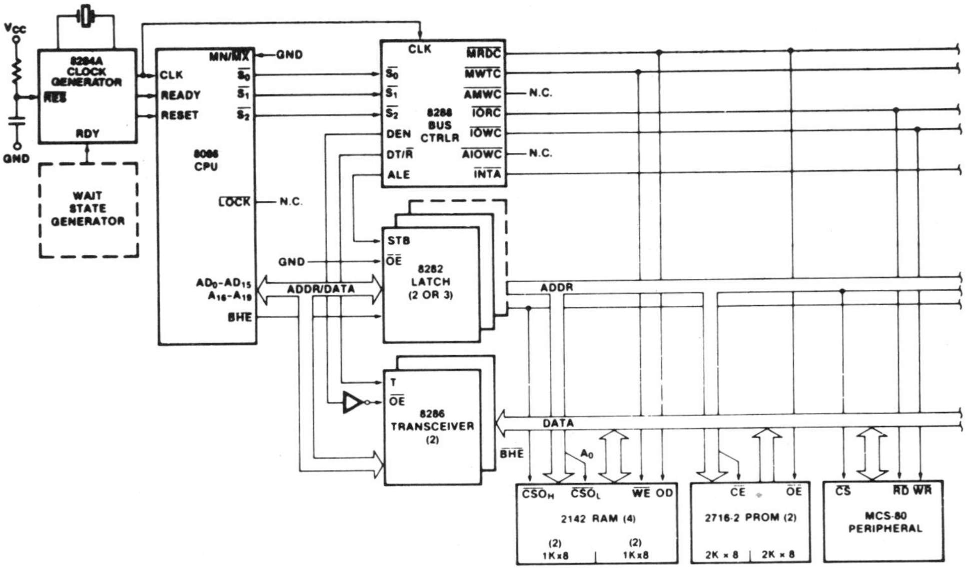

Figure 4b. Maximum Mode IAPX 86/10 Typical Configuration

157

BUS OPERATION

The 86/10 has a combined address and data bus commonly referred to as a time multiplexed bus. This technique provides the most efficient use of pins on the processor while permitting the use of a standard 40-lead package. This "local bus" can be buffered directly and used throughout the system with address latching provided throughout the system and I/O modules. In addition, the bus can also be demultiplexed at the processor with a single set of address latches if a standard non-multiplexed bus is desired for the system.

Each processor bus cycle consists of at least four CLK cycles. These are referred to as T_1, T_2, T_3 and T_4 (see Figure 5). The address is emitted from the processor during T_1 and data transfer occurs on the bus during T_3 and T_4. T_2 is used primarily for changing the direction of the bus during read operations. In the event that a "NOT READY" indication is given by the addressed device, "Wait" states (T_w) are inserted between T_3 and T_4. Each inserted "Wait" state is of the same duration as a CLK cycle. Periods can occur between 8086 bus cycles.

Status bits S_3 through S_7 are multiplexed with high-order address bits and the $\overline{BHE}$ signal, and are therefore valid during T_2 through T_4. S_3 and S_4 indicate which segment register (see Instruction Set description) was used for this bus cycle in forming the address, according to the following table:

S_4	S_3	CHARACTERISTICS
0 (LOW)	0	Alternate Data (extra segment)
0	1	Stack
1 (HIGH)	0	Code or None
1	1	Data

S_5 is a reflection of the PSW interrupt enable bit. S_6=0 and S_7 is a spare status bit.

These are referred to as "idle" states (T_I) or inactive CLK cycles. The processor uses these cycles for internal housekeeping.

During T_1 of any bus cycle the ALE (Address Latch Enable) signal is emitted (by either the processor or the 8288 bus controller, depending on the MN/MX strap). At the trailing edge of this pulse, a valid address and certain status information for the cycle may be latched.

Status bits $\overline{S}_0$, $\overline{S}_1$, and $\overline{S}_2$ are used, in maximum mode, by the bus controller to identify the type of bus transaction according to the following table:

$\overline{S}_2$	$\overline{S}_1$	$\overline{S}_0$	CHARACTERISTICS
0 (LOW)	0	0	Interrupt Acknowledge
0	0	1	Read I/O
0	1	0	Write I/O
0	1	1	Halt
1 (HIGH)	0	0	Instruction Fetch
1	0	1	Read Data from Memory
1	1	0	Write Data to Memory
1	1	1	Passive (no bus cycle)

I/O ADDRESSING

In the 86/10, I/O operations can address up to a maximum of 64K I/O byte registers or 32K I/O word registers. The I/O address appears in the same format as the memory address on bus lines A_{15}-A_0. The address lines A_{19}-A_{16} are zero in I/O operations. The variable I/O instructions which use register DX as a pointer have full address capability while the direct I/O instructions directly address one or two of the 256 I/O byte locations in page 0 of the I/O address space.

I/O ports are addressed in the same manner as memory locations. Even addressed bytes are transferred on the D_7-D_0 bus lines and odd addressed bytes on D_{15}-D_8. Care must be taken to assure that each register within an 8-bit peripheral located on the lower portion of the bus be addressed as even.

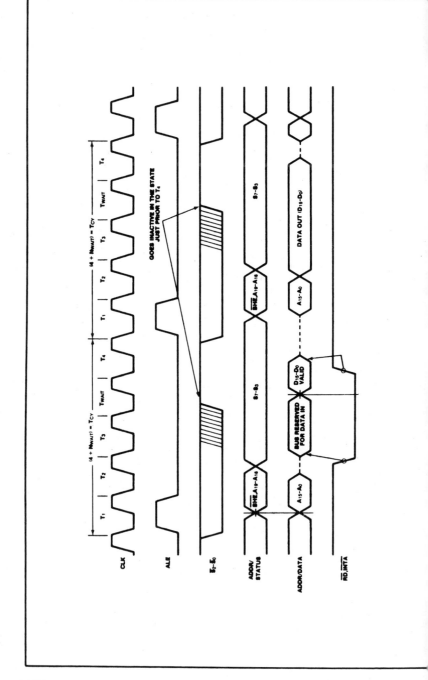

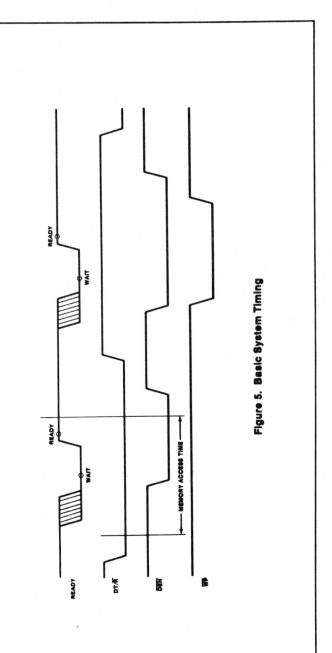

Figure 5. Basic System Timing

EXTERNAL INTERFACE

PROCESSOR RESET AND INITIALIZATION

Processor initialization or start up is accomplished with activation (HIGH) of the RESET pin. The 8086 RESET is required to be HIGH for greater than 4 CLK cycles. The 8086 will terminate operations on the high-going edge of RESET and will remain dormant as long as RESET is HIGH. The low-going transition of RESET triggers an internal reset sequence for approximately 10 CLK cycles. After this interval the 8086 operates normally beginning with the instruction in absolute location FFFF0H (see Figure 3B). The details of this operation are specified in the Instruction Set description of the MCS-86 Family User's Manual. The RESET input is internally synchronized to the processor clock. At initialization the HIGH-to-LOW transition of RESET must occur no sooner than 50 μs after power-up, to allow complete initialization of the 8086.

NMI may not be asserted prior to the 2nd CLK cycle following the end of RESET.

INTERRUPT OPERATIONS

Interrupt operations fall into two classes; software or hardware initiated. The software initiated interrupts and software aspects of hardware interrupts are specified in the Instruction Set description. Hardware interrupts can be classified as non-maskable or maskable.

sequence, which is used to "vector" through the appropriate element to the new interrupt service program location.

NON-MASKABLE INTERRUPT (NMI)

The processor provides a single non-maskable interrupt pin (NMI) which has higher priority than the maskable interrupt request pin (INTR). A typical use would be to activate a power failure routine. The NMI is edge-triggered on a LOW-to-HIGH transition. The activation of this pin causes a type 2 interrupt. (See Instruction Set description.)

NMI is required to have a duration in the HIGH state of greater than two CLK cycles, but is not required to be synchronized to the clock. Any high-going transition of NMI is latched on-chip and will be serviced at the end of the current instruction or between whole moves of a block-type instruction. Worst case response to NMI would be for multiply, divide, and variable shift instructions. There is no specification on the occurrence of the low-going edge; it may occur before, during, or after the servicing of NMI. Another high-going edge triggers another response if it occurs after the start of the NMI procedure. The signal must be free of logical spikes in general and be free of bounces on the low-going edge to avoid triggering extraneous responses.

MASKABLE INTERRUPT (INTR)

The 86/10 provides a single interrupt request input (INTR)

Interrupts result in a transfer of control to a new program location. A 256-element table containing address pointers to the interrupt service-program locations resides in absolute locations 0 through 3FFH (see Figure 3b), which are reserved for this purpose. Each element in the table is 4 bytes in size and corresponds to an interrupt "type". An interrupting device supplies an 8-bit type number, during the interrupt acknowledge

which can be masked internally by software with the resetting of the interrupt enable FLAG status bit. The interrupt request signal is level triggered. It is internally synchronized during each clock cycle on the high-going edge of CLK. To be responded to, INTR must be present (HIGH) during the clock period preceding the end of the current instruction or the end of a whole move for a block-type instruction. During the interrupt response sequence further interrupts are disabled. The enable bit is reset as part of the response to any interrupt (INTR, NMI, software interrupt or single-step), although the

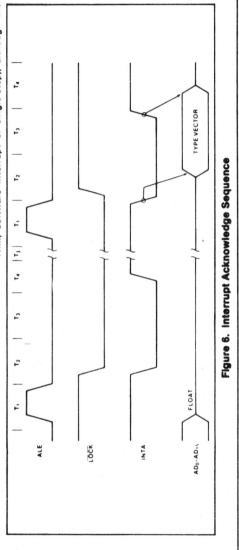

Figure 6. Interrupt Acknowledge Sequence

FLAGS register which is automatically pushed onto the stack reflects the state of the processor prior to the interrupt. Until the old FLAGS register is restored the enable bit will be zero unless specifically set by an instruction.

During the response sequence (figure 6) the processor executes two successive (back-to-back) interrupt acknowledge cycles. The 8086 emits the LOCK signal from T_2 of the first bus cycle until T_2 of the second. A local bus "hold" request will not be honored until the end of the second bus cycle. In the second bus cycle a byte is fetched from the external interrupt system (e.g., 8259A PIC) which identifies the source (type) of the interrupt. This byte is multiplied by four and used as a pointer into the interrupt vector lookup table. An INTR signal left HIGH will be continually responded to within the limitations of the enable bit and sample period. The INTERRUPT RETURN instruction includes a FLAGS pop which returns the status of the original interrupt enable bit when it restores the FLAGS.

HALT

When a software "HALT" instruction is executed the processor indicates that it is entering the "HALT" state in one of two ways depending upon which mode is strapped. In minimum mode, the processor issues one ALE with no qualifying bus control signals. In Maximum Mode, the processor issues appropriate HALT status on $\overline{S}_2\overline{S}_1\overline{S}_0$ and the 8288 bus controller issues one ALE. The 8086 will not leave the "HALT" state when a local bus

to become active. It must remain active for at least 5 CLK cycles. The WAIT instruction is re-executed repeatedly until that time. This activity does not consume bus cycles. The processor remains in an idle state while waiting. All 8086 drivers go to 3-state OFF if bus "Hold" is entered. If interrupts are enabled, they may occur while the processor is waiting. When this occurs the processor fetches the WAIT instruction one extra time, processes the interrupt, and then re-fetches and re-executes the WAIT instruction upon returning from the interrupt.

BASIC SYSTEM TIMING

Typical system configurations for the processor operating in minimum mode and in maximum mode are shown in Figures 4a and 4b, respectively. In minimum mode, the MN/$\overline{MX}$ pin is strapped to V_{CC} and the processor emits bus control signals in a manner similar to the 8085. In maximum mode, the MN/$\overline{MX}$ pin is strapped to V_{SS} and the processor emits coded status information which the 8288 bus controller uses to generate MULTIBUS compatible bus control signals. Figure 5 illustrates the signal timing relationships.

AX	AH	AL	ACCUMULATOR
BX	BH	BL	BASE
CX	CH	CL	COUNT
DX	DH	DL	DATA

"hold" is entered while in "HALT". In this case, the processor reissues the HALT indicator. An interrupt request or RESET will force the 8086 out of the "HALT" state.

READ/MODIFY/WRITE (SEMAPHORE) OPERATIONS VIA LOCK

The LOCK status information is provided by the processor when directly consecutive bus cycles are required during the execution of an instruction. This provides the processor with the capability of performing read/modify/write operations on memory (via the Exchange Register With Memory instruction, for example) without the possibility of another system bus master receiving intervening memory cycles. This is useful in multiprocessor system configurations to accomplish "test and set lock" operations. The LOCK signal is activated (forced LOW) in the clock cycle following the one in which the software "LOCK" prefix instruction is decoded by the EU. It is deactivated at the end of the last bus cycle of the instruction following the "LOCK" prefix instruction. While LOCK is active a request on a RQ/GT pin will be recorded and then honored at the end of the LOCK.

EXTERNAL SYNCHRONIZATION VIA TEST

As an alternative to the interrupts and general I/O capabilities, the 8086 provides a single software-testable input known as the TEST signal. At any time the program may execute a WAIT instruction. If at that time the TEST signal is inactive (HIGH), program execution becomes suspended while the processor waits for TEST

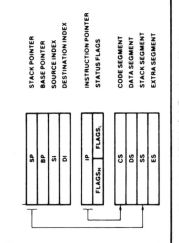

Figure 7. IAPX 86/10 Register Model

SYSTEM TIMING — MINIMUM SYSTEM

The read cycle begins in T_1 with the assertion of the Address Latch Enable (ALE) signal. The trailing (low-going) edge of this signal is used to latch the address information, which is valid on the local bus at this time, into the 8282/8283 latch. The BHE and A_0 signals address the low, high, or both bytes. From T_1 to T_4 the M/IO signal indicates a memory or I/O operation. At T_2 the address is removed from the local bus and the bus goes to a high impedance state. The read control signal is also asserted at T_2. The read (RD) signal causes the addressed device to enable its data bus drivers to the local bus. Some time later valid data will be available on the bus and the addressed device will drive the READY line HIGH. When the processor returns the read signal to a HIGH level, the addressed device will again 3-state its bus drivers. If a transceiver (8286/8287) is required to buffer the 8086 local bus, signals DT/$\overline{R}$ and $\overline{DEN}$ are provided by the 8086.

A write cycle also begins with the assertion of ALE and the emission of the address. The M/$\overline{IO}$ signal is again asserted to indicate a memory or I/O write operation. In the T_2 immediately following the address emission the processor emits the data to be written into the addressed location. This data remains valid until the middle of T_4. During T_2, T_3, and T_W the processor asserts the write control signal. The write ($\overline{WR}$) signal becomes active at the beginning of T_2 as opposed to the read which is delayed somewhat into T_2 to provide time for the bus to float.

The $\overline{BHE}$ and A_0 signals are used to select the proper byte(s) of the memory/IO word to be read or written according to the following table:

read ($\overline{RD}$) signal and the address bus is floated. (See Figure 6.) In the second of two successive INTA cycles, a byte of information is read from bus lines D_7–D_0 as supplied by the interrupt system logic (i.e., 8259A Priority Interrupt Controller). This byte identifies the source (type) of the interrupt. It is multiplied by four and used as a pointer into an interrupt vector lookup table, as described earlier.

BUS TIMING—MEDIUM SIZE SYSTEMS

For medium size systems the MN/$\overline{MX}$ pin is connected to V_{SS} and the 8288 Bus Controller is added to the system as well as an 8282/8283 latch for latching the system address, and a 8286/8287 transceiver to allow for bus loading greater than the 8086 is capable of handling. Signals ALE, $\overline{DEN}$, and DT/$\overline{R}$ are generated by the 8288 instead of the processor in this configuration although their timing remains relatively the same. The 8086 status outputs ($\overline{S}_2$, $\overline{S}_1$, and $\overline{S}_0$) provide type-of-cycle information and become

8288 inputs. This bus cycle information specifies read (code, data, or I/O), write (data or I/O), interrupt acknowledge, or software halt. The 8288 thus issues control signals specifying memory read or write, I/O read or write, or interrupt acknowledge. The 8288 provides two types of write strobes, normal and advanced, to be applied as required. The normal write strobes have data valid at the leading edge of write. The advanced write strobes have the same timing as read strobes, and hence data isn't valid at the leading edge of write. The 8286/8287 transceiver receives the usual T and OE inputs from the 8288's DT/$\overline{R}$ and DEN.

The pointer into the interrupt vector table, which is passed during the second INTA cycle, can derive from an 8259A located on either the local bus or the system bus. If the master 8259A Priority Interrupt Controller is positioned on the local bus, a TTL gate is required to disable the 8286/8287 transceiver when reading from the master 8259A during the interrupt acknowledge sequence and software "poll".

$\overline{BHE}$	A0	CHARACTERISTICS
0	0	Whole word
0	1	Upper byte from/ to odd address
1	0	Lower byte from/ to even address
1	1	None

I/O ports are addressed in the same manner as memory location. Even addressed bytes are transferred on the D_7–D_0 bus lines and odd addressed bytes on D_{15}–D_8.

The basic difference between the interrupt acknowledge cycle and a read cycle is that the interrupt acknowledge signal ($\overline{INTA}$) is asserted in place of the

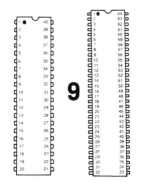

9

Intel 8088 Spec Sheets

---

iAPX 88/10
8-BIT HMOS MICROPROCESSOR
8088/8088-2

- ■ 8-Bit Data Bus Interface
- ■ 16-Bit Internal Architecture
- ■ Direct Addressing Capability to 1 Mbyte of Memory
- ■ Direct Software Compatibility with iAPX 86/10 (8086 CPU)
- ■ 14-Word by 16-Bit Register Set with Symmetrical Operations
- ■ 24 Operand Addressing Modes
- ■ Byte, Word, and Block Operations
- ■ 8-Bit and 16-Bit Signed and Unsigned Arithmetic in Binary or Decimal, Including Multiply and Divide
- ■ Compatible with 8155-2, 8755A-2 and 8185-2 Multiplexed Peripherals
- ■ Two Clock Rates:
  5 MHz for 8088   8 MHz for 8088-2

The Intel® iAPX 88/10 is a new generation, high performance microprocessor implemented in N-channel, depletion load, silicon gate technology (HMOS), and packaged in a 40-pin CerDIP package. The processor has attributes of both 8- and 16-bit microprocessors. It is directly compatible with iAPX 86/10 software and 8080/8085 hardware and peripherals.

The material in this chapter is by courtesy of Intel Corporation, copyright 1977.

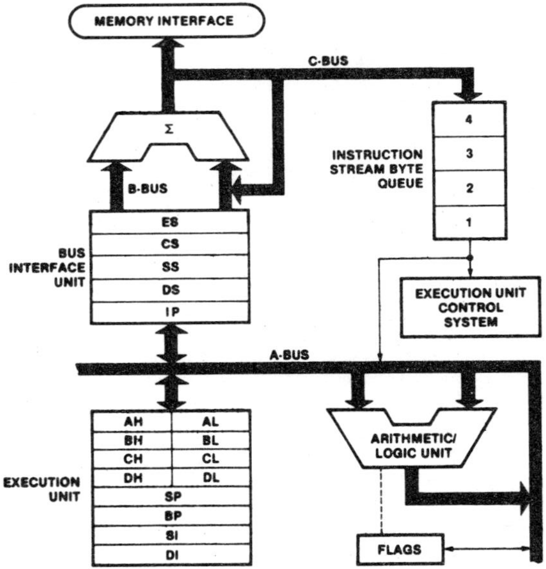

Figure 1. IAPX 88/10 CPU Functional Block Diagram

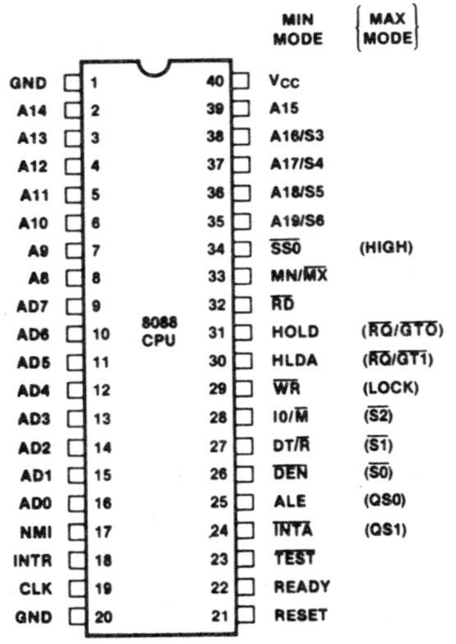

Figure 2. IAPX 88/10 Pin Configuration

Table 1. Pin Description

The following pin function descriptions are for 8088 systems in either minimum or maximum mode. The "local bus" in these descriptions is the direct multiplexed bus interface connection to the 8088 (without regard to additional bus buffers).

Symbol	Pin No.	Type	Name and Function
AD7–AD0	9-16	I/O	**Address Data Bus:** These lines constitute the time multiplexed memory/IO address (T1) and data (T2, T3, Tw, and T4) bus. These lines are active HIGH and float to 3-state OFF during interrupt acknowledge and local bus "hold acknowledge".
A15–A8	2-8, 39	O	**Address Bus:** These lines provide address bits 8 through 15 for the entire bus cycle (T1–T4). These lines do not have to be latched by ALE to remain valid. A15–A8 are active HIGH and float to 3-state OFF during interrupt acknowledge and local bus "hold acknowledge".
A19/S6, A18/S5, A17/S4, A16/S3	34-38	O	**Address/Status:** During T1, these are the four most significant address lines for memory operations. During I/O operations, these lines are LOW. During memory and I/O operations, status information is available on these lines during T2, T3, Tw, and T4. The status of the interrupt enable flag bit (S5) is updated at the beginning of each clock cycle. S4 and S3 are encoded as shown. This information indicates which segment register is presently being used for data accessing. These lines float to 3-state OFF during local bus "hold acknowledge".

S4	S3	CHARACTERISTICS
0 (LOW)	0	Alternate Data
0	1	Stack
1 (HIGH)	0	Code or None
1	1	Data

S6 is 0 (LOW)

170

RD	32	O	**Read:** Read strobe indicates that the processor is performing a memory or I/O read cycle, depending on the state of the IO/M̄ pin or S2. This signal is used to read devices which reside on the 8088 local bus. RD̄ is active LOW during T2, T3 and Tw of any read cycle, and is guaranteed to remain HIGH in T2 until the 8088 local bus has floated. This signal floats to 3-state OFF in "hold acknowledge".
READY	22	I	**READY:** is the acknowledgement from the addressed memory or I/O device that it will complete the data transfer. The RDY signal from memory or I/O is synchronized by the 8284 clock generator to form READY. This signal is active HIGH. The 8088 READY input is not synchronized. Correct operation is not guaranteed if the set up and hold times are not met.
INTR	18	I	**Interrupt Request:** is a level triggered input which is sampled during the last clock cycle of each instruction to determine if the processor should enter into an interrupt acknowledge operation. A subroutine is vectored to via an interrupt vector lookup table located in system memory. It can be internally masked by software resetting the interrupt enable bit. INTR is internally synchronized. This signal is active HIGH.
TEST	23	I	**TEST:** input is examined by the "wait for test" instruction. If the TEST input is LOW, execution continues, otherwise the processor waits in an "idle" state. This input is synchronized internally during each clock cycle on the leading edge of CLK.
NMI	17	I	**Non-Maskable Interrupt:** is an edge triggered input which causes a type 2 interrupt. A subroutine is vectored to via an interrupt vector lookup table located in system memory. NMI is not maskable internally by software. A transition from a LOW to HIGH initiates the interrupt at the end of the current instruction. This input is internally synchronized.

Table 1. Pin Description (Continued)

Symbol	Pin No.	Type	Name and Function
RESET	21	I	**RESET**: causes the processor to immediately terminate its present activity. The signal must be active HIGH for at least four clock cycles. It restarts execution, as described in the instruction set description, when RESET returns LOW. RESET is internally synchronized.
CLK	19	I	**Clock**: provides the basic timing for the processor and bus controller. It is asymmetric with a 33% duty cycle to provide optimized internal timing.
V$_{CC}$	40		**V$_{CC}$**: is the +5V ±10% power supply pin.
GND	1, 20		**GND**: are the ground pins.
MN/$\overline{\text{MX}}$	33	I	**Minimum/Maximum**: indicates what mode the processor is to operate in. The two modes are discussed in the following sections.

The following pin function descriptions are for the 8088 minimum mode (i.e., MN/MX = V$_{CC}$). Only the pin functions which are unique to minimum mode are described; all other pin functions are as described above.

IO/$\overline{\text{M}}$	28	O	**Status Line**: is an inverted maximum mode $\overline{S2}$. It is used to distinguish a memory access from an I/O access. IO/$\overline{\text{M}}$ becomes valid in the T4 preceding a bus cycle and remains valid until the final T4 of the cycle (I/O=HIGH, M=LOW). IO/$\overline{\text{M}}$ floats to 3-state OFF in local bus "hold acknowledge".
$\overline{\text{WR}}$	29	O	**Write**: strobe indicates that the processor is performing a write memory or write I/O cycle, depending on the state of the IO/$\overline{\text{M}}$ signal. $\overline{\text{WR}}$ is active for T2, T3, and Tw of any write cycle. It is active LOW, and floats to 3-state OFF in local bus "hold acknowledge".
$\overline{\text{INTA}}$	24	O	**INTA**: is used as a read strobe for interrupt acknowledge cycles. It is active LOW during T2, T3, and Tw of each interrupt acknowledge cycle.

Name	Pin	Type	Description
ALE	25	O	**Address Latch Enable:** is provided by the processor to latch the address into the 8282/8283 address latch. It is a HIGH pulse active during clock low of T1 of any bus cycle. Note that ALE is never floated.
DT/R̄	27	O	**Data Transmit/Receive:** is needed in a minimum system that desires to use an 8286/8287 data bus transceiver. It is used to control the direction of data flow through the transceiver. Logically, DT/R̄ is equivalent to S̄1 in the maximum mode, and its timing is the same as for IO/M̄ (T=HIGH, R=LOW). This signal floats to 3-state OFF in local "hold acknowledge".
DEN̄	26	O	**Data Enable:** is provided as an output enable for the 8286/8287 in a minimum system which uses the transceiver. DEN̄ is active LOW during each memory and I/O access, and for INTĀ cycles. For a read or INTĀ cycle, it is active from the middle of T2 until the middle of T4, while for a write cycle, it is active from the beginning of T2 until the middle of T4. DEN̄ floats to 3-state OFF during local bus "hold acknowledge".
HOLD, HLDA	30,31	I, O	**HOLD:** indicates that another master is requesting a local bus "hold". To be acknowledged, HOLD must be active HIGH. The processor receiving the "hold" request will issue HLDA (HIGH) as an acknowledgement, in the middle of a T4 or Ti clock cycle. Simultaneous with the issuance of HLDA the processor will float the local bus and control lines. After HOLD is detected as being LOW, the processor lowers HLDA, and when the processor needs to run another cycle, it will again drive the local bus and control lines. Hold is not an asynchronous input. External synchronization should be provided if the system cannot otherwise guarantee the set up time.
SSŌ	34	O	**Status line:** is logically equivalent to S̄0 in the maximum mode. The combination of SSŌ, IO/M̄ and DT/R̄ allows the system to completely decode the current bus cycle status.

IO/M̄	DT/R̄	SSŌ	CHARACTERISTICS
1 (HIGH)	0	0	Interrupt Acknowledge
	0	1	Read I/O port
	1	0	Write I/O port
	1	1	Halt
0 (LOW)	0	0	Code access
	0	1	Read memory
	1	0	Write memory
	1	1	Passive

Table 1. Pin Description (Continued)

Symbol	Pin No.	Type	Name and Function
RESET	21	I	**RESET:** causes the processor to immediately terminate its present activity. The signal must be active HIGH for at least four clock cycles. It restarts execution, as described in the instruction set description, when RESET returns LOW. RESET is internally synchronized.
CLK	19	I	**Clock:** provides the basic timing for the processor and bus controller. It is asymmetric with a 33% duty cycle to provide optimized internal timing.
V$_{CC}$	40		V$_{CC}$: is the +5V ±10% power supply pin.
GND	1, 20		**GND:** are the ground pins.
MN/$\overline{MX}$	33	I	**Minimum/Maximum:** indicates what mode the processor is to operate in. The two modes are discussed in the following sections.

The following pin function descriptions are for the 8088 minimum mode (i.e., MN/MX = V$_{CC}$). Only the pin functions which are unique to minimum mode are described; all other pin functions are as described above.

IO/$\overline{M}$	28	O	**Status Line:** is an inverted maximum mode $\overline{S2}$. It is used to distinguish a memory access from an I/O access. IO/$\overline{M}$ becomes valid in the T4 preceding a bus cycle and remains valid until the final T4 of the cycle (I/O=HIGH, M=LOW). IO/$\overline{M}$ floats to 3-state OFF in local bus "hold acknowledge".
$\overline{WR}$	29	O	**Write:** strobe indicates that the processor is performing a write memory or write I/O cycle, depending on the state of the IO/$\overline{M}$ signal. WR is active for T2, T3, and Tw of any write cycle. It is active LOW, and floats to 3-state OFF in local bus "hold acknowledge".
$\overline{INTA}$	24	O	**INTA:** is used as a read strobe for interrupt acknowledge cycles. It is active LOW during T2, T3, and Tw of each interrupt acknowledge cycle.

Signal	Pin	Type	Description
ALE	25	O	**Address Latch Enable:** is provided by the processor to latch the address into the 8282/8283 address latch. It is a HIGH pulse active during clock low of T1 of any bus cycle. Note that ALE is never floated.
DT/R̄	27	O	**Data Transmit/Receive:** is needed in a minimum system that desires to use an 8286/8287 data bus transceiver. It is used to control the direction of data flow through the transceiver. Logically, DT/R̄ is equivalent to S̄1 in the maximum mode, and its timing is the same as for IO/M̄ (T=HIGH, R=LOW). This signal floats to 3-state OFF in local "hold acknowledge".
DEN̄	26	O	**Data Enable:** is provided as an output enable for the 8286/8287 in a minimum system which uses the transceiver. DEN̄ is active LOW during each memory and I/O access, and for INTĀ cycles. For a read or INTĀ cycle, it is active from the middle of T2 until the middle of T4, while for a write cycle, it is active from the beginning of T2 until the middle of T4. DEN̄ floats to 3-state OFF during local bus "hold acknowledge".
HOLD, HLDA	30,31	I, O	**HOLD:** indicates that another master is requesting a local bus "hold". To be acknowledged, HOLD must be active HIGH. The processor receiving the "hold" request will issue HLDA (HIGH) as an acknowledgement, in the middle of a T4 or Tl clock cycle. Simultaneous with the issuance of HLDA the processor will float the local bus and control lines. After HOLD is detected as being LOW, the processor lowers HLDA, and when the processor needs to run another cycle, it will again drive the local bus and control lines. Hold is not an asynchronous input. External synchronization should be provided if the system cannot otherwise guarantee the set up time.
SSO̅	34	O	**Status line:** is logically equivalent to S̄0 in the maximum mode. The combination of SSO̅, IO/M̄ and DT/R̄ allows the system to completely decode the current bus cycle status.

Table 1. Pin Description (Continued)

Symbol	Pin No.	Type	Name and Function
LOCK	29	O	LOCK: indicates that other system bus masters are not to gain control of the system bus while LOCK is active (LOW). The LOCK signal is activated by the "LOCK" prefix instruction and remains active until the completion of the next instruction. This signal is active LOW, and floats to 3-state off in "hold acknowledge".
QS1, QS0	24, 25	O	Queue Status: provide status to allow external tracking of the internal 8088 instruction queue. The queue status is valid during the CLK cycle after which the queue operation is performed.
—	34	O	Pin 34 is always high in the maximum mode.

QS1	QS0	CHARACTERISTICS
0 (LOW)	0	No operation
0	1	First byte of opcode from queue
1 (HIGH)	0	Empty the queue
1	1	Subsequent byte from queue

FUNCTIONAL DESCRIPTION

Memory Organization

The processor provides a 20-bit address to memory which locates the byte being referenced. The memory is organized as a linear array of up to 1 million bytes, addressed as 00000(H) to FFFFF(H). The memory is logically divided into code, data, extra data, and stack segments of up to 64K bytes each, with each segment falling on 16-byte boundaries. (See Figure 3.)

All memory references are made relative to base addresses contained in high speed segment registers. The segment types were chosen based on the addressing needs of programs. The segment register to be selected is automatically chosen according to the rules of the following table. All information in one segment type share the same logical attributes (e.g. code or data). By structuring memory into relocatable areas of similar characteristics and by automatically selecting segment registers, programs are shorter, faster, and more structured.

Word (16-bit) operands can be located on even or odd address boundaries. For address and data operands, the least significant byte of the word is stored in the lower valued address location and the most significant byte in the next higher address location. The BIU will automatically execute two fetch or write cycles for 16-bit operands.

Certain locations in memory are reserved for specific

CPU operations. (See Figure 4.) Locations from addresses FFFF0H through FFFFFH are reserved for operations including a jump to the initial system initialization routine. Following RESET, the CPU will always begin execution at location FFFF0H where the jump must be located. Locations 00000H through 003FFH are reserved for interrupt operations. Four-byte pointers consisting of a 16-bit segment address and a 16-bit offset address direct program flow to one of the 256 possible interrupt service routines. The pointer elements are assumed to have been stored at their respective places in reserved memory prior to the occurrence of interrupts.

Minimum and Maximum Modes

The requirements for supporting minimum and maximum 8088 systems are sufficiently different that they cannot be done efficiently with 40 uniquely defined pins. Consequently, the 8088 is equipped with a strap pin (MN/MX) which defines the system configuration. The definition of a certain subset of the pins changes, dependent on the condition of the strap pin. When the MN/MX pin is strapped to GND, the 8088 defines pins 24 through 31 and 34 in maximum mode. When the MN/MX pin is strapped to V$_{CC}$, the 8088 generates bus control signals itself on pins 24 through 31 and 34.

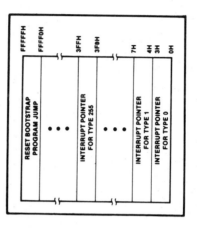

Figure 4. Reserved Memory Locations

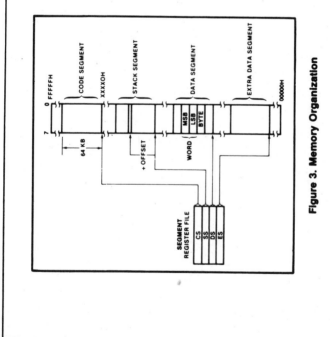

Figure 3. Memory Organization

178

Memory Reference Need	Segment Register Used	Segment Selection Rule
Instructions	CODE (CS)	Automatic with all instruction prefetch.
Stack	STACK (SS)	All stack pushes and pops. Memory references relative to BP base register except data references.
Local Data	DATA (DS)	Data references when: relative to stack, destination of string operation, or explicitly overridden.
External (Global) Data	EXTRA (ES)	Destination of string operations: Explicitly selected using a segment override.

The minimum mode 8088 can be used with either a multiplexed or demultiplexed bus. The multiplexed bus configuration is compatible with the MCS-85™ multiplexed bus peripherals (8155, 8156, 8355, 8755A, and 8185). This configuration (See Figure 5) provides the user with a minimum chip count system. This architecture provides the 8088 processing power in a highly integrated form.

The demultiplexed mode requires one latch (for 64K addressability) or two latches (for a full megabyte of addressing). A third latch can be used for buffering if the address bus loading requires it. An 8286 or 8287 transceiver can also be used if data bus buffering is required. (See Figure 6.) The 8088 provides DEN and DT/R to control the transceiver, and ALE to latch the addresses. This configuration of the minimum mode provides the standard demultiplexed bus structure with heavy bus buffering and relaxed bus timing requirements.

The maximum mode employs the 8288 bus controller. (See Figure 7.) The 8288 decodes status lines S0, S1, and S2, and provides the system with all bus control signals. Moving the bus control to the 8288 provides better source and sink current capability to the control lines, and frees the 8088 pins for extended large system features. Hardware lock, queue status, and two request/grant interfaces are provided by the 8088 in maximum mode. These features allow co-processors in local bus and remote bus configurations.

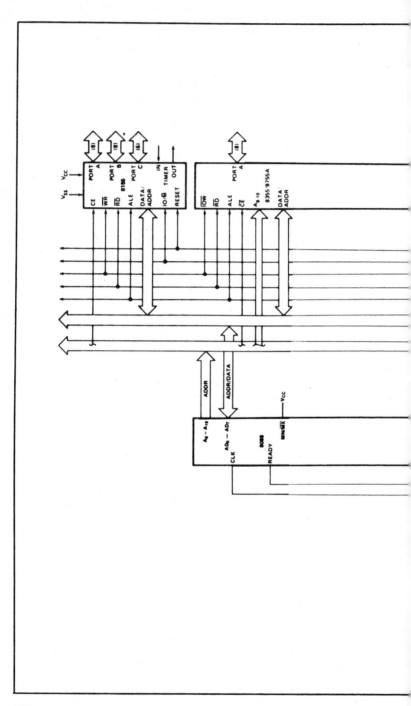

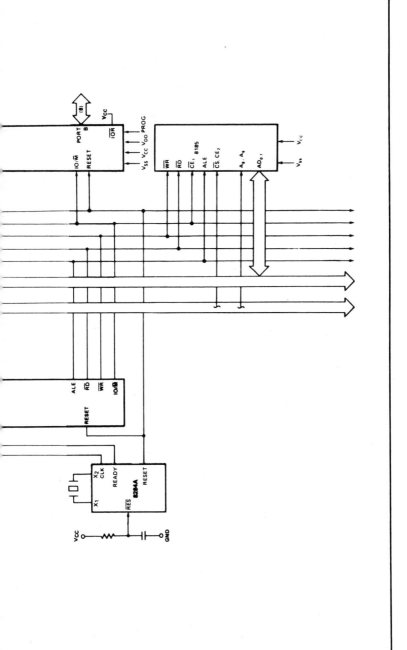

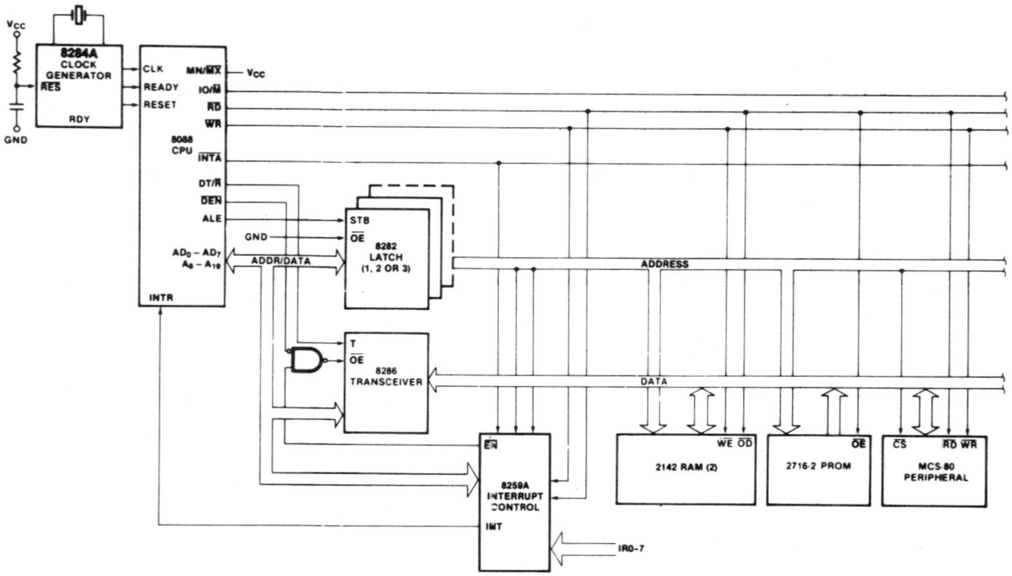

Figure 6. Demultiplexed Bus Configuration

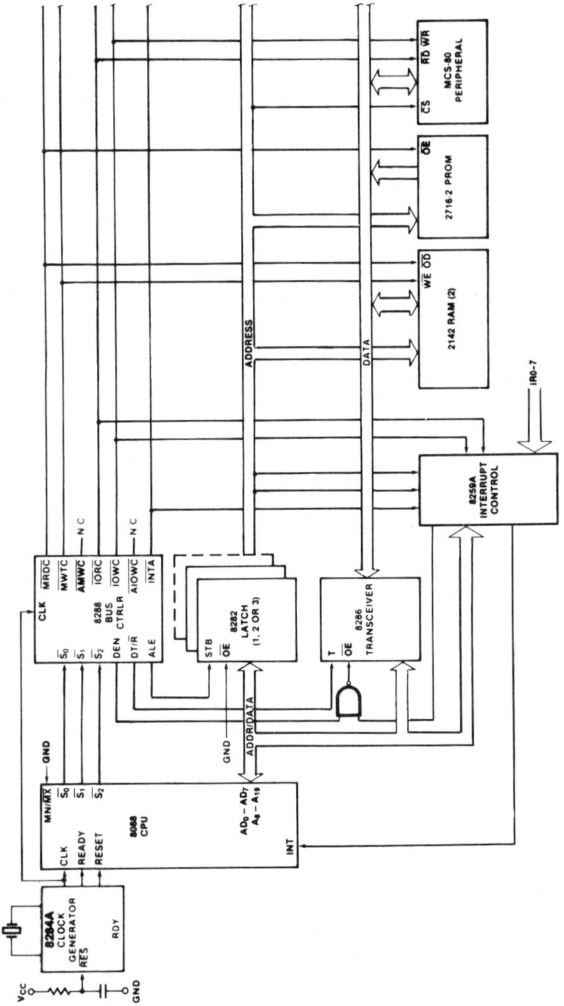

Figure 7. Fully Buffered System Using Bus Controller

183

Bus Operation

The 8088 address/data bus is broken into three parts — the lower eight bit address/data bits (AD0–AD7), the middle eight address bits (A8–A15), and the upper four address bits (A16–A19). The address/data bits and the highest four address bits are time multiplexed. This technique provides the most efficient use of pins on the processor, permitting the use of a standard 40 lead package. The middle eight address bits are not multiplexed, i.e. they remain valid throughout each bus cycle. In addi-

tion, the bus can be demultiplexed at the processor with a single address latch if a standard, non-multiplexed bus is desired for the system.

Each processor bus cycle consists of at least four CLK cycles. These are referred to as T1, T2, T3, and T4. (See Figure 8). The address is emitted from the processor during T1 and data transfer occurs on the bus during T3 and T4. T2 is used primarily for changing the direction of the bus during read operations. In the event that a "NOT READY" indication is given by the addressed device.

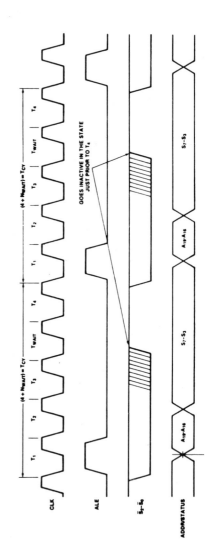

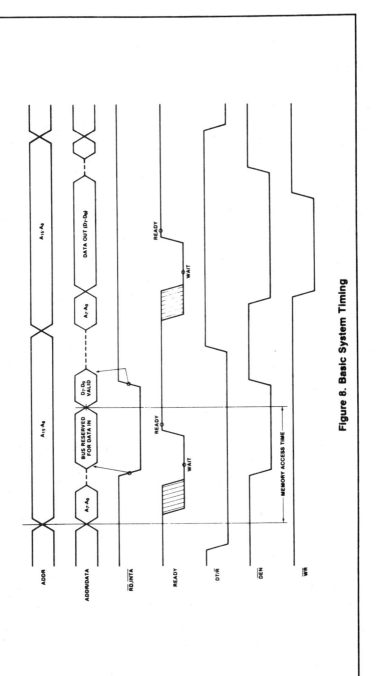

Figure 8. Basic System Timing

185

"wait" states (Tw) are inserted between T3 and T4. Each inserted "wait" state is of the same duration as a CLK cycle. Periods can occur between 8088 driven bus cycles. These are referred to as "idle" states (Ti), or inactive CLK cycles. The processor uses these cycles for internal housekeeping.

During T1 of any bus cycle, the ALE (address latch enable) signal is emitted (by either the processor or the 8288 bus controller, depending on the MN/$\overline{\text{MX}}$ strap). At the trailing edge of this pulse, a valid address and certain status information for the cycle may be latched.

Status bits $\overline{S0}$, $\overline{S1}$, and $\overline{S2}$ are used by the bus controller, in maximum mode, to identify the type of bus transaction according to the following table:

$\overline{S}_2$	$\overline{S}_1$	$\overline{S}_0$	CHARACTERISTICS
0 (LOW)	0	0	Interrupt Acknowledge
0	0	1	Read I/O
0	1	0	Write I/O
0	1	1	Halt
1 (HIGH)	0	0	Instruction Fetch
1	0	1	Read Data from Memory
1	1	0	Write Data to Memory
1	1	1	Passive (no bus cycle)

Status bits S3 through S6 are multiplexed with high order address bits and are therefore valid during T2 through T4.

EXTERNAL INTERFACE

Processor Reset and Initialization

Processor initialization or start up is accomplished with activation (HIGH) of the RESET pin. The 8088 RESET is required to be HIGH for greater than four clock cycles. The 8088 will terminate operations on the high-going edge of RESET and will remain dormant as long as RESET is HIGH. The low-going transition of RESET triggers an internal reset sequence for approximately 7 clock cycles. After this interval the 8088 operates normally, beginning with the instruction in absolute location FFF0H. (See Figure 4.) The RESET input is internally synchronized to the processor clock. At initialization, the HIGH to LOW transition of RESET must occur no sooner than 50 μs after power up, to allow complete initialization of the 8088.

If INTR is asserted sooner than nine clock cycles after the end of RESET, the processor may execute one instruction before responding to the interrupt.

All 3-state outputs float to 3-state OFF during RESET. Status is active in the idle state for the first clock after RESET becomes active and then floats to 3-state OFF.

Interrupt Operations

Interrupt operations fall into two classes: software or hardware initiated. The software initiated interrupts and software aspects of hardware interrupts are specified in the instruction set description in the iAPX 88 Book or the

S3 and S4 indicate which segment register was used for this bus cycle in forming the address according to the following table:

S4	S3	CHARACTERISTICS
0 (LOW)	0	Alternate Data (extra segment)
0	1	Stack
1 (HIGH)	0	Code or None
1	1	Data

S5 is a reflection of the PSW interrupt enable bit. S6 is always equal to 0.

I/O Addressing

In the 8088, I/O operations can address up to a maximum of 64K I/O registers. The I/O address appears in the same format as the memory address on bus lines A15-A0. The address lines A19-A16 are zero in I/O operations. The variable I/O instructions, which use register DX as a pointer, have full address capability, while the direct I/O instructions directly address one or two of the 256 I/O byte locations in page 0 of the I/O address space. I/O ports are addressed in the same manner as memory locations.

Designers familiar with the 8085 or upgrading an 8085 design should note that the 8085 addresses I/O with an 8-bit address on both halves of the 16-bit address bus. The 8088 uses a full 16-bit address on its lower 16 address lines.

iAPX 86, 88 User's Manual. Hardware interrupts can be classified as nonmaskable or maskable.

Interrupts result in a transfer of control to a new program location. A 256 element table containing address pointers to the interrupt service program locations resides in absolute locations 0 through 3FFH (see Figure 4), which are reserved for this purpose. Each element in the table is 4 bytes in size and corresponds to an interrupt "type." An interrupting device supplies an 8-bit type number, during the interrupt acknowledge sequence, which is used to vector through the appropriate element to the new interrupt service program location.

Non-Maskable Interrupt (NMI)

The processor provides a single non-maskable interrupt (NMI) pin which has higher priority than the maskable interrupt request (INTR) pin. A typical use would be to activate a power failure routine. The NMI is edge-triggered on a LOW to HIGH transition. The activation of this pin causes a type 2 interrupt.

NMI is required to have a duration in the HIGH state of greater than two clock cycles, but is not required to be synchronized to the clock. Any higher going transition of NMI is latched on-chip and will be serviced at the end of the current instruction or between whole moves (2 bytes in the case of word moves) of a block type instruction. Worst case response to NMI would be for multiply, divide, and variable shift instructions. There is no specification on the occurrence of the low-going edge; it may occur before, during, or after the servicing of NMI. Another high-going edge triggers another response if it occurs after the start of the NMI procedure. The signal must be free of logical spikes in general and be free of bounces on the low-going edge to avoid triggering extraneous responses.

Maskable Interrupt (INTR)

The 8088 provides a single interrupt request input (INTR) which can be masked internally by software with the resetting of the interrupt enable (IF) flag bit. The interrupt request signal is level triggered. It is internally synchronized during each clock cycle on the high-going edge of CLK. To be responded to, INTR must be present (HIGH) during the clock period preceding the end of the current instruction or the end of a whole move for a block type instruction. During interrupt response sequence, further interrupts are disabled. The enable bit is reset as part of the response to any interrupt (INTR, NMI, software interrupt, or single step), although the FLAGS register which is automatically pushed onto the stack reflects the state of the processor prior to the interrupt. Until the old FLAGS register is restored, the enable bit will be zero unless specifically set by an instruction.

During the response sequence (See Figure 9), the processor executes two successive (back to back) interrupt acknowledge cycles. The 8088 emits the LOCK signal (maximum mode only) from T2 of the first bus cycle until T2 of the second. A local bus "hold" request will not be

and sample period. The interrupt return instruction includes a flags pop which returns the status of the original interrupt enable bit when it restores the flags.

HALT

When a software HALT instruction is executed, the processor indicates that it is entering the HALT state in one of two ways, depending upon which mode is strapped. In minimum mode, the processor issues ALE, delayed by one clock cycle, to allow the system to latch the halt status. Halt status is available on IO/$\overline{M}$, DT/$\overline{R}$, and $\overline{SSO}$. In maximum mode, the processor issues appropriate HALT status on $\overline{S2}$, $\overline{S1}$, and $\overline{S0}$, and the 8288 bus controller issues one ALE. The 8088 will not leave the HALT state when a local bus hold is entered while in HALT. In this case, the processor reissues the HALT indicator at the end of the local bus hold. An interrupt request or RESET will force the 8088 out of the HALT state.

Read/Modify/Write (Semaphore) Operations via LOCK

The LOCK status information is provided by the processor when consecutive bus cycles are required during the execution of an instruction. This allows the processor to perform read/modify/write operations on memory (via the "exchange register with memory" instruction), without another system bus master receiving intervening memory cycles. This is useful in multi-

honored until the end of the second bus cycle. In the second bus cycle, a byte is fetched from the external interrupt system (e.g., 8259A PIC) which identifies the source (type) of the interrupt. This byte is multiplied by four and used as a pointer into the interrupt vector lookup table. An INTR signal left HIGH will be continually responded to within the limitations of the enable bit

processor system configurations to accomplish "test and set lock" operations. The $\overline{\text{LOCK}}$ signal is activated (LOW) in the clock cycle following decoding of the LOCK prefix instruction. It is deactivated at the end of the last bus cycle of the instruction following the LOCK prefix. While $\overline{\text{LOCK}}$ is active, a request on a $\overline{\text{RQ}}/\overline{\text{GT}}$ pin will be recorded, and then honored at the end of the LOCK.

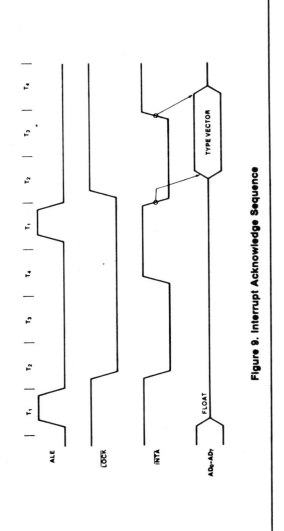

Figure 9. Interrupt Acknowledge Sequence

189

External Synchronization via TEST

As an alternative to interrupts, the 8088 provides a single software-testable input pin (TEST). This input is utilized by executing a WAIT instruction. The single WAIT instruction is repeatedly executed until the TEST input goes active (LOW). The execution of WAIT does not consume bus cycles once the queue is full.

If a local bus request occurs during WAIT execution, the 8088 3-states all output drivers. If interrupts are enabled, the 8088 will recognize interrupts and process them. The WAIT instruction is then refetched, and reexecuted.

Basic System Timing

In minimum mode, the MN/$\overline{MX}$ pin is strapped to V_{CC} and the processor emits bus control signals compatible with the 8085 bus structure. In maximum mode, the MN/$\overline{MX}$ pin is strapped to GND and the processor emits coded status information which the 8288 bus controller uses to generate MULTIBUS compatible bus control signals.

System Timing — Minimum System

(See Figure 8.)

The read cycle begins in T1 with the assertion of the address latch enable (ALE) signal. The trailing (low going) edge of this signal is used to latch the address information, which is valid on the address/data bus (AD0–AD7)

a byte of information is read from the data bus, as supplied by the interrupt system logic (i.e. 8259A priority interrupt controller). This byte identifies the source (type) of the interrupt. It is multiplied by four and used as a pointer into the interrupt vector lookup table, as described earlier.

Bus Timing — Medium Complexity Systems

(See Figure 10.)

For medium complexity systems, the MN/$\overline{MX}$ pin is connected to GND and the 8288 bus controller is added to the system, as well as an 8282/8283 latch for latching the system address, and an 8286/8287 transceiver to allow for bus loading greater than the 8088 is capable of handling. Signals ALE, $\overline{DEN}$, and DT/$\overline{R}$ are generated by the 8288 instead of the processor in this configuration, although their timing remains relatively the same. The 8088 status outputs ($\overline{S2}$, $\overline{S1}$, and $\overline{S0}$) provide type of cycle information and become 8288 inputs. This bus cycle information specifies read (code, data, or I/O), write (data or I/O), interrupt acknowledge, or software halt. The 8288 thus issues control signals specifying memory read or write, I/O read or write, or interrupt acknowledge. The 8288 provides two types of write strobes, normal and advanced, to be applied as required. The normal write strobes have data valid at the leading edge of write. The advanced write strobes have the same timing as read strobes, and hence, data is not

at this time, into the 8282/8283 latch. Address lines A8 through A15 do not need to be latched because they remain valid throughout the bus cycle. From T1 to T4 the IO/M̄ signal indicates a memory or I/O operation. At T2 the address is removed from the address/data bus and the bus goes to a high impedance state. The read control signal is also asserted at T2. The read (RD) signal causes the addressed device to enable its data bus drivers to the local bus. Some time later, valid data will be available on the bus and the addressed device will drive the READY line HIGH. When the processor returns the read signal to a HIGH level, the addressed device will again 3-state its bus drivers. If a transceiver (8286/8287) is required to buffer the 8088 local bus, signals DT/R̄ and DEN are provided by the 8088.

A write cycle also begins with the assertion of ALE and the emission of the address. The IO/M̄ signal is again asserted to indicate a memory or I/O write operation. In T2, immediately following the address emission, the processor emits the data to be written into the addressed location. This data remains valid until at least the middle of T4. During T2, T3, and Tw, the processor asserts the write control signal. The write (WR) signal becomes active at the beginning of T2, as opposed to the read, which is delayed somewhat into T2 to provide time for the bus to float.

The basic difference between the interrupt acknowledge cycle and a read cycle is that the interrupt acknowledge (INTA) signal is asserted in place of the read (RD) signal and the address bus is floated. (See Figure 9.). In the second of two successive INTA cycles,

valid at the leading edge of write. The 8286/8287 transceiver receives the usual T and OE inputs from the 8288's DT/R̄ and DEN outputs.

The pointer into the interrupt vector table, which is passed during the second INTA cycle, can derive from an 8259A located on either the local bus or the system bus. If the master 8289A priority interrupt controller is positioned on the local bus, a TTL gate is required to disable the 8286/8287 transceiver when reading from the master 8259A during the interrupt acknowledge sequence and software "poll".

The 8088 Compared to the 8086

The 8088 CPU is an 8-bit processor designed around the 8086 internal structure. Most internal functions of the 8088 are identical to the equivalent 8086 functions. The 8088 handles the external bus the same way the 8086 does with the distinction of handling only 8 bits at a time. Sixteen-bit operands are fetched or written in two consecutive bus cycles. Both processors will appear identical to the software engineer, with the exception of execution time. The internal register structure is identical and all instructions have the same end result. The differences between the 8088 and 8086 are outlined below. The engineer who is unfamiliar with the 8086 is referred to the iAPX 86, 88 User's Manual, Chapters 2 and 4, for function description and instruction set information. Internally, there are three differences between the 8088 and the 8086. All changes are related to the 8-bit bus interface.

The hardware interface of the 8088 contains the major differences between the two CPUs. The pin assignments are nearly identical, however, with the following functional changes:

- A8–A15 — These pins are only address outputs on the 8088. These address lines are latched internally and remain valid throughout a bus cycle in a manner similar to the 8085 upper address lines.

- $\overline{BHE}$ has no meaning on the 8088 and has been eliminated.

- $\overline{SSO}$ provides the $\overline{SO}$ status information in the minimum mode. This output occurs on pin 34 in minimum mode only. DT/$\overline{R}$, IO/$\overline{M}$, and $\overline{SSO}$ provide the complete bus status in minimum mode.

- IO/$\overline{M}$ has been inverted to be compatible with the MCS-85 bus structure.

- ALE is delayed by one clock cycle in the minimum mode when entering HALT, to allow the status to be latched with ALE.

- The queue length is 4 bytes in the 8088, whereas the 8086 queue contains 6 bytes, or three words. The queue was shortened to prevent overuse of the bus by the BIU when prefetching instructions. This was required because of the additional time necessary to fetch instructions 8 bits at a time.

- To further optimize the queue, the prefetching algorithm was changed. The 8088 BIU will fetch a new instruction to load into the queue each time there is a 1 byte hole (space available) in the queue. The 8086 waits until a 2-byte space is available.

- The internal execution time of the instruction set is affected by the 8-bit interface. All 16-bit fetches and writes from/to memory take an additional four clock cycles. The CPU is also limited by the speed of instruction fetches. This latter problem only occurs when a series of simple operations occur. When the more sophisticated instructions of the 8088 are being used, the queue has time to fill and the execution proceeds as fast as the execution unit will allow.

The 8088 and 8086 are completely software compatible by virtue of their identical execution units. Software that is system dependent may not be completely transferable, but software that is not system dependent will operate equally as well on an 8088 or an 8086.

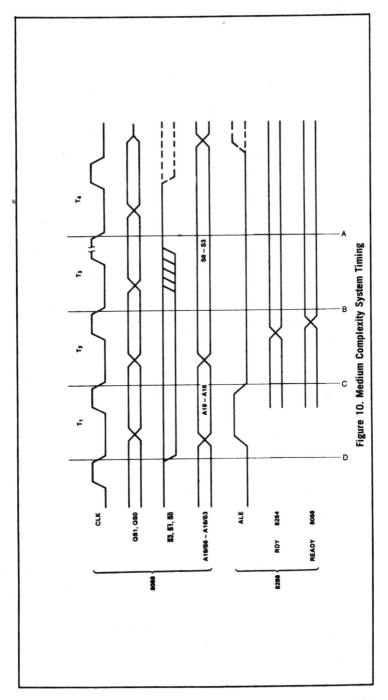

Figure 10. Medium Complexity System Timing

193

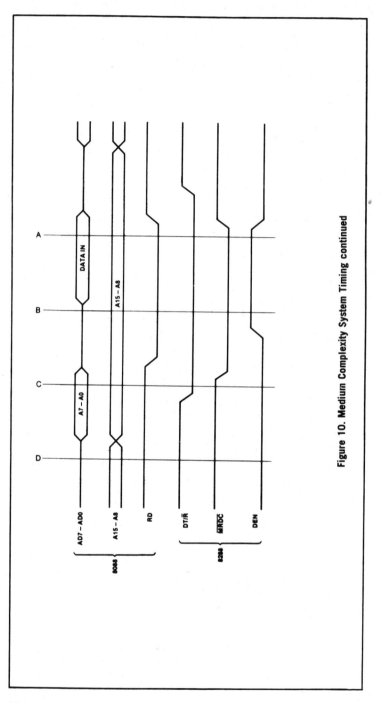

Figure 10. Medium Complexity System Timing continued

194

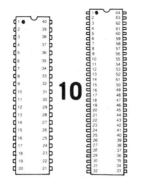

10

Motorola 68000 Spec Sheets

The MC68000 is the first in a family of advanced microprocessors from Motorola. Utilizing VLSI technology, the MC68000 is a fully-imlememented 16-bit microprocessor with 32-bit registers, a rich basic instruction set, and versatile addressing modes.

The MC68000 possesses an asynchronous bus structure with a 24-bit address bus and a 16-bit data bus.

The resources available to the MC68000 user consist of the following:
- ■ 17 32-Bit Data and Address Registers
- ■ 16 Megabyte Direct Addressing Range
- ■ 56 Powerful Instruction Types
- ■ Operations on Five Main Data Types
- ■ Memory Mapped I/O
- ■ 14 Addressing Modes

Material in this chapter is courtesy of Motorola, Inc.

As shown in the programming model (Figure 1-1), the MC68000 offers seventeen 32-bit registers, a 32-bit program counter, and a 16-bit status register. The first eight registers (D0-D7) are used as data registers for byte (8-bit), word (16-bit), and long word (32-bit) operations. The second set of seven registers (A0-A6) and the system stack pointer may be used as software stack pointers and base address registers. In addition, the registers may be used for word and long word operations. All of the 17 registers may be used as index registers.

The status register (Figure 1-2) contains the interrupt mask (eight levels available) as well as the condition codes: extend (X), negative (N), zero (Z), overflow (V), and carry (C). Additional status bits indicate that the processor is in a trace (T) mode and in a supervisor (S) or user state.

1.1 DATA TYPES AND ADDRESSING MODES

Five basic data types are supported. These data types are:

- Bits
- BCD Digits (4 bits)
- Bytes (8 bits)
- Words (16 bits)
- Long Words (32 bits)

In addition, operations on other data types such as memory addresses, status word data, etc., are provided in the instruction set.

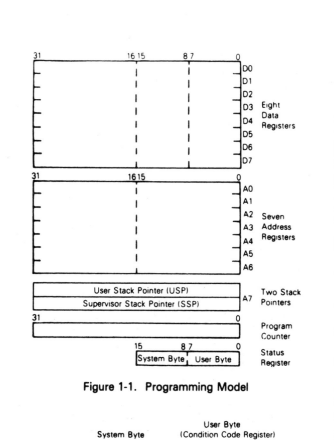

Figure 1-1. Programming Model

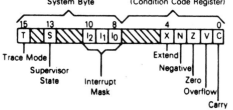

Figure 1-2. Status Register

The 14 address modes, shown in Table 1-1, include six basic types:

- Register Direct
- Register Indirect
- Absolute
- Program Counter Relative
- Immediate
- Implied

Included in the register indirect addressing modes is the capability to do postincrementing, predecrementing, offsetting, and indexing. The program counter relative mode can also be modified via indexing and offsetting.

Table 1-1. Addressing Modes

Mode	Generation
Register Direct Addressing	
Data Register Direct	$EA = Dn$
Address Register Direct	$EA = An$
Absolute Data Addressing	
Absolute Short	$EA = (Next\ Word)$
Absolute Long	$EA = (Next\ Two\ Words)$
Program Counter Relative Addressing	
Relative with Offset	$EA = (PC) + d_{16}$
Relative with Index and Offset	$EA = (PC) + (Xn) + d_8$
Register Indirect Addressing	
Register Indirect	$EA = (An)$
Postincrement Register Indirect	$EA = (An),\ An \leftarrow An + N$
Predecrement Register Indirect	$An \leftarrow An - N,\ EA = (An)$

Register Indirect with Offset	EA = (An) + d₁₆
Indexed Register Indirect with Offset	EA = (An) + (Xn) + d₈
Immediate Data Addressing	
Immediate	DATA = Next Word(s)
Quick Immediate	Inherent Data
Implied Addressing	
Implied Register	EA = SR, USP, SP, PC

NOTES:

EA	=	Effective Address
An	=	Address Register
Dn	=	Data Register
Xn	=	Address or Data Register Used as Index Register
SR	=	Status Register
PC	=	Program Counter
( )	=	Contents of
d₈	=	8-Bit Offset (Displacement)
d₁₆	=	16-Bit Offset (Displacement)
N	=	1 for byte, 2 for word, and 4 for long word. If An is
		the stack pointer and the operand size is byte, N = 2
		to keep
		the stack pointer on a word boundary.
←	=	Replaces

1.2 INSTRUCTION SET OVERVIEW

The MC68000 instruction set is shown in Table 1-2. Some additional instructions are variations, or subsets, of these and they appear in Table 1-3. Special emphasis has been given to the instruction set's support of structured high-level languages to facilitate ease of programming. Each instruction, with few exceptions, operates on bytes, words, and long words and most instructions can use any of the 14 addressing modes. Combining instruction types, data types, and addressing modes, over 1000 useful instructions are provided. These instructions include signed and unsigned, multiply and divide, "quick" arithmetic operations, BCD arithmetic, and expanded operations (through traps).

Table 1-2. Instruction Set Summary

Mnemonic	Description
ADBC	Add Decimal With Extend
ADD	Add
AND	Logical And
ASL	Arithmetic Shift Left
ASR	Arithmetic Shift Right
BCC	Branch Conditionally
BCHG	Bit Test and Change
BCLR	Bit Test and Clear
BRA	Branch Always
BSET	Bit Test and Set
BSR	Branch to Subroutine
BTST	Bit Test
CHK	Check Register Against Bounds
CLR	Clear Operand
CMP	Compare
DBcc	Test Condition, Decrement and Branch
DIVS	Signed Divide
DIVU	Unsigned Divide
EOR	Exclusive Or
EXG	Exchange Registers
EXT	Sign Extend
JMP	Jump
JSR	Jump to Subroutine
LEA	Load Effective Address
LINK	Link Stack
LSL	Logical Shift Left
LSR	Logical Shift Right

Mnemonic	Description
MOVE	Move
MULS	Signed Multiply
MULU	Unsigned Multiply
NBCD	Negate Decimal with Extend
NEG	Negate
NOP	No Operation
NOT	One's Complement
OR	Logical Or
PEA	Push Effective Address
RESET	Reset External Devices
ROL	Rotate Left without Extend
ROR	Rotate Right without Extend
ROXL	Rotate Left with Extend
ROXR	Rotate Right with Extend
RTE	Return from Exception
RTR	Return and Restore
RTS	Return from Subroutine
SBCD	Subtract Decimal with Extend
SCC	Set Conditional
STOP	Stop
SUB	Subtract
SWAP	Swap Data Register Halves
TAS	Test and Set Operand
TRAP	Trap
TRAPV	Trap on Overflow
TST	Test
UNLK	Unlink

Table 1-3. Variations of Instruction Types

Instruction Type	Variation	Description
ADD	ADD	Add
	ADDA	Add Address
	ADDQ	Add Quick
	ADDI	Add Immediate
	ADDX	Add with Extend
AND	AND	Logical And
	ANDI	And Immediate
	ANDI to CCR	And Immediate to Condition Codes
	ANDI to SR	And Immediate to Status Register
CMP	CMP	Compare
	CMPA	Compare Address
	CMPM	Compare Memory
	CMPI	Compare Immediate
EOR	EOR	Exclusive Or
	EORI	Exclusive Or Immediate
	EORI to CCR	Exclusive Or Immediate to Condition Codes
	EORI to SR	Exclusive Or Immediate to Status Register

Instruction Type	Variation	Description
MOVE	MOVE	Move
	MOVEA	Move Address
	MOVEM	Move Multiple Registers
	MOVEP	Move Peripheral Data
	MOVEQ	Move Quick
	MOVE from SR	Move from Status Register
	MOVE to SR	Move to Status Register
	MOVE to CCR	Move to Condition Codes
	MOVE USP	Move User Stack Pointer
NEG	NEG	Negate
	NEGX	Negate with Extend
OR	OR	Logical Or
	ORI	Or Immediate
	ORI to CCR	Or Immediate to Condition Codes
	ORI to SR	Or Immediate to Status Register
SUB	SUB	Subtract
	SUBA	Subtract Address
	SUBI	Subtract Immediate
	SUBQ	Subtract Quick
	SUBX	Subtract with Extend

DATA ORGANIZATION AND ADDRESSING CAPABILITIES

This section contains a description of the registers and the data organization of the MC68000.

2.1 OPERAND SIZE

Operand sizes are defined as follows: a byte equals 8 bits, a word equals 16 bits, and a long word equals 32 bits. The operand size for each instruction is either explicitly encoded in the instruction or implicitly defined by the instruction operation. Implicit instructions support some subset of all three sizes.

2.2 DATA ORGANIZATION IN REGISTERS

The eight data registers support data operands of 1, 8, 16, or 32 bits. The seven address registers together with the stack pointers support address operands of 32 bits.

2.2.1 Data Registers

Each data register is 32 bits wide. Byte operands occupy the low order 8 bits, word operands the low order 16 bits, and long word operands the entire 32 bits. The least significant bit is addressed as bit zero; the most significant bit is addressed as bit 31.

When a data register is used as either a source or destination operand, only the appropriate low order portion is changed; the remaining high order portion is neither used nor changed.

2.2.2 Address Registers

Each address register and the stack pointer is 32 bits wide and holds a full 32-bit address. Address registers do not support the sized operands. Therefore, when an address register is used as a source operand, either the low order word or the entire long word operand is used depending upon the operation size. When an address register is used as the destination operand, the entire register is affected regardless of the operation size. If the operation size is word, any other operands are sign extended to 32 bits before the operation is performed.

2.3 DATA ORGANIZATION IN MEMORY

Bytes are individually addressable with the high order byte having an even address the same as the word, as shown in Figure 2-1. The low order byte has an odd address that is one count higher than the word address. Instructions and multibyte data are accessed only on word (even byte) boundaries. If a long word datum is located at address n (n even), then the second word of that datum is located at address n + 2.

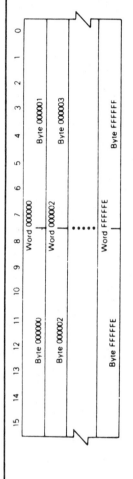

Figure 2-1. Word Organization in Memory

The data types supported by the MC68000 are: bit data, integer data of 8, 16, or 32 bits, 32-bit addresses and binary coded decimal data. Each of these data types is put in memory, as shown in Figure 2-2. The numbers indicate the order in which the data would be accessed from the processor.

2.4 ADDRESSING

Instructions for the MC68000 contain two kinds of information: the type of function to be performed and the location of the operand(s) on which to perform that function. The methods used to locate (address) the operand(s) are explained in the following paragraphs.

Instructions specify an operand location in one of three ways:

Register Specification — the number of the register is given in the register field of their instruction.

Effective Address — use of the different effective addressing modes.

Implicit Reference — the definition of certain instructions implies the use of specific registers.

2.5 INSTRUCTION FORMAT

Instructions are from one to five words in length as shown in Figure 2-3. The length of the instruction and the operation to be performed is specified by the first word of the instruction which is called the operation word. The remaining words further specify the operands. These words are either immediate operands or extensions to the effective address mode specified in the operation word.

2.6 PROGRAM/DATA REFERENCES

The MC68000 separates memory references into two classes: program references and data references. Program references, as the name implies, are references to that section of memory that contains the program being executed. Data references refer to that section of memory that contains data. Operand reads are from the data space except in the case of the program counter relative addressing mode. All operand writes are to the data space.

2.7 REGISTER SPECIFICATION

The register field within an instruction specifies the register to be used. Other fields within the instruction specify whether the register selected is an address or data register and how the register is to be used.

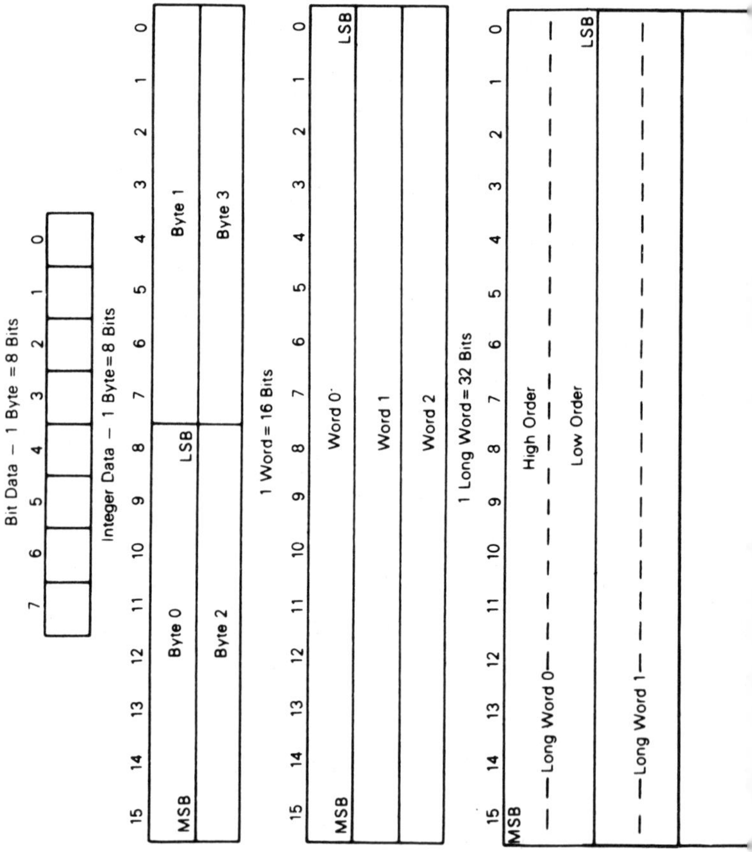

Bit Data — 1 Byte = 8 Bits

7	6	5	4	3	2	1	0

Integer Data — 1 Byte = 8 Bits

15	14	13	12	11	10	9	8	7	6	5	4	3	2	1	0
MSB			Byte 0				LSB			Byte 1					
			Byte 2							Byte 3					

1 Word = 16 Bits

15	14	13	12	11	10	9	8	7	6	5	4	3	2	1	0
MSB							Word 0								LSB
							Word 1								
							Word 2								

1 Long Word = 32 Bits

15	14	13	12	11	10	9	8	7	6	5	4	3	2	1	0
MSB	— — Long Word 0—						High Order							—	
	— — Long Word 1—						Low Order							—	LSB

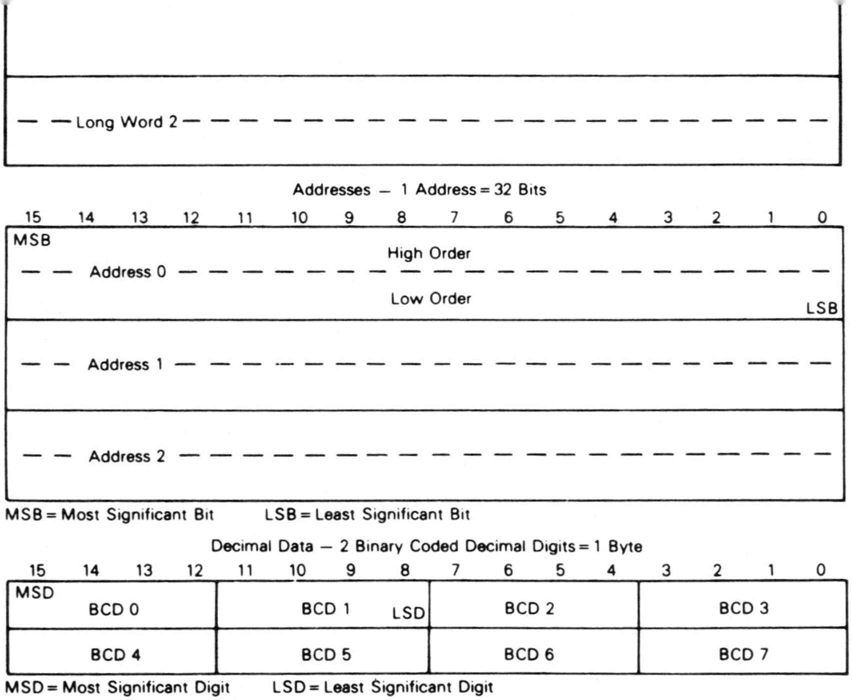

Figure 2-2. Memory Data Organization

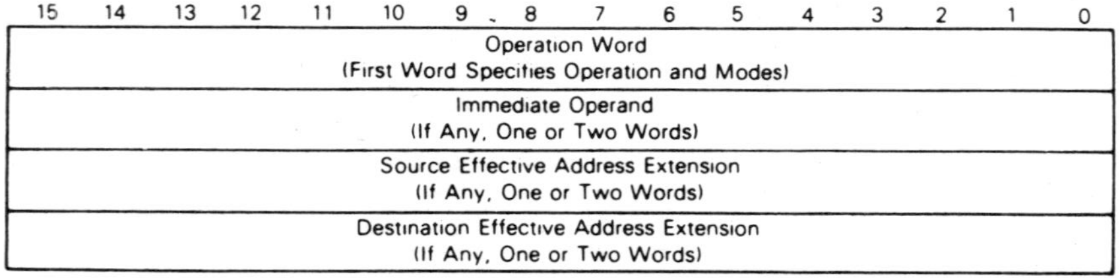

15	14	13	12	11	10	9	8	7	6	5	4	3	2	1	0

Operation Word
(First Word Specifies Operation and Modes)

Immediate Operand
(If Any, One or Two Words)

Source Effective Address Extension
(If Any, One or Two Words)

Destination Effective Address Extension
(If Any, One or Two Words)

Figure 2-3. Instruction Operation Word General Format

2.8 EFFECTIVE ADDRESS

Most instructions specify the location of an operand by using the effective address field in the operation word. For example, Figure 2-4 shows the general format of the single-effective-address instruction operation word. The effective address is composed of two 3-bit fields: the mode field and the register field. The value in the mode field selects the different address modes. The register field contains the number of a register.

The effective address field may require additional information to fully specify the operand. This additional information, called the effective address extension, is contained in the following word or words and is considered part of the instruction, as shown in Figure 2-3. The effective address modes are grouped into three categories: register direct, memory addressing, and special.

15	14	13	12	11	10	9	8	7	6	5	4	3	2	1	0
x	x	x	x	x	x	x	x	x	x		Mode			Register	

Effective Address

Figure 2-4. Single-Effective-Address Instruction Operation Word

2.8.1 Register Direct Modes

These effective addressing modes specify that the operand is in one of 16 multifunction registers.

2.8.1.1 DATA REGISTER DIRECT. The operand is in the data register specified by the effective address register field.

2.8.1.2 ADDRESS REGISTER DIRECT. The operand is in the address register specified by the effective address register field.

2.8.2 Memory Address Modes

These effective addressing modes specify that the operand is in memory and provide the specific address of the operand.

2.8.2.1 ADDRESS REGISTER INDIRECT. The address of the operand is in the address register specified by the register field. The reference is classified as a data reference with the exception of the jump and jump-to-subroutine instructions.

2.8.2.2 ADDRESS REGISTER INDIRECT WITH POSTINCREMENT. The address of the operand is in the address register specified by the register field. After the operand address is used, it is incremented by one, two, or four depending upon whether the size of the operand is byte, word, or long word. If the address register is the stack pointer and the operand size is byte, the address is incremented by two rather than one to keep the stack pointer on a word boundary. The reference is classified as a data reference.

2.8.2.3 ADDRESS REGISTER INDIRECT WITH PREDECREMENT. The address of the operand is in the address register specified by the register field. Before the operand address is used, it is decremented by one, two, or four depending upon whether the operand size is byte, word, or long word. If the address register is the stack pointer and the operand size is byte, the address is decremented by two rather than one to keep the stack pointer on a word boundary. The reference is classified as a data reference.

2.8.2.4 ADDRESS REGISTER INDIRECT WITH DISPLACEMENT. This addressing mode requires one word of extension. The address of the operand is the sum of the address in the address register and the sign-extended 16-bit displacement integer in the extension word. The reference is classified as a data reference with the exception of the jump and jump-to-subroutine instructions.

2.8.2.5 ADDRESS REGISTER INDIRECT WITH INDEX. This addressing mode requires one word of extension. The address of the operand is the sum of the address in the address register, the sign-extended displacement integer in the low order eight bits of the extension word, and the contents of the index register. The reference is classified as a data reference with the exception of the jump and jump-to-subroutine instructions.

2.8.3 Special Address Modes

The special address modes use the effective address register field to specify the special addressing mode instead of a register number.

2.8.3.1 ABSOLUTE SHORT ADDRESS. This addressing mode requires one word of extension. The address of the operand is the extension word. The 16-bit address is sign extended before it is used. The reference is classified as a data reference with the exception of the jump and jump-to-subroutine instructions.

2.8.3.2 ABSOLUTE LONG ADDRESS. This addressing mode requires two words of extension. The address of the operand is developed by the concatenation of the extension words. The high order part of the address is the first extension word; the low order part of the address is the second extension word. The reference is classified as a data reference with the exception of the jump and jump-to-subroutine instructions.

2.8.3.3 PROGRAM COUNTER WITH DISPLACEMENT. This addressing mode requires one word of extension. The address of the operand is the sum of the address in the program counter and the sign-extended 16-bit displacement integer in the extension word. The value in the program counter is the address of the extension word. The reference is classified as a program reference.

2.8.3.4 PROGRAM COUNTER WITH INDEX. This addressing mode requires one word of extension. The address is the sum of the address in the program counter, the sign-extended displacement integer in the lower eight bits of the extension word, and the contents of the index register. The value in the program counter is the address of the extension word. This reference is classified as a program reference.

2.8.3.5 IMMEDIATE DATA. This addressing mode requires either one or two words of extension depending on the size of the operation.

Byte Operation — operand is low order byte of extension word

Word Operation — operand is extension word

Long Word Operation — operand is in the two extension words, high order 16 bits are in the first extension word, low order 16 bits are in the second extension word.

2.8.3.6 IMPLICIT REFERENCE. Some instructions make implicit reference to the program counter (PC), the system stack pointer (SP), the supervisor stack pointer (SSP), the user stack pointer (USP), or the status register (SR). A selected set of instructions may reference the status register by means of the effective address field. These are:

ANDI to CCR	EORI to SR	MOVE to CCR
ANDI to SR	ORI to CCR	MOVE to SR
EORI to CCR	ORI to SR	MOVE from SR

2.9 EFFECTIVE ADDRESS ENCODING SUMMARY

Table 2-1 is a summary of the effective addressing modes discussed in the previous paragraphs.

Table 2-1. Effective Address Encoding Summary

Addressing Mode	Mode	Register
Data Register Direct	000	Register Number
Address Register Direct	001	Register Number
Address Register Indirect	010	Register Number
Address Register Indirect with Postincrement	011	Register Number
Address Register Indirect with Predecrement	100	Register Number
Address Register Indirect with Displacement	101	Register Number

Addressing Mode	Mode	Register
Address Register Indirect with Index	110	Register Number
Absolute Short	111	000
Absolute Long	111	001
Program Counter with Displacement	111	010
Program Counter with Index	111	011
Immediate	111	100

2.10 SYSTEM STACK

The system stack is used implicitly by many instructions; user stacks and queues may be created and maintained through the addressing modes. Address register seven (A7) is the system stack pointer (SP). The system stack pointer is either the supervisor stack pointer (SSP) or the user stack pointer (USP), depending on the state of the S bit in the status register. If the S bit indicates supervisor state, SSP is the active system stack pointer and the USP cannot be referenced as an address register. If the S bit indicates user state, the USP is the active system stack pointer, and the SSP cannot be referenced. Each system stack fills from high memory to low memory.

INSTRUCTION SET SUMMARY

This section contains an overview of the form and structure of the MC68000 instruction set. The instructions form a set of tools that include all the machine functions to perform the following operations:

Data Movement   Bit Manipulation
Integer Arithmetic   Binary Coded Decimal
Logical   Program Control
Shift and Rotate   System Control

The complete range of instruction capabilities combined with the flexible addressing modes described previously provide a very flexible base for program development.

3.1 DATA MOVEMENT OPERATIONS

The basic method of data acquisition (transfer and storage) is provided by the move (MOVE) instruction. The move instruction and the effective addressing modes allow both address and data manipulation. Data move instructions allow byte, word, and long word operands to be transferred from memory to memory, memory to register, register to memory, and register to register. Address move instructions allow word and long word operand transfers and ensure that only legal address manipulations are executed. In addition to the general move instruction there are several special data movement instructions: move multiple registers (MOVEM), move peripheral data (MOVEP), exchange registers (EXG), load effective address (LEA), push effective address (PEA), link stack (LINK), unlink stack (UNLK), and move quick (MOVEQ). Table 3-1 is a summary of the data movement operations.

Table 3-1. Data Movement Operations

Instruction	Operand Size	Operation
EXG	32	Rx ←→ Ry
LEA	32	EA → An
LINK	—	An → – (SP) SP → An SP + displacement → SP
MOVE	8, 16, 32	s → d
MOVEM	16, 32	(EA) → An, Dn An, Dn → EA

Instruction	Operand Size	Operation
MOVEP	16, 32	(EA) → Dn Dn → (EA)
MOVEQ	8	#xxx → Dn
PEA	32	EA → – (SP)
SWAP	32	Dn[31:16] ←→ Dn[15:0]
UNLK	—	An → Sp (SP) + → An

NOTES:

s = source
d = destination
[ ] = bit number

– ( ) = indirect with predecrement
( ) + = indirect with postdecrement
= immediate data

215

3.2 INTEGER ARITHMETIC OPERATIONS

The arithmetic operations include the four basic operations of add (ADD), subtract (SUB), multiply (MUL), and divide (DIV) as well as arithmetic compare (CMP), clear (CLR), and negate (NEG). The add and subtract instructions are available for both address and data operations, with data operations accepting all operand sizes. Address operations are limited to legal address size operands (16 or 32 bits). Data, address, and memory compare operations are also available. The clear and negate instructions may be used on all sizes of data operands.

The multiply and divide operations are available for signed and unsigned operands using word multiply to produce a long word product, and a long word dividend with word divisor to produce a word quotient with a word remainder.

Multiprecision and mixed size arithmetic can be accomplished using a set of extended instructions. These instructions are: add extended (ADDX), subtract extended (SUBX), sign extend (EXT), and negate binary with extend (NEGX).

A test operand (TST) instruction that will set the condition codes as a result of a compare of the operand with zero is also available. Test and set (TAS) is a synchronization instruction useful in multiprocessor systems. Table 3-2 is a summary of the integer arithmetic operations.

Table 3-2. Integer Arithmetic Operations

Instruction	Operand Size	Operation
ADD	8, 16, 32	Dn + (EA) → Dn (EA) + Dn → (EA) (EA) + #xxx → (EA)
	16, 32	An + (EA) → An
ADDX	8, 16, 32	Dx + Dy + X → Dx
	16, 32	-(Ax) + -(Ay) + X → (Ax)
CLR	8, 16, 32	0 → EA
CMP	8, 16, 32	Dn - (EA) (EA) - #xxx
	16, 32	(Ax)+ - (Ay) - An - (EA)
DIVS	32 ÷ 16	Dn ÷ (EA) → Dn
DIVU	32 ÷ 16	Dn ÷ (EA) → Dn
EXT	8 → 16 16 → 32	(Dn)8 → Dn16 (Dn)16 → Dn32
MULS	16 × 16 → 32	Dn × (EA) → Dn
MULU	16 × 16 → 32	Dn × (EA) → Dn
NEG	8, 16, 32	0 - (EA) → (EA)
NEGX	8, 16, 32	0 - (EA) - X → (EA)
SUB	8, 16, 32	Dn - (EA) → Dn (EA) - Dn → (EA) (EA) - #xxx → (EA)
	16, 32	An - (EA) → An
SUBX	8, 16, 32	Dx - Dy - X → Dx -(Ax) - -(Ay) - X → (Ax)
TAS	8	[EA] - 0, 1 → EA[7]
TST	8, 16, 32	(EA) - 0

NOTES:
[ ] = bit number
- ( ) = indirect with predecrement
( ) + = indirect with postdecrement
= immediate data

3.3 LOGICAL OPERATIONS

Logical operation instructions AND, OR, EOR, and NOT are available for all sizes of integer data operands. A similar set of immediate instructions (ANDI, ORI, and EORI) provide these logical operations with all sizes of immediate data. Table 3-3 is a summary of the logical operations.

Table 3-3. Logical Operations

Instruction	Operand Size	Operation
AND	8, 16, 32	Dn∧(EA) → Dn (EA)∧Dn → (EA) (EA)∧#xxx → (EA)
OR	8, 16, 32	Dn v (EA) → Dn (EA) v Dn → (EA) (EA) v #xxx → (EA)
EOR	8, 16, 32	(EA) ⊕ Dy → (EA) (EA) ⊕ #xxx → (EA)
NOT	8, 16, 32	~ (EA) → (EA)

NOTES:

~ = invert   V = logical OR
# = immediate data   ⊕ = logical exclusive OR
∧ = logical AND

3.4 SHIFT AND ROTATE OPERATIONS

Shift operations in both directions are provided by the arithmetic instructions ASR and ASL and logical shift instructions LSR and LSL. The rotate instructions (with and without extend) available are ROXR, ROXL, ROR, and ROL. All shift and rotate operations can be performed in either registers or memory. Register shifts and rotates support all operand sizes and allow a shift count specified in a data register.

Memory shifts and rotates are for word operands only and allow only single-bit shifts or rotates.

Table 3-4 is a summary of the shift and rotate operations.

Table 3-4. Shift and Rotate Operations

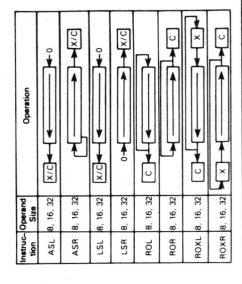

Instruction	Operand Size	Operation
ASL	8, 16, 32	
ASR	8, 16, 32	
LSL	8, 16, 32	
LSR	8, 16, 32	
ROL	8, 16, 32	
ROR	8, 16, 32	
ROXL	8, 16, 32	
ROXR	8, 16, 32	

3.5 BIT MANIPULATION OPERATIONS

Bit manipulation operations are accomplished using the following instructions: bit test (BTST), bit test and set (BSET), bit test and clear (BCLR), and bit test and change (BCHG). Table 3-5 is a summary of the bit manipulation operations. (Z is bit 2 of the status register.)

Table 3-5. Bit Manipulation Operations

Instruction	Operand Size	Operation
BTST	8, 32	~ bit of (EA) → Z
BSET	8, 32	~ bit of (EA) → Z 1 → bit of EA
BCLR	8, 32	~ bit of (EA) → Z 0 → bit of EA
BCHG	8, 32	~ bit of (EA) → Z ~ bit of (EA) → bit of EA

NOTE: ~ = invert

3.6 BINARY CODED DECIMAL OPERATIONS

Multiprecision arithmetic operations on binary coded decimal numbers are accomplished using the following instructions: add decimal with extend (ABCD), subtract decimal with extend (SBCD), and negate decimal with extend (NBCD). Table 3-6 is a summary of the binary coded decimal operations.

Table 3-6. Binary Coded Decimal Operations

Instruction	Operand Size	Operation
ABCD	8	$Dx_{10} + Dy_{10} + X \rightarrow Dx$ $-(Ax)_{10} + -(Ay)_{10} + x \rightarrow (Ax)$
SBCD	8	$Dx_{10} - Dy_{10} - X \rightarrow Dx$ $-(Ax)_{10} - -(Ay)_{10} - X \rightarrow (Ax)$
NBCD	8	$0 - (EA)_{10} - X \rightarrow (EA)$

NOTE: $-( )$ = indirect with predecrement

3.7 PROGRAM CONTROL OPERATIONS

Program control operations are accomplished using a series of conditional and unconditional branch instructions and return instructions. These instructions are summarized in Table 3-7.

The conditional instructions provide setting and branching for the following conditions:

CC — carry clear
CS — carry set
EQ — equal
F — never true
GE — greater or equal
GT — greater than
HI — high
LE — less or equal
LS — low or same
LT — less than
MI — minus
NE — not equal
PL — plus
T — always true
VC — no overflow
VS — overflow

Table 3-7. Program Control Operations

Instruction	Operation
Conditional	
B$_{CC}$	Branch Conditionally (14 Conditions) 8- and 16-Bit Displacement
DB$_{CC}$	Test Condition, Decrement, and Branch 16-Bit Displacement
S$_{CC}$	Set Byte Conditionally (16 Conditions)
Unconditional	
BRA	Branch Always 8- and 16-Bit Displacement
BSR	Branch to Subroutine 8- and 16-Bit Displacement
JMP	Jump
JSR	Jump to Subroutine
Returns	
RTR	Return and Restore Condition Codes
RTS	Return from Subroutine

3.8 SYSTEM CONTROL OPERATIONS

System control operations are accomplished by using privileged instructions, trap generating instructions, and instructions that use or modify the status register. These instructions are summarized in Table 3-8.

Table 3-8. System Control Operations

Instruction	Operation
Privileged	
ANDI to SR	Logical AND to Status Register
EORI to SR	Logical EOR to Status Register
MOVE EA to SR	Load New Status Register
MOVE USP	Move User Stack Pointer
ORI to SR	Logical OR to Status Register
RESET	Reset External Devices
RTE	Return from Exception
STOP	Stop Program Execution
Trap Generating	
CHK	Check Data Register Against Upper Bounds
TRAP	Trap
TRAPV	Trap on Overflow
Status Register	
ANDI to CCR	Logical AND to Condition Codes
EORI to CCR	Logical EOR to Condition Codes
MOVE EA to CCR	Load New Condition Codes
MOVE SR to EA	Store Status Register
ORI to CCR	Logical OR to Condition Codes

SIGNAL AND BUS OPERATION DESCRIPTION

This section contains a brief description of the input and output signals. A discussion of bus operation during the various machine cycles and operations is also given.

NOTE

The terms **assertion** and **negation** will be used extensively. This is done to avoid confusion when dealing with a mixture of "active-low" and "active-high" signals. The term assert or assertion is used to indicate that a signal is active or true, independent of whether that level is represented by a high or low voltage. The term negate or negation is used to indicate that a signal is inactive or false.

4.1 SIGNAL DESCRIPTION

The input and output signals can be functionally organized into the groups shown in Figure 4-1. The following paragraphs provide a brief description of the signals and a reference (if applicable) to other paragraphs that contain more detail about the function being performed.

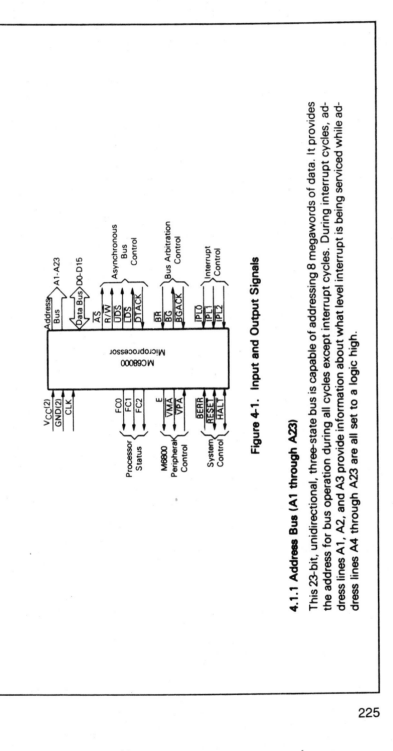

Figure 4-1. Input and Output Signals

4.1.1 Address Bus (A1 through A23)

This 23-bit, unidirectional, three-state bus is capable of addressing 8 megawords of data. It provides the address for bus operation during all cycles except interrupt cycles. During interrupt cycles, address lines A1, A2, and A3 provide information about what level interrupt is being serviced while address lines A4 through A23 are all set to a logic high.

4.1.2 Data Bus (D0 through D15)

This 16-bit, bidirectional, three-state bus is the general purpose data path. It can transfer and accept data in either word or byte length. During an interrupt acknowledge cycle, the external device supplies the vector number on data lines D0-D7.

4.1.3 Asynchronous Bus Control

Asynchronous data transfers are handled using the following control signals: address strobe, read/write, upper and lower data strobes, and data transfer acknowledge. These signals are explained in the following paragraphs.

4.1.3.1 ADDRESS STROBE (AS). This signal indicates that there is a valid address on the address bus.

4.1.3.2 READ/WRITE (R/W̄). This signal defines the data bus transfer as a read or write cycle. The R/W̄ signal also works in conjunction with the data strobes as explained in the following paragraph.

4.1.3.3 UPPER AND LOWER DATA STROBE (ŪDS̄, L̄DS̄). These signals control the flow of data on the data bus, as shown in Table 4-1. When the R/W̄ line is high, the processor will read from the data bus as indicated. When the R/W̄ line is low, the processor will write to the data bus as shown.

Table 4-1. Data Strobe Control of Data Bus

UDS	LDS	R/W	D8-D15	D0-D7
High	High	–	No Valid Data	No Valid Data
Low	Low	High	Valid Data Bits 8-15	Valid Data Bits 0-7
High	Low	High	No Valid Data	Valid Data Bits 0-7
Low	High	High	Valid Data Bits 8-15	No Valid Data
Low	Low	Low	Valid Data Bits 8-15	Valid Data Bits 0-7
High	Low	Low	Valid Data Bits 0-7*	Valid Data Bits 0-7
Low	High	Low	Valid Data Bits 8-15	Valid Data Bits 8-15*

*These conditions are a result of current implementation and may not appear on future devices.

4.1.3.4 DATA TRANSFER ACKNOWLEDGE (DTACK). This input indicates that the data transfer is completed. When the processor recognizes DTACK during a read cycle, data is latched and the bus cycle terminated. When DTACK is recognized during a write cycle, the bus cycle is terminated. (Refer to **4.4 ASYNCHRONOUR VERSUS SYNCHRONOUS OPERATION**).

4.1.4 Bus Arbitration Control

The three signals, bus request, bus grant, and bus grant acknowledge, form a bus arbitration circuit to determine which device will be the bus master device.

4.1.4.1 BUS REQUEST (BR). This input is wire ORed with all other devices that could be bus masters. This input indicates to the processor that some other device desires to become the bus master.

4.1.4.2 BUS GRANT (BG). This output indicates to all other potential bus master devices that the processor will release bus control at the end of the current bus cycle.

4.1.4.3 BUS GRANT ACKNOWLEDGE (BGACK). This input indicates that some other device has become the bus master. This signal should not be asserted until the following four conditions are met:

1. a bus grant has been received,

2. address strobe is inactive which indicates that the microprocessor is not using the bus,

3. data transfer acknowledge is inactive which indicates that neither memory nor peripherals are using the bus, and

4. bus grant acknowledge is inactive which indicates that no other device is still claiming bus mastership.

4.1.5 Interrupt Control (IPL0, IPL1, IPL2)

These input pins indicate the encoded priority level of the device requesting an interrupt. Level seven is the highest priority while level zero indicates that no interrupts are requested. Level seven cannot be masked. The least significant bit is given in $\overline{\text{IPL0}}$ and the most significant bit is contained in $\overline{\text{IPL2}}$. These lines must remain stable until the processor signals interrupt acknowledge (FC0-FC2 are all high) to insure that the interrupt is recognized.

4.1.6 System Control

The system control inputs are used to either reset or halt the processor and to indicate to the processor that bus errors have occurred. The three system control inputs are explained in the following paragraphs.

4.1.6.1 BUS ERROR ($\overline{\text{BERR}}$). This input informs the processor that there is a problem with the cycle currently being executed. Problems may be a result of:

1. nonresponding devices,
2. interrupt vector number acquisition failure,
3. illegal access request as determined by a memory management unit, or
4. other application dependent errors.

The bus error signal interacts with the halt signal to determine if the current bus cycle should be re-executed or if exception processing should be performed.

Refer to **4.2.4 Bus Error and Halt Operation** for additional information about the interaction of the bus error and halt signals.

4.1.6.2 RESET ($\overline{\text{RESET}}$). This bidirectional signal line acts to reset (start a system initialization sequence) the processor in response to an external reset signal. An internally generated reset (result of a $\overline{RESET}$ instruction) causes all external devices to be reset and the internal state of the processor is not affected. A total system reset (processor and external devices) is the result of external $\overline{HALT}$ and $\overline{RESET}$ signals applied at the same time. Refer to **4.2.5 Reset Operation** for further information.

4.1.6.3 HALT ($\overline{HALT}$). When this bidirectional line is driven by an external device, it will cause the processor to stop at the completion of the current bus cycle. When the processor has been halted using this input, all control signals are inactive and all three-state lines are put in their high-impedance state (refer to Table 4-3). Refer to **4.2.4 Bus Error and Halt Operation** for additional information about the interaction between the $\overline{HALT}$ and bus error signals.

When the processor has stopped executing instructions, such as in a double bus fault condition (refer to **4.2.4.4 DOUBLE BUS FAULTS**), the $\overline{HALT}$ line is driven by the processor to indicate to external devices that the processor has stopped.

4.1.7 M6800 Peripheral Control

These control signals are used to allow the interfacing of synchronous M6800 peripheral devices with the asynchronous MC68000. These signals are explained in the following paragraphs.

4.1.7.1 ENABLE (E). This signal is the standard enable signal common to all M6800 type peripheral devices. The period for this output is ten MC68000 clock periods (six clocks low, four clocks high). Enable is generated by an internal ring counter which may come up in any state (i.e., at power on, it is impossible to guarantee phase relationship of E to CLK). E is a free-running clock and runs regardless of the state of the bus on the MPU.

4.1.7.2 VALID PERIPHERAL ADDRESS (VPA). This input indicates that the device or region addressed is an M6800 Family device and that data transfer should be synchronized with the enable (E) signal. This input also indicates that the processor should use automatic vectoring for an interrupt. Refer to **SECTION 6 INTERFACE WITH M6800 PERIPHERALS.**

4.1.7.3 VALID MEMORY ADDRESS (VMA). This output is used to indicate to M6800 peripheral devices that there is a valid address on the address bus and the processor is synchronized to enable. This signal only responds to a valid peripheral address (VPA) input which indicates that the peripheral is an M6800 Family device.

4.1.8 Processor Status (FC0, FC1, FC2)

These function code outputs indicate the state (user or supervisor) and the cycle type currently being executed, as shown in Table 4-2. The information indicated by the function code outputs is valid whenever address strobe (AS) is active.

Table 4-2. Function Code Outputs

Function Code Output			Cycle Type
FC2	FC1	FC0	
Low	Low	Low	(Undefined, Reserved)
Low	Low	High	User Data
Low	High	Low	User Program
Low	High	High	(Undefined, Reserved)
High	Low	Low	(Undefined, Reserved)
High	Low	High	Supervisor Data
High	High	Low	Supervisor Program
High	High	High	Interrupt Acknowledge

4.1.9 Clock (CLK)

The clock input is a TTL-compatible signal that is internally buffered for development of the internal clocks needed by the processor. The clock input should not be gated off at any time and the clock signal must conform to minimum and maximum pulse width times.

4.1.10 Signal Summary

Table 4-3 is a summary of all the signals discussed in the previous paragraphs.

Table 4-3. Signal Summary

Signal Name	Mnemonic	Input/Output	Active State	Hi-Z On HALT	Hi-Z On BGACK
Address Bus	A1-A23	Output	High	Yes	Yes
Data Bus	D0-D15	Input/Output	High	Yes	Yes
Address Strobe	$\overline{AS}$	Output	Low	No	Yes
Read/Write	$R/\overline{W}$	Output	Read-High Write-Low	No	Yes
Upper and Lower Data Stobes	$\overline{UDS}$, $\overline{LDS}$	Output	Low	No	Yes
Data Transfer Acknowledge	$\overline{DTACK}$	Input	Low	No	No
Bus Request	$\overline{BR}$	Input	Low	No	No
Bus Grant	$\overline{BG}$	Output	Low	No	No
Bus Grant Acknowledge	$\overline{BGACK}$	Input	Low	No	No
Interrupt Priority Level	$\overline{IPL0}$, $\overline{IPL1}$, $\overline{IPL2}$	Input	Low	No	No
Bus Error	$\overline{BERR}$	Input	Low	No	No

Reset	RESET	Input/Output	Low	No[1]	No[1]
Halt	HALT	Input/Output	Low	No[1]	No[1]
Enable	E	Output	High	No	No
Valid Memory Address	VMA	Output	Low	No	Yes
Valid Peripheral Address	VPA	Input	Low	No	No
Function Code Output	FC0, FC1, FC2	Output	High	No[2]	Yes
Clock	CLK	Input	High	No	No
Power Input	VCC	Input	—	—	—
Ground	GND	Input	—	—	—

NOTES:
1. Open drain
2. Function codes are placed in high-impedance state during HALT for R9M, T6E, and BF4 mask sets

4.2 BUS OPERATION

The following paragraphs explain control signal and bus operation during data transfer operations, bus arbitration, bus error and halt conditions, and reset operation.

4.2.1 Data Transfer Operations

Transfer of data between devices involves the following leads:
1. address bus A1 through A23,
2. data bus D0 through D15, and
3. control signals.

The address and data buses are separate parallel buses used to transfer data using an asynchronous bus structure. In all cycles, the bus master assumes responsibility for deskewing all signals it issues at both the start and end of a cycle. In addition, the bus master is responsible for deskewing the acknowledge and data signals from the slave device.

The following paragraphs explain the read, write, and read-modify-write cycles. The indivisible read-modify-write cycle is the method used by the MC68000 for interlocked multiprocessor communications.

4.2.1.1 READ CYCLE. During a read cycle, the processor receives data from the memory or a peripheral device. The processor reads bytes of data in all cases. If the instruction specifies a word (or double word) operation, the processor reads both upper and lower bytes simultaneously by asserting both upper and lower data strobes. When the instruction specifies byte operation, the processor uses an internal A0 bit to determine which byte to read and then issues the data strobe required for that byte. For byte operations, when the A0 bit equals zero, the upper data strobe is issued. When the A0 bit equals one, the lower data strobe is issued. When the data is received, the processor correctly positions it internally.

A word read cycle flowchart is given in Figure 4-2. A byte read cycle flowchart is given in Figure 4-4. Read cycle timing is given in Figure 4-3.

SLAVE

BUS MASTER

Address the Device

1) Set R/W̄ to Read

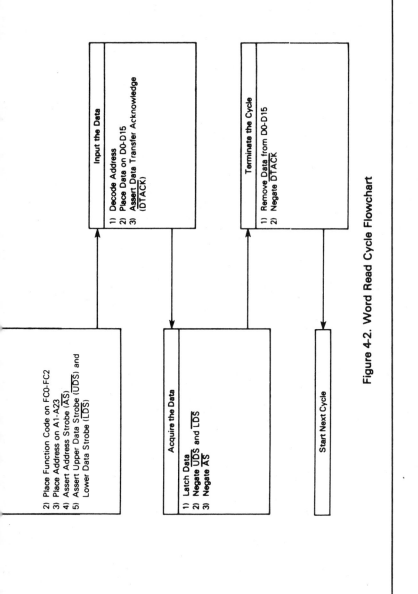

Figure 4-2. Word Read Cycle Flowchart

2) Place Function Code on FC0-FC2
3) Place Address on A1-A23
4) Assert Address Strobe ($\overline{AS}$)
5) Assert Upper Data Strobe ($\overline{UDS}$) and Lower Data Strobe ($\overline{LDS}$)

Input the Data

1) Decode Address
2) Place Data on D0-D15
3) Assert Data Transfer Acknowledge ($\overline{DTACK}$)

Acquire the Data

1) Latch Data
2) Negate $\overline{UDS}$ and $\overline{LDS}$
3) Negate $\overline{AS}$

Terminate the Cycle

1) Remove Data from D0-D15
2) Negate $\overline{DTACK}$

Start Next Cycle

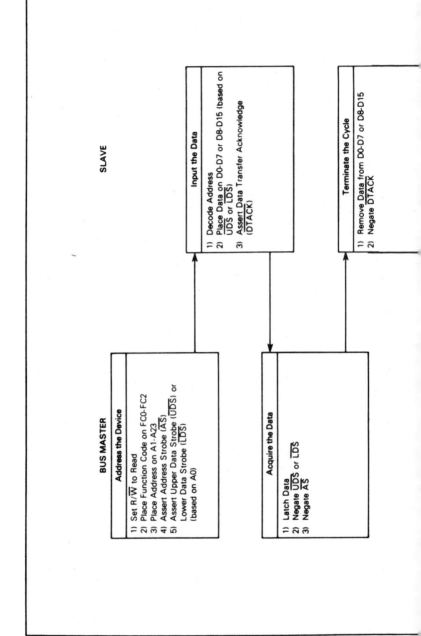

SLAVE

BUS MASTER

Address the Device

1) Set R/$\overline{W}$ to Read
2) Place Function Code on FC0-FC2
3) Place Address on A1-A23
4) Assert Address Strobe ($\overline{AS}$)
5) Assert Upper Data Strobe ($\overline{UDS}$) or
   Lower Data Strobe ($\overline{LDS}$)
   (based on A0)

Input the Data

1) Decode Address
2) Place Data on D0-D7 or D8-D15 (based on
   $\overline{UDS}$ or $\overline{LDS}$)
3) Assert Data Transfer Acknowledge
   ($\overline{DTACK}$)

Acquire the Data

1) Latch Data
2) Negate $\overline{UDS}$ or $\overline{LDS}$
3) Negate $\overline{AS}$

Terminate the Cycle

1) Remove Data from D0-D7 or D8-D15
2) Negate $\overline{DTACK}$

236

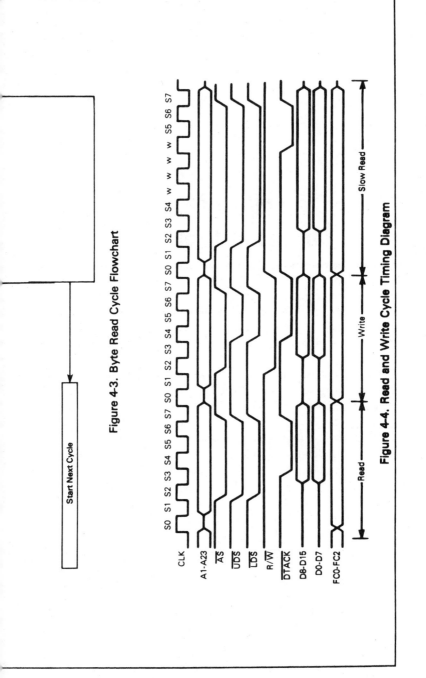

Start Next Cycle

Figure 4-3. Byte Read Cycle Flowchart

Figure 4-4. Read and Write Cycle Timing Diagram

237

Appendix A
Address Decoder
Circuits and Techniques

A microprocessor, like any programmable digital computer, will access a particular memory location by placing a binary address on the *address bus*. In most microprocessors, especially the 8-bit variety, the address bus is sixteen bits long (A0-A15), so it will be able to uniquely address up to 65,536 different memory locations. In computer parlance, this means "64K" of memory, with "K" nominally meaning 1000, but actually indicating 1024 (which is 2^{10}). In order to address any given location or I/O port, however, we must be able to detect when the microcomputer has placed its address on the address bus. That is the function of the address decoder circuit.

Several different circuits are shown in this appendix, and they are representative of the class. But we do not intend to imply that they are the be-all and end-all of address decoders. These circuits work, but the idea in this and the following appendices is to teach you the principles so that you can apply other IC devices, as required.

One of our circuits is based upon the 7442 integrated circuit (Fig. A-1). This TTL device performs the function of a BCD-to-one-of-ten-decoder. This means that it has four inputs weighted in the binary coded decimal scheme, and ten unique outputs—one for each of the ten digits of the decimal number system. The inputs of the 7442 are TTL-compatible, and will respond according to the weights normal for the binary coded decimal (BCD) 1-2-4-8 system, as shown on the next page.

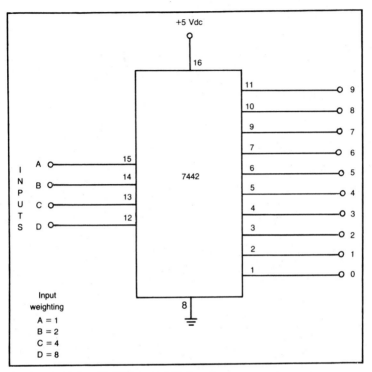

Fig. A-1. 7442 four-bit BCD-to-1-of-10-decoder.

Designation	BCD Weight	7442 Pin-in
A	1	15
B	2	14
C	4	13
D	8	12

The 7442 has ten outputs, and all are active-LOW. The 7442 output pin-outs are shown below:

BCD Number	Decimal Number	7442 Pin-out
0000	0	1
0001	1	2
0010	2	3
0011	3	4
0100	4	5
0101	5	6
0110	6	7

BCD Number	Decimal Number	7442 Pin-out
0111	7	9
1000	8	10
1001	9	11

Thus, a single 7442 device can be used as a four-bit decoder. Of course, a four-bit decoder may seem a little useless on a microcomputer that has a sixteen-bit address bus, but not so. For many applications, the entire address bus is not used. Also, it is possible to cascade 7442s in order to accommodate longer word lengths.

Figure A-2 shows an application for the 7442 decoder in which only four bits are used. This circuit can be used on any Z80 circuit to make the I/O address decoder. On the Z80, the port number (000 to 255) is passed along the lower eight bits of the address bus during either input or output operations. If the user does not anticipate any more than ten different I/O ports on the computer, or, alternatively, on the printed circuit card where the decoder is used, then it may be appropriate to use this circuit. It is based on the 7442 device described above. In this case, however, we connect bits A0 through A3 of the address bus to the 7442 inputs. The address codes are as follows:

A3	A2	A1	A0	Port No.	7442 Pin
0	0	0	0	0	1
0	0	0	1	1	2
0	0	1	0	2	3
0	0	1	1	3	4
0	1	0	0	4	5
0	1	0	1	5	6

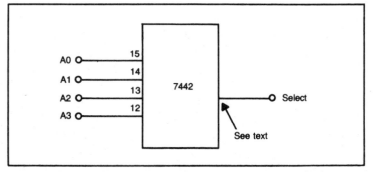

Fig. A-2. 7442 as a simple address decoder for low-order four bits of address bus.

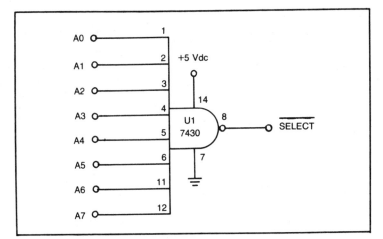

Fig. A-3. 7430 eight-input NAND gate (TTL).

A3	A2	A1	A0	Port No.	7442 Pin
0	1	1	0	6	7
0	1	1	1	7	9
1	0	0	0	8	10
1	0	0	1	9	11

Thus, the $\overline{\text{SELECT}}$ signals are generated by the 7442 outputs in response to addresses applied to the four-bit BCD input. We will discuss further applications of the 7442 device later in this appendix, and in Appendix B (Generating Device-Select Pulses).

As mentioned earlier, there are several different devices that can be used for making address decoders. Figure A-3 shows the TTL eight-input NAND gate called the 7430. This device obeys the following protocol:

If any one input is LOW, then the output is HIGH.

All eight inputs must be HIGH for the output to be LOW.

The device can be used directly, without additional chips, only for the address FF (hex), which is the same as 11111111 in binary. At this address, all eight lines of the address bus will be HIGH at the same time, which according to condition No. 2 (above), is what will satisfy the 7430 and produce a LOW output. For all other addresses, there will be at least one line LOW.

The idea when using the 7430 device, is to conspire to produce a HIGH at each input if and only if the correct address is present on the bus. For those lines which will be LOW at the correct address, therefore, we will require inverters. Figure A-4 shows a typical 7430 circuit in which inverters are used. In this particular example, the correct address is 01001000 (48 hex). This means that the A3 and A6 lines will be HIGH, while all other lines are LOW when the address is present on the bus. For all of these lines (A0, A1, A2, A4, A5, and A7), we will need inverters that will present a HIGH on the 7430 input when the address bus line is LOW.

Still another method is shown in Fig. A-5. Here we use a collection of open-collector inverters to accomplish the chore. An open-collector TTL device has a special output circuit that consists of merely a transistor with no collector load. The designer provides a collector load in the form of a pull-up resistor between the TTL output and the +5 Vdc power supply. There are several devices in the TTL line which feature open-collector outputs; both inverting and noninverting types are available. The most common are the hex inverters (7405, 7406, 7407, 7416, and 7417), but there are also octal devices on the market. A "hex" inverter contains six independent inverter stages, while the octal type contains eight inverters.

Recall the operation of the inverter. When the input is HIGH, the output is LOW, but if the input is LOW, the output will be HIGH. If we use the so-called "Wired-OR" connection of Fig. A-5, we will tie all of the outputs together. If any one of them is LOW, the output will be LOW; all of the open-collector outputs must be HIGH to

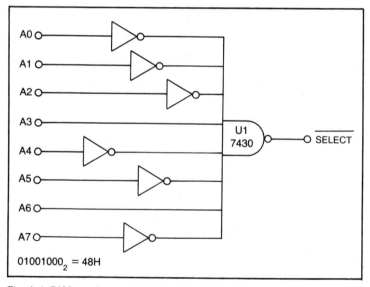

Fig. A-4. 7430 used as an eight-bit address decoder.

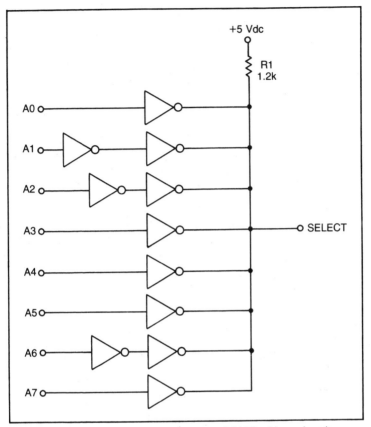

Fig. A-5. Open-collector inverters used as an eight-bit address decoder.

make SELECT HIGH. Since a LOW on the inverter input is needed to make the output HIGH, we must apply all LOWs to the circuit in order to make the SELECT signal active. The only natural address which does this is 00 (hex), or 00000000 in binary. In some cases, this is all that is needed, for we will place such items as I/O ports in Z80 based systems at location 00. But in other cases, we will have to invert the address bus line applied to certain inputs before the circuit will work. The address which is recognized by the circuit in Fig. A-5 is 01000110 (i.e., 46H).

One last technique is shown in Fig. A-6. Here we depend upon either the TTL 7485 circuit, or, the CMOS 4063 circuit. Both are pin-for-pin compatible with each other (except for drive capacity, which is lower on the CMOS device), and are known as four-bit-binary-comparators. These devices will examine two four-bit bi-

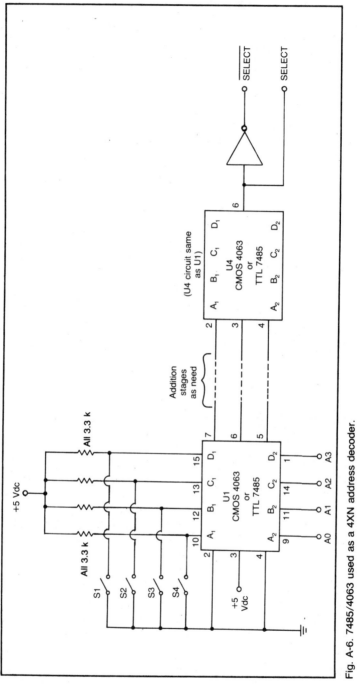

Fig. A-6. 7485/4063 used as a 4XN address decoder.

nary words, labeled *A* and *B*, and then issue a HIGH on whichever of three possible outputs is true: *A* equals *B*, *A* is greater than *B*, or *A* is less than *B*. In our circuit, we will use only the *A=B* output, which will go HIGH if and only if words *A* and *B* are identical.

In our little example of Fig. A-6, we will apply the address bus signals to the "A" inputs of the 7485/4063, and program the "B" inputs for the desired address. The programming job can be done either with switches and pull-up resistors, as shown, if flexibility is desired, or, by hard-wiring inputs to either ground or a pull-up resistor.

The 7485/4063 devices are cascadable. We can connect the outputs of one device to the "cascading inputs" of the next device in sequence. This is shown in Fig. A-6. We gain four bits per stage, so four 7485/4063 devices will be needed for a sixteen-bit address bus.

COMBINING DECODERS

The address decoder circuits we have so far considered are all eight bit or less, with the possible exception of cascaded 7485/4063 devices. We rarely have just an eight-bit address in anything other than input/output ports, so we'll have to learn how to convert sixteen-bit addresses into SELECT or $\overline{\text{SELECT}}$ signals. Figure A-7 shows a method. If the SELECT signals are active-LOW (i.e., $\overline{\text{SELECT}}$), then we can use an n-bit NOR gate in order to combine

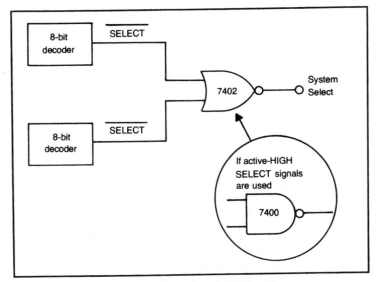

Fig. A-7. Combining 8-bit decoders to decode 16-bit addresses.

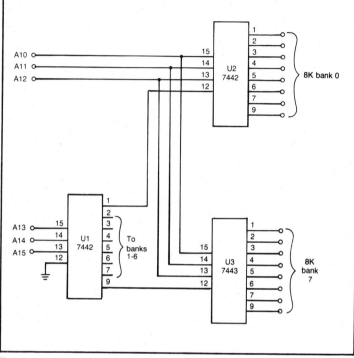

Fig. A-8. Memory banking.

the outputs of the lesser decoders, where n is the number of eight-bit segments. In the case of a sixteen-bit address bus, therefore, we will have to combine the outputs of two eight-bit decoders in the manner shown in Fig. A-7. In this case, a 7402 NOR-gate is used.

If the SELECT signals are active-HIGH, then use a NAND gate instead of the NOR gate used previously. In the case of the NOR version, the SYSTEM SELECT is active-HIGH, but is generated from active-LOW $\overline{\text{SELECT}}$ signals. If the NAND gate is used, then an active-LOW $\overline{\text{SYSTEM SELECT}}$ is generated from active-HIGH SELECT signals.

Of course, we can always make a SELECT signal into a $\overline{\text{SELECT}}$, or vice versa, by using a simple inverter. The problem becomes compounded a little in system signals, however, because the device will be required to drive a larger number of TTL inputs. There are devices in the TTL catalogs, however, which will easily handle the requirements.

246

BANK SELECT STRATEGIES

The use of a unique decoder for each memory location is absurd, and is never done. Instead, we bank memory into groups of 1K, 4K, 8K, 16K, and so forth (often according to the size of chips available to us). In Fig. A-8, we see a scheme for banking 8K of memory. Each bank will have the address lines for locations 0 through 8192, and all of these lines are connected in parallel (i.e., bits A0-A12). The high three bits, A10 through A12, also go to the A, B, and C inputs of a 7442 (discussed earlier), one for each bank. The D inputs of the 7442 devices go to the outputs of another 7442, which decodes address lines A13, A14, and A15. When a bank is selected by the combined address, the appropriate 7442 output will go LOW. Each of the "bank" 7442's (i.e., U2, U3, etc.) is divided into 1K lines (does that suggest that a 2102 is used for memory?) that each will go LOW when the appropriate sub-bank is called for by the CPU.

Appendix B
Generating Device-Select Pulses

The purpose of a device-select pulse is to turn on and off memory, an I/O port, or some peripheral. The generation of the device-select signal is a critical chore in any interfacing effort. The critical elements that go into making up the device select signal are the control signals plus the output of an address decoder (either SELECT or $\overline{\text{SELECT}}$). This latter requirement is necessary because the device select pulse must be uniquely generated, and not come on (i.e., go active) during any but the correct situations. Of course, since the control signals protocols for the different microprocessor chips are slightly different from one another, it is also true that the exact device-select protocol will vary from chip to chip. In this appendix, however, we will consider the protocols for the Z80 and 6502 since we operate on the premise that these chips are more or less representative of large segments of the market. Since Z80 and 6502 make up the chips in a large percentage of microcomputers sold (6502 is in Apple, for example), this is a reasonable selection.

Figure B-1 shows the device-select pulse circuit for a 6502-based microcomputer. Recall that there are two control signals on the 6502, Phase-2 clock and R/$\overline{\text{W}}$ ("read/not-write"). On the 6502, all peripheral, memory, and I/O action is to occur in the Phase-2 clock cycle, i.e. when Phase-2 clock is HIGH. The R/$\overline{\text{W}}$ is HIGH for a read or input, and LOW for a write or output operation. Thus, we have the following true for these two forms of operation:

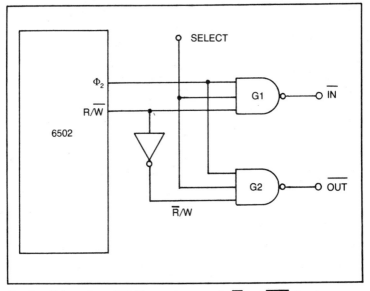

Fig. B-1. Using 3-input NAND gates to generate $\overline{\text{IN}}$ and $\overline{\text{OUT}}$ signals.

1. The Phase-2 clock and the R/$\overline{\text{W}}$ will both be HIGH for a read or input operation:

2. The Phase-2 clock will be HIGH, and the R/$\overline{\text{W}}$ will be LOW for a write or output operation.

The circuit in Fig. B-1 is based on the three-input NAND gate. Let's recall the rules of operation for a NAND gate:

1. If any one output is LOW, then the output is HIGH.

2. All three inputs must be HIGH for the output to be LOW.

Since there are three inputs on each NAND gate, we can accommodate both of the control signals and a SELECT signal from the address decoder circuit (see Appendix A). The operation for the input or read operation is as follows: SELECT, Phase-2 clock and R/$\overline{\text{W}}$ will all be HIGH when the operation is active, so the output of G1 will drop LOW, forming an active-LOW $\overline{\text{IN}}$ signal.

When a write or output operation is called for, we find that the Phase-2 clock, SELECT signal are HIGH, and the R/$\overline{\text{W}}$ is LOW. Since the NAND gate wants to see a HIGH, we must invert the R/$\overline{\text{W}}$ signal to form a $\overline{\text{R/W}}$ signal. This signal will meet the criteria of all three inputs HIGH on the NAND gate if and only if all signals are described above.

A Z80 device-select pulse circuit is shown in Fig. B-2. Recall the protocol for the Z80 signal. The $\overline{\text{IORQ}}$ will go LOW for any input/output operation. An output is designated by the coincidence of the $\overline{\text{IORQ}}$ and the write ($\overline{\text{WR}}$) signals. Both are active-LOW, so will be LOW only when an output operation is called for. Similarly, an input is designated by the coincidence of the $\overline{\text{IORQ}}$ and the $\overline{\text{RD}}$ signal. For memory operations, the $\overline{\text{MREQ}}$ signal replaces $\overline{\text{IORQ}}$, but the read and write functions remain the same.

The circuit in Fig. B-2 is a device select generator for the Z80 microprocessor. The active component is a 7442 BCD-to-one-of-ten-decoder. This IC has ten unique outputs, one for each digit of the decimal numbers system. The outputs are active-LOW, so will drop LOW if and only if the chip sees a binary coded decimal (BCD) four-bit word applied to the inputs of the correct form. The 7442 inputs are weighted in the familiar 1-2-4-8 manner of the BCD system. The pin-outs for the 7442 are as follows:

Binary Input	Decimal Digit	7442 Pin
0000	0	1
0001	1	2
0010	2	3
0011	3	4
0100	4	5

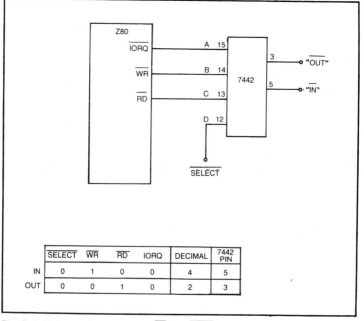

	SELECT	WR	RD	IORQ	DECIMAL	7442 PIN
IN	0	1	0	0	4	5
OUT	0	0	1	0	2	3

Fig. B-2. Using 7442 to generate $\overline{\text{IN}}$ and $\overline{\text{OUT}}$ signals.

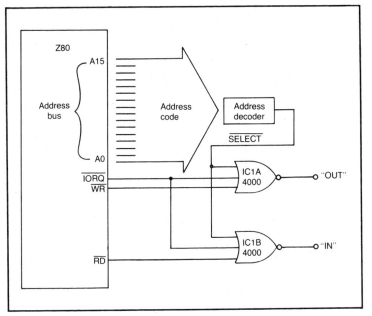

Fig. B-3. NOR Gates to generate IN and OUT signals.

Binary Input	Decimal Digit	7442 Pin
0101	5	6
0110	6	7
0111	7	9
1000	8	10
1001	9	11

Thus, when the code for decimal "4" (i.e., binary 0100) appears on the input lines, the "4" output, pin no. 5, will drop LOW; all other pins are HIGH. We can use this operation to form a device-select pulse generator by connecting the control signal pins of the Z80 to three of the inputs, and the $\overline{\text{SELECT}}$ signal from an active-LOW output address decoder to the fourth input.

The 7442 inputs are weighted as shown in the pin-in table below:

BCD weight	D = 8	C = 4	B = 2	A = 1
7442 pin	12	13	14	15

In the circuit of Fig. B-2, we connect the $\overline{\text{IORQ}}$ to the A input (weight 1), the $\overline{\text{WR}}$ signal to the "B" input (weight 2), the $\overline{\text{RD}}$ signal to the "C" input (weight 4) and the $\overline{\text{SELECT}}$ signal to the "D" input (weight 8). Thus, a BCD "0100" (decimal 4) will indicate an IN operation, while OUT is indicated by BCD 0010 (decimal 2). We find, therefore, pin no. 5 of the 7442 drops LOW for input operations and pin no. 3 drops LOW for output operations. These form $\overline{\text{IN}}$ and $\overline{\text{OUT}}$ signals, respectively.

A second variation of the device-select for a Z80 chip is shown in Fig. B-3. In this case, since all of the control signals are active-LOW instead of active-HIGH (compare Fig. B-1), we use NOR gates instead of NAND gates. Otherwise, the operation is quite similar to Fig. B-1. In this case, however, all three inputs are LOW for the output of either gate to be HIGH.

Appendix C
Input/Output Devices

An input/output port is the communications port between the computer and the outside world. An input port, therefore, brings data into the computer from the outside world. The output port, on the other hand, transmits data from the computer to the outside world. In this section, we will discuss some practical devices of both types and demonstrate how they are used.

OUTPUT PORT

The output port, according to our definition, will transmit data from the inside of the computer to the outside world. The typical output port must be latched (believe it or not, there has been at least one computer that did not use latched output ports! The data disappeared from the port immediately after the output instruction was executed!). Thus, a successful output port device will have the capability to *latch*, i.e., remember data after the execution of the cycle. A likely candidate for this service is the type-D flip-flop shown in Fig. C-1. Let's recall the basic rules of the type-D flip-flop.

1. The Q-output will follow the D-input only when the clock line (CLK) is active (HIGH in most cases);

2. When the clock (CLK) line becomes inactive, the Q-output will remain at the last valid state prior to the transition of the clock line.

Thus, when the clock (CLK) line of type-D flip-flop shown in

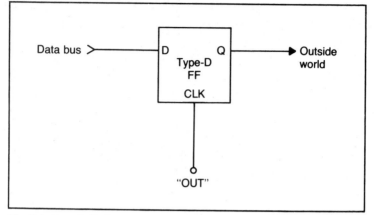

Fig. C-1. Type-D flip-flop.

Fig. C-1 goes HIGH, data is transferred from the D-input to the Q-output. This data will remain on the Q-output when the CLK line drops LOW again, so the data is said to be remembered, or "latched."

There are TTL and CMOS integrated circuits that are called *data latches*. These devices contain banks of four or eight type-D flip-flops. In most cases, the latch flip-flops will not have a NOT-Q output, using only the Q-output that represents the input data (the NOT-Q output will complement the input data). Examples of data latches from the TTL line are the 7475 device, which contains four type-D flip-flops arranged in two banks of two each, and the 74100 device which consists of eight flip-flops arranged in two banks of four each. Figure C-2 shows a 74100 data latch configured to operate as an output port (eight bit). In this case, there are two CLK lines, pins 12 and 23, tied together to form a single "OUT" control signal. When this signal goes HIGH (the active state), the data on the eight input lines will be transferred to the output lines. By connecting the eight input lines to bit DB0 through DB7 of the data bus in the microcomputer, we obtain an eight-bit parallel output port; the output lines of the 74100 device becomes bits B0 through B7 of the port.

The OUT signal used in Fig. C-2 must be generated by the computer, and must be totally unique for *that* and that port alone. This signal must never be active for any other reason than that the computer program has called for that port to become active. For generation of the IN and OUT device select pulses, see Appendix B. If you are unaware of the method for creating this signal, then read (or reread) that appendix. Other output port devices that combine the input and output functions in one chip are discussed later.

INPUT PORT

The job of the input port is to bring data from the outside world into the computer. There is also a special constraint placed on the input port. Unlike the output port, which connects only a single TTL input per bit of the data bus (i.e., minimum loading of the bus), the input port will connect TTL output lines to the data bus. If any one bit is LOW, for example, it will drag down the corresponding bit of the data bus erroneously. In order to overcome this problem, we will require a device that has a *tri-state output* (see Fig. C-3).

Normal TTL devices have two-state outputs. Any output can only be HIGH or LOW, there is no in between (that is the nature of all binary devices; a switch, after all, can only be on or off). The tri-state output provides one additional state: disconnected. Where the HIGH state provides a low impedance to V+, the LOW state provides a low impedance to ground (or V− in CMOS devices), the third state is disconnected (i.e.,there is a high impedance to both

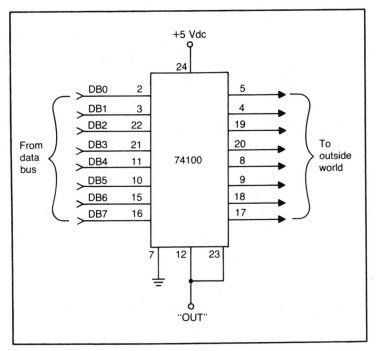

Fig. C-2. 74100 dual four-bit (quad) latch.

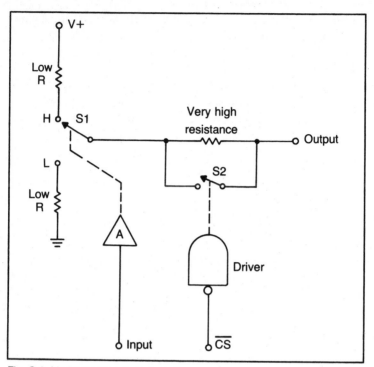

Fig. C-3. Model for tri-state logic devices.

V+ and ground). Figure C-3 shows a model circuit that represents the tri-state output TTL device.

Switch S1 in Fig. C-3 represents the action of the circuit with respect to the input. In this example, the stage is a noninverting buffer, as represented by the stage marked "A". The switch (S1) will be connected to the "H" side of the circuit when the input is HIGH, and the "L" side when the input is LOW. A second switch, S2, however, determines whether or not the output is connected to the package output terminals. When the *chip select* terminal is LOW, switch S2 is closed, so the output terminal of the device is connected to the output circuit. If, however, the $\overline{CS}$ terminal is HIGH, then the switch is open and there is a high impedance between the output terminal and the internal output circuitry.

The advantage of the tri-state output device is that it allows the computer to disconnect the input port from the data bus whenever it is not in use. The output circuitry of the device will be connected to the data bus only when an input operation is being executed. Unlike the output port, the input port device is not latched.

Figure C-4 shows a common input device, the 74125 TTL integrated circuit. Each 74125 contains four independent tri-state noninverting buffer stages, so two are required for an eight-bit input port. There is also a 74126 device available, which is the same thing only with inverting internal buffers. In order to make an input port with these chips it is necessary to use two of them, and connect all eight chip select lines together at a common point to form an "IN" device select line. Like the OUT counterpart discussed earlier, the $\overline{\text{IN}}$ signal must be active only when the computer commands that particular input port to become active (see Appendix B). The 74125 device uses active-LOW chip select ($\overline{\text{CS}}$) control lines, so the $\overline{\text{IN}}$ signal will turn on the input port when it drops LOW. A simple inverter circuit will make the $\overline{\text{IN}}$ into an IN signal if desired (or needed).

INTEL 8226/8216 FOUR-BIT PARALLEL BIDIRECTIONAL BUS DRIVERS

There are a number of integrated circuits on the market that were intended specifically as input/output devices for microcomputers. One of the easiest to apply and earliest of these special purpose I/O devices is the Intel Corporation's 8216 and 8226 devices. These twin devices differ only in that the 8216 is noninvert-

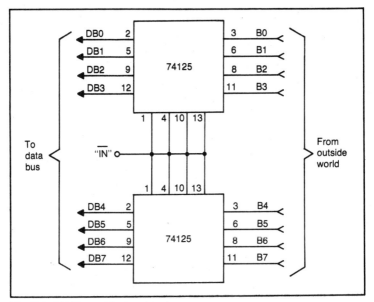

Fig. C-4. 74125 used for input port.

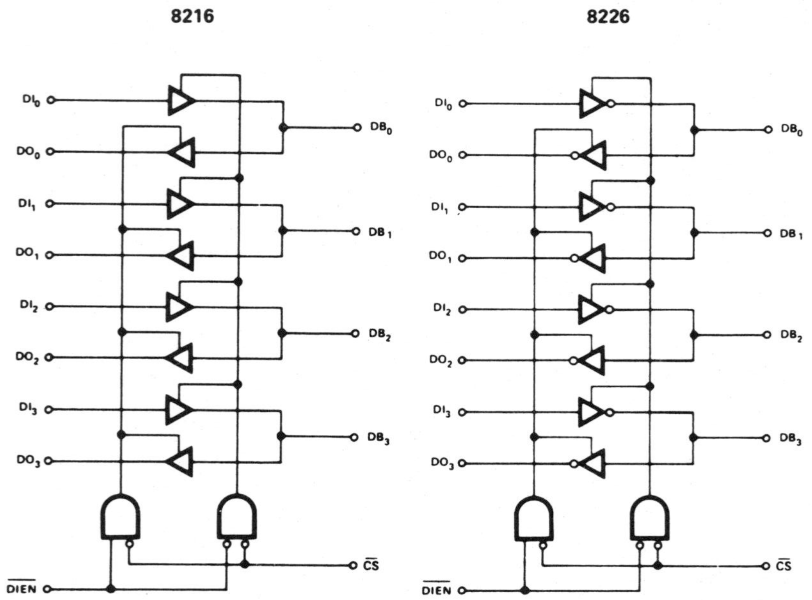

Figure 2. Pin Configuration

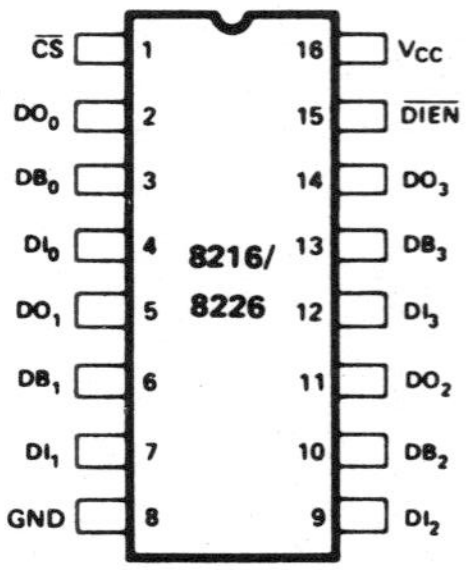

DB$_0$-DB$_3$	DATA BUS BI DIRECTIONAL	
DI$_0$-DI$_3$	DATA INPUT	
DO$_0$-DO$_3$	DATA OUTPUT	
DIEN	DATA IN ENABLE DIRECTION CONTROL	
CS	CHIP SELECT	

Figure 1. Block Diagrams

Ⓐ

FUNCTIONAL DESCRIPTION

Microprocessors like the 8080 are MOS devices and are generally capable of driving a single TTL load. The same is true for MOS memory devices. While this type of drive is sufficient in small systems with few components, quite often it is necessary to buffer the microprocessor and memories when adding components or expanding to a multi-board system.

The 8216/8226 is a four bit bidirectional bus driver specifically designed to buffer microcomputer system components.

Bidirectional Driver

Each buffered line of the four bit driver consists of two separate buffers that are tri-state in nature to achieve direct bus interface and bidirectional capability. On one side of the driver the output of one buffer and the input of another are tied together (DB), this side is used to interface to the system side components such as memories, I/O, etc., because its interface is direct TTL compatible and it has high drive (50mA). On the other side of the driver the inputs and outputs are separated to provide maximum flexibility. Of course, they can be tied together so that the driver can

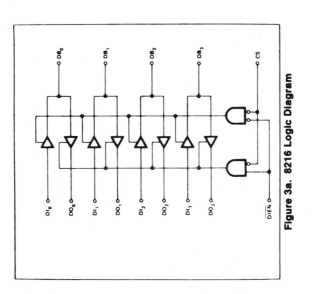

Figure 3a. 8216 Logic Diagram

Fig. C-5. 8216/8226 bidirectional bus driver (courtesy of Intel Corporation).

259

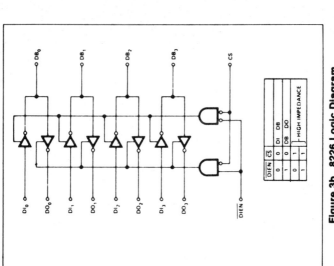

DIEN	CS		
0	0	DI	DB
1	0	DB	DO
0	1	HIGH IMPEDANCE	
1	1	HIGH IMPEDANCE	

Figure 3b. 8226 Logic Diagram

be used to buffer a true bi-directional bus such as the 8080 Data Bus. The DO outputs on this side of the driver have a special high voltage output drive capability (3.65V) so that direct interface to the 8080 and 8008 CPUs is achieved with an adequate amount of noise immunity (350mV worst case).

Control Gating DIEN, CS

The CS input is actually a device select. When it is "high" the output drivers are all forced to their high-impedance state. When it is at "zero" the device is selected (enabled) and the direction of the data flow is determined by the DIEN input.

The DIEN input controls the direction of data flow (see Figure 3) for complete truth table. This direction control is accomplished by forcing one of the pair of buffers into its high impedance state and allowing the other to transmit its data. A simple two gate circuit is used for this function

The 8216/8226 is a device that will reduce component count in microcomputer systems and at the same time enhance noise immunity to assure reliable, high performance operation.

B

ABSOLUTE MAXIMUM RATINGS*

Temperature Under Bias	0°C to 70°C
Storage Temperature	-65°C to +150°C
All Output and Supply Voltages	-0.5V to +7V
All Input Voltages	-1.0V to +5.5V
Output Currents	125 mA

*NOTICE: Stresses above those listed under "Absolute Maximum Ratings" may cause permanent damage to the device. This is a stress rating only and functional operation of the device at these or any other conditions above those indicated in the operational sections of this specification is not implied. Exposure to absolute maximum rating conditions for extended periods may affect device reliability.

D.C. CHARACTERISTICS (T_A = 0°C to +70°C, V_{CC} = +5V ± 5%)

Symbol	Parameter	Limits			Unit	Conditions
		Min.	Typ.	Max.		
I_{F1}	Input Load Current $\overline{DIEN}$, $\overline{CS}$		-0.15	-.5	mA	V_F = 0.45
I_{F2}	Input Load Current All Other Inputs		-0.08	-.25	mA	V_F = 0.45
I_{R1}	Input Leakage Current $\overline{DIEN}$, $\overline{CS}$			80	μA	V_R = 5.25V
I_{R2}	Input Leakage Current DI Inputs			40	μA	V_R = 5.25V
V_C	Input Forward Voltage Clamp			-1	V	I_C = -5mA

Fig. C-5. 8216/8226 bidirectional bus driver (courtesy of Intel Corporation). (Continued from page 260.)

Symbol	Parameter		Limits			Unit	Conditions
			Min.	Typ.	Max.		
V_{IL}	Input "Low" Voltage				.95	V	
V_{IH}	Input "High" Voltage		2.0			V	
$|I_O|$	Output Leakage Current (3-State)	DO DB			20 100	µA	$V_O = 0.45V/5.25V$
I_{CC}	Power Supply Current	8216 8226		95 85	130 120	mA	
V_{OL1}	Output "Low" Voltage			0.3	.45	V	DO Outputs I_{OL}=15mA DB Outputs I_{OL}=25mA
V_{OL2}	Output "Low" Voltage	8216 8226		0.5 0.5	.6 .6	V	DB Outputs I_{OL}=55mA DB Outputs I_{OL}=50mA
V_{OH1}	Output "High" Voltage		3.65	4.0		V	DO Outputs I_{OH} = –1mA
V_{OH2}	Output "High" Voltage		2.4	3.0		V	DB Outputs I_{OH} = –10mA
I_{OS}	Output Short Circuit Current		–15 –30	–35 –75	–65 –120	mA mA	DO Outputs $V_O \cong 0V$, DB Outputs V_{CC}=5.0V

NOTE:
Typical values are for $T_A = 25°C$, $V_{CC} = 5.0V$.

CAPACITANCE[5] (V_{BIAS} = 2.5V, V_{CC} = 5.0V, T_A = 25°C, f = 1 MHz)

Symbol	Parameter	Min.	Typ.[1]	Max.	Unit
C_{IN}	Input Capacitance		4	8	pF
C_{OUT1}	Output Capacitance		6	10	pF
C_{OUT2}	Output Capacitance		13	18	pF

A.C. CHARACTERISTICS (T_A = 0°C to +70°C, V_{CC} = +5V ± 5%)

Symbol	Parameter	Min.	Typ.[1]	Max.	Unit	Conditions
T_{PD1}	Input to Output Delay DO Outputs		15	25	ns	C_L=30pF, R_1=300Ω, R_2=600Ω
T_{PD2}	Input to Output Delay DB Outputs					C_L=300pF, R_1=90Ω
	8216		19	30	ns	
	8226		16	25	ns	R_2 = 180Ω
T_E	Output Enable Time				ns	(Note 2)
	8216		42	65	ns	

Fig. C-5. 8216/8226 bidirectional bus driver (courtesy of Intel Corporation). (Continued from page 261.)

Symbol	Parameter	Limits			Unit	Conditions
		Min.	Typ.[1]	Max.		
	8226					
T_D	Output Disable Time		16	35	ns	(Note 4)
			36	54	ns	(Note 3)

NOTE:

Input pulse amplitude of 2.5V.

Input rise and fall times of 5 ns between 1 and 2 volts.

Output loading is 5 mA and 10 pF.

Speed measurements are made at 1.5 volt levels.

NOTES:

1. Typical values are for $T_A = 25°C$, $V_{CC} = 5.0V$.
2. DO Outputs, $C_L = 30pF$, $R_1 = 300/10$ KΩ, $R_2 = 180/1K\Omega$; DB Outputs, $C_L = 300pF$, $R_1 = 90/10$ KΩ, $R_2 = 180/1$ KΩ.
3. DO Outputs, $C_L = 30pF$, $R_1 = 300/10$ KΩ, $R_2 = 600/1K$; DB Outputs, $C_L = 300pF$ $R_1 = 90/10$ KΩ, $R_2 = 180/1$ KΩ.
4. DO Outputs, $C_L = 5pF$, $R_1 = 300/10K\Omega$, $R_2 = 600/1$ KΩ; DB Outputs, $C_L = 5pF$, $R_1 = 90/10$ KΩ, $R_2 = 180/1$ KΩ.
5. This parameter is periodically sampled and not 100% tested.

A.C. TESTING LOAD CIRCUIT

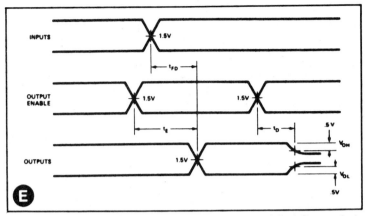

Fig. C-5. 8216/8226 bidirectional bus driver (courtesy of Intel Corporation). (Continued from page 263.)

ing, while the 8226 is inverting; otherwise, all other functions are the same. Figure C-5 shows the specification sheet for these devices. The internal block diagram and pin-outs for the 8216/8226 are shown in Fig. C-5A.

The 8216/8226 devices are tri-state output and can drive up to 50 milliampere loads at normal TTL levels. Originally, the 8216/8226 were designed to work with the Intel 8080 microprocessor, but they are sufficiently universal to work with almost any other microprocessor on the market, although some additional external chips may be required.

The secret to bidirectionality in the 8216/8226 is that each stage contains a pair of buffers (or, in the case of the 8226 a pair of inverters), one facing each direction. The data bus lines, DB_0 through DB_3, are connected to the input of one device and the output of the other. In addition to the data bus lines, there are also input lines marked DI_0 through DI_3, and output lines marked DO_0 through DO_3. A chip select ($\overline{CS}$) signal provides an active-LOW terminal that connects the tri-state outputs of the stages to the outside world. The $\overline{DIEN}$ line is labeled *data in enable direction control*. When $\overline{DIEN}$ is LOW, the DI terminals are connected to the data bus, so the device functions as an input port. Similarly, when $\overline{DIEN}$ is HIGH, the DO terminals are connected to the data bus and the device functions as an output port. Operation with $\overline{CS}$ and $\overline{DIEN}$ are given in Fig. C-5B. Electrical ratings of the 8216/8226 devices are shown in Figs. C-5C and C-5D. The timing diagram is shown in Fig. C-5E.

Two 8216/8226 devices are needed for an eight-bit input/

8080 Data Bus Buffer

The 8080 CPU Data Bus is capable of driving a single TTL load and is more than adequate for small, single board systems. When expanding such a system to more than one board to increase I/O or Memory size, it is necessary to provide a buffer. The 8216/8226 is a device that is exactly fitted to this application.

Shown in Figure 2 are a pair of 8216/8226 connected directly to the 8080 Data Bus and associated control signals. The buffer is bidirectional in nature and serves to isolate the CPU data bus.

On the system side, the DB lines interface with standard semiconductor I/O and Memory components and are completely TTL compatible. The DB lines also provide a high drive capability (50mA) so that an extremely large system can be dirven along with possible bus termination networks.

On the 8080 side the DI and DO lines are tied together and are directly connected to the 8080 Data Bus for bidirectional operation. The DO outputs of the 8216/8226 have a high voltage output capability of 3.65 volts which allows direct connection to the 8080 whose minimum input voltage is 3.3 volts. It also gives a very adequate noise margin of 350mV (worst case).

The DIEN inputs to 8216/8226 is connected directly to the

The 8216/8226 can be used in a wide variety of other buffering functions in microcomputer systems such as Address Bus Drivers, Drivers to peripheral devices such as printers, and as Drivers for long length cables to other peripherals or systems.

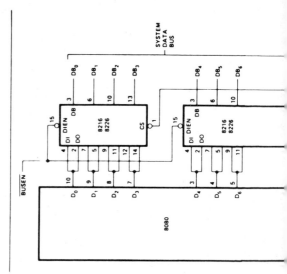

8080. $\overline{\text{DIEN}}$ is tied to DBIN so that proper bus flow is maintained, and $\overline{\text{CS}}$ is tied to $\overline{\text{BUSEN}}$ so that the system side Data Bus will be 3-stated when a Hold request has been acknowledged during a DMA activity.

Memory and I/O Interface to a Bidirectional Bus

In large microcomputer systems it is often necessary to provide Memory and I/O with their own buffers and at the same time maintain a direct, common interface to a bidirectional Data Bus. The 8216/8226 has separated data in and data out lines on one side and a common bidirectional set on the other to accommodate such a function.

Shown in Figure 3 is an example of how the 8216/8226 is used in this type of application.

The interface to Memory is simple and direct. The memories used are typically Intel® 8102, 8102A, 8101 or 8107B-4 and have separate data inputs and outputs. The DI and DO lines of the 8216/8226 tie to them directly and under control of the $\overline{\text{MEMR}}$ signal, which is connected to the $\overline{\text{DIEN}}$ input, an interface to the bidirectional Data Bus is maintained.

The interface to I/O is similar to Memory. The I/O devices used are typically Intel® 8255s, and can be used for both input and output ports. The $\overline{\text{I/O R}}$ signal is connected directly to the $\overline{\text{DIEN}}$ input so that proper data flow from the I/O device to the Data Bus is maintained.

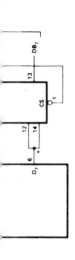

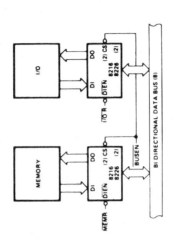

Figure 2. 8080 Data Bus Buffer

Figure 3. Memory and I/O Interface to a Bidirectional Bus

Fig. C-6. Applications of the 8216/8226 (courtesy of Intel Corporation).

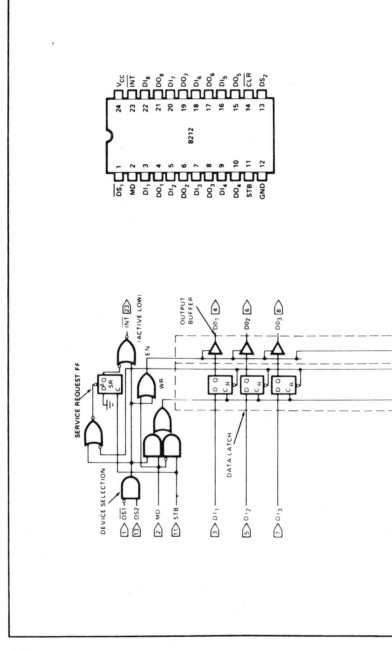

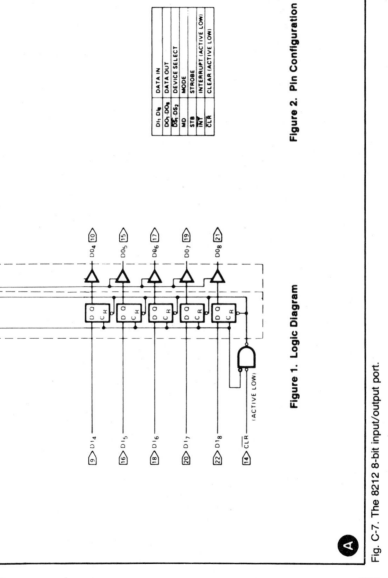

Figure 1. Logic Diagram

DI_1, DI_8	DATA IN
DO_1, DO_8	DATA OUT
DS_1, DS_2	DEVICE SELECT
MD	MODE
STB	STROBE
$\overline{INT}$	INTERRUPT (ACTIVE LOW)
$\overline{CLR}$	CLEAR (ACTIVE LOW)

Figure 2. Pin Configuration

Fig. C-7. The 8212 8-bit input/output port.

FUNCTIONAL DESCRIPTION

Data Latch

The 8 flip-flops that make up the data latch are of a "D" type design. The output (Q) of the flip-flop will follow the data input (D) while the clock input (C) is high. Latching will occur when the clock (C) returns low.

The latched data is cleared by an asynchronous reset input ($\overline{CLR}$). (Note: Clock (C) Overrides Reset ($\overline{CLR}$).)

Output Buffer

The outputs of the data latch (Q) are connected to 3-state, non-inverting output buffers. These buffers have a common control line (EN); this control line either enables the buffer to transmit the data from the outputs of the data latch (Q) or disables the buffer, forcing the output into a high impedance state. (3-state)

The high impedance state allows the designer to connect the 8212 directly onto the microprocessor bidirectional data bus.

Control Logic

The 8212 has control inputs $\overline{DS1}$, DS2, MD and STB. These inputs are used to control device selection, data latching, output buffer state and service request flip-flop.

Service Request Flip-Flop

The (SR) flip-flop is used to generate and control interrupts in microcomputer systems. It is asynchronously set by the $\overline{CLR}$ input (active low). When the (SR) flip-flop is set it is in the non-interrupting state.

The output of the (SR) flip-flop (Q) is connected to an inverting input of a "NOR" gate. The other input to the "NOR" gate is non-inverting and is connected to the device selection logic (DS1 · DS2). The output of the "NOR" gate ($\overline{INT}$) is active low (interrupting state) for connection to active low input priority generating circuits.

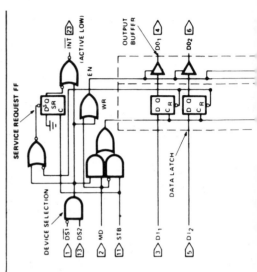

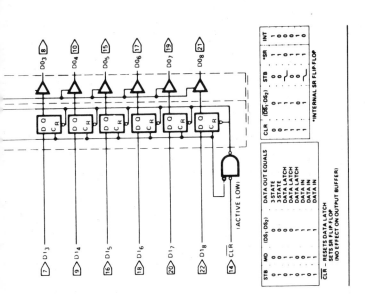

DO3 [8]
DO4 [10]
DO5 [15]
DO6 [17]
DO7 [19]
DO8 [21]

DI3 [7]
DI4 [9]
DI5 [16]
DI6 [18]
DI7 [20]
DI8 [22]

CLR [14] (ACTIVE LOW)

STB	MD	(DS₁ · DS₂)	DATA OUT EQUALS
0	0	0	3 STATE
0	0	1	3 STATE
0	1	0	DATA LATCH
0	1	1	DATA LATCH
1	0	0	DATA LATCH
1	0	1	DATA IN
0	1	0	DATA IN
1	1	1	DATA IN

CLR – RESETS DATA LATCH
SETS SR FLIP FLOP
(NO EFFECT ON OUTPUT BUFFER)

CLR	(DS₁, DS₂)	STB	*SR	INT
0			1	0
0			1	0
1	0	0	0	0
1	0	1	0	0
1	1	0	1	1
1	1	1	1	1
1			0	0

*INTERNAL SR FLIP-FLOP

DS1, DS2 (Device Select)

These 2 inputs are used for device selection. When $\overline{DS1}$ is low and DS2 is high ($\overline{DS1} \cdot DS2$) the device is selected. In the selected state the output buffer is enabled and the service request flip-flop (SR) is asynchronously set.

MD (Mode)

This input is used to control the state of the output buffer and to determine the source of the clock input (C) to the data latch.

When MD is high (output mode) the output buffers are enabled and the source of clock (C) to the data latch is from the device selection logic ($\overline{DS1} \cdot DS2$).

When MD is low (input mode) the output buffer state is determined by the device selection logic ($\overline{DS1} \cdot DS2$) and the source of clock (C) to the data latch is the STB (Strobe) input.

STB (Strobe)

This input is used as the clock (C) to the data latch for the input mode MD = 0) and to synchronously reset the service request flip-flop (SR).

Note that the SR flip-flop is negative edge triggered.

B

Fig. C-7. The 8212 8-bit input/output port. (Continued from page 269.)

ABSOLUTE MAXIMUM RATINGS*

Temperature Under Bias Plastic .... 0°C to +70°C
Storage Temperature .... -65°C to +160°C
All Output or Supply Voltages .... -0.5 to +7 Volts
All Input Voltages .... -1.0 to 5.5 Volts
Output Currents 100mA

D.C. CHARACTERISTICS (T$_A$=0°C to +75°C, V$_{CC}$= +5V ± 5%)

Symbol	Parameter	Limits Min.	Limits Typ.	Limits Max.	Unit	Test Conditions
I$_F$	Input Load Current, ACK, DS$_2$, CR, DI$_1$-DI$_8$ Inputs			-.25	mA	V$_F$ = .45V
I$_F$	Input Load Current MD Input			-.75	mA	V$_F$ = .45V
I$_F$	Input Load Current DS$_1$ Input			-1.0	mA	V$_F$ = .45V
I$_R$	Input Leakage Current, ACK, DS, CR, DI$_1$-DI$_8$ Inputs			10	µA	V$_R$ ≤ V$_{CC}$
I$_R$	Input Leakage Current MO Input			30	µA	V$_R$ ≤ V$_{CC}$
I$_R$	Input Leakage Current DS$_1$ Input			40	µA	V$_R$ ≤ V$_{CC}$
V$_C$	Input Forward Voltage Clamp			-1	V	I$_C$ = -5mA
V$_{IL}$	Input "Low" Voltage			.85	V	
V$_{IH}$	Input "High" Voltage	2.0			V	
V$_{OL}$	Output "Low" Voltage			.45	V	I$_{OL}$ = 15mA

Symbol	Parameter	Min		Max		Unit	Test Conditions
V_{OH}	Output "High" Voltage	3.65	4.0			V	$I_{OH} = -1mA$ $V_O = 0V$, $V_{CC} = 5V$
I_{sc}	Short Circuit Output Current	-15		-75		mA	
$|I_{OL}|$	Output Leakage Current High Impedance State			20		µA	$V_O = .45V/5.25V$
I_{cc}	Power Supply Current			90	130	mA	

CAPACITANCE*

$(F = 1MHz, V_{BIAS} = 2.5V, V_{CC} = +5V, T_A = +25°C)$

Symbol	Test	Limits	
		Typ.	Max.
C_{IN}	DS_1 MD Input Capacitance	9pF	12pF
C_{IN}	DS_2, $\overline{CLR}$, STB, DI_1-DI_8 Input Capacitance	5pF	9pF
C_{OUT}	DO_1-DO_8 Output Capacitance	8pF	12pF

*This parameter is sampled and not 100% tested.

A.C. TESTING LOAD CIRCUIT

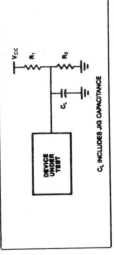

C_L INCLUDES JIG CAPACITANCE

SWITCHING CHARACTERISTICS

Conditions of Test

Input Pulse Amplitude = 2.5V
Input Rise and Fall Times 5ns
Between 1V and 2V Measurements made at 1.5V
with 15mA and 30pF Test Load

NOTE:
1.

Test	C_L*	R_1	R_2
t_{PD}, t_{WE}, t_R, t_S, t_C	30pF	300Ω	600Ω
t_E, ENABLE↑	30pF	10KΩ	1KΩ
t_E, ENABLE↓	30pF	300Ω	600Ω
t_E, DISABLE↑	5pF	300Ω	600Ω
t_E, DISABLE↓	5pF	10KΩ	1KΩ

*Includes probe and jig capacitance.

Fig. C-7. The 8212 8-bit input/output port. (Continued from page 271.)

A.C. CHARACTERISTICS ($T_A = 0°C$ to $+70°C$, $V_{CC} = +5V \pm 5\%$)

Symbol	Parameter	Limits			Unit	Test Conditions
		Min.	Typ.	Max.		
t_{PW}	Pulse Width	30			ns	
t_{PD}	Data to Output Delay			30	ns	Note 1
t_{WE}	Write Enable to Output Delay			40	ns	Note 1
t_{SET}	Data Set Up Time	15			ns	
t_H	Data Hold Time	20			ns	
t_R	Reset to Output Delay			40	ns	Note 1
t_S	Set to Output Delay			30	ns	Note 1
t_E	Output Enable/Disable Time			45	ns	Note 1
t_C	Clear to Output Delay			55	ns	Note 1

APPLICATIONS
Basic Schematic Symbols

Two examples of ways to draw the 8212 on system schematics—(1) the top being the detailed view showing pin numbers, and (2) the bottom being the symbolic view showing the system input or output as a system bus (bus containing 8 parallel lines). The output to the data bus is symbolic in referencing 8 parallel lines.

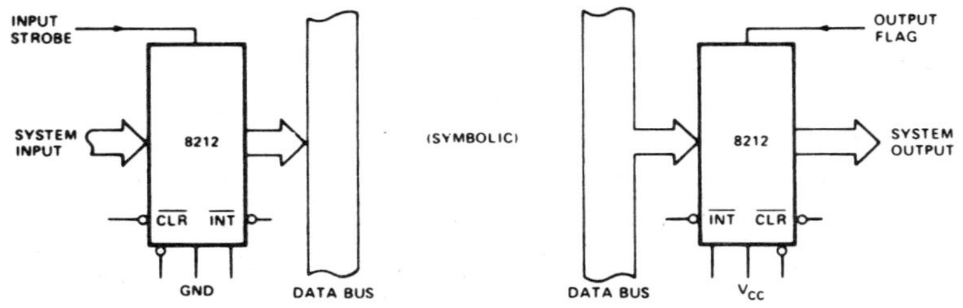

Figure 3. Basic Schematic Symbols

Gated Buffer (3-State)

The simplest use of the 8212 is that of a gated buffer. By tying the mode signal low and the strobe input high, the data latch is acting as a straight through gate. The output buffers are then enabled from the device selection logic $\overline{DS1}$ and DS2.

When the device selection logic is false, the outputs are 3-state.

When the device selection logic is true, the input data from the system is directly transferred to the output. The input data load is 250 micro amps. The output data can sink 15 milli amps. The minimum high output is 3.65 volts.

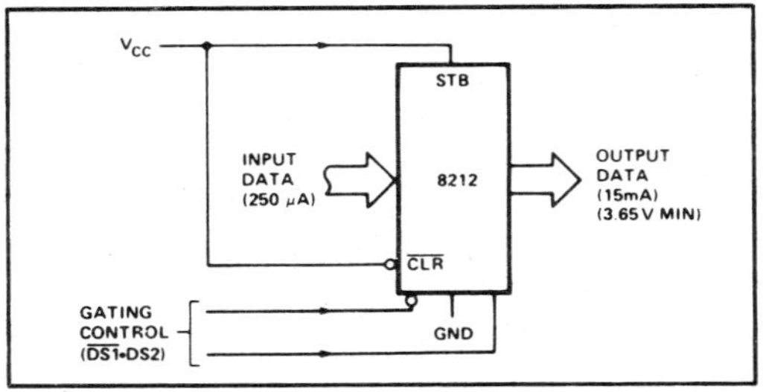

Figure 4. Gated Buffer

Fig. C-7. The 8212 8-bit input/output port. (Continued from page 273.)

BiDirectional Bus Driver

A pair of 8212's wired (back-to-back) can be used as a symmetrical drive, bidirectional bus driver. The devices are controlled by the data bus input control which is connected to $\overline{DS1}$ on the first 8212 and to DS2 on the second. One device is active, and acting as a straight through buffer the other is in 3-state mode. This is a very useful circuit in small system design.

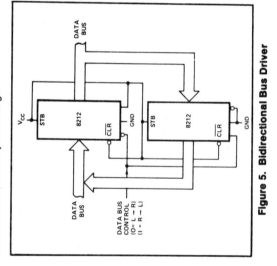

Figure 5. Bidirectional Bus Driver

Interrupt Instruction Port

The 8212 can be used to gate the interrupt instruction, normally RESTART instructions, onto the data bus. The device is enabled from the interrupt acknowledge signal from the microprocessor and from a port selection signal. This signal is normally tied to ground. ($\overline{DS1}$ could be used to multiplex a variety of interrupt instruction ports onto a common bus).

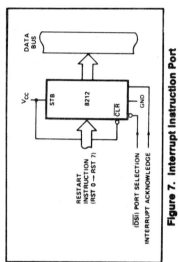

Figure 7. Interrupt Instruction Port

Output Port (With Hand-Shaking)

The 8212 can be used to transmit data from the data bus to a system output. The output strobe could be a hand-shaking signal such as "reception of data" from the device that the system is outputting to. It in turn, can interrupt the system signifying the reception of data. The selection of the port comes from the device selection logic. ($\overline{DS1} \cdot DS2$)

276

Interrupting Input Port

This use of an 8212 is that of a system input port that accepts a strobe from the system input source, which in turn clears the service request flip-flop and interrupts the processor. The processor then goes through a service routine, identifies the port, and causes the device selection logic to go true — enabling the system input data onto the data bus.

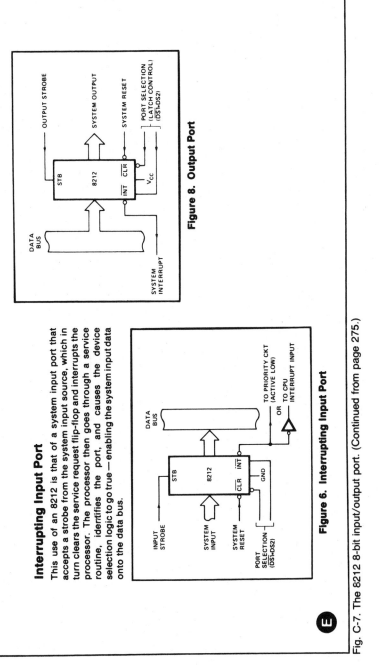

Figure 8. Output Port

Figure 6. Interrupting Input Port

Fig. C-7. The 8212 8-bit input/output port. (Continued from page 275.)

808A Status Latch

Here the 8212 is used as the status latch for an 8080A microcomputer system. The input to the 8212 latch is directly from the 8080A data bus. Timing shows that when the SYNC signal is true, which is connected to the DS2 input and the phase 1 signal is true, which is a TTL level coming from the clock generator; then, the status data will be latched into the 8212.

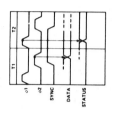

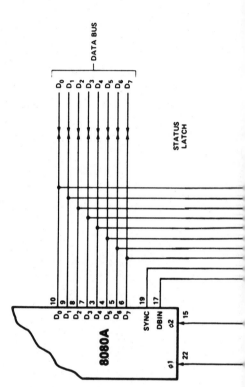

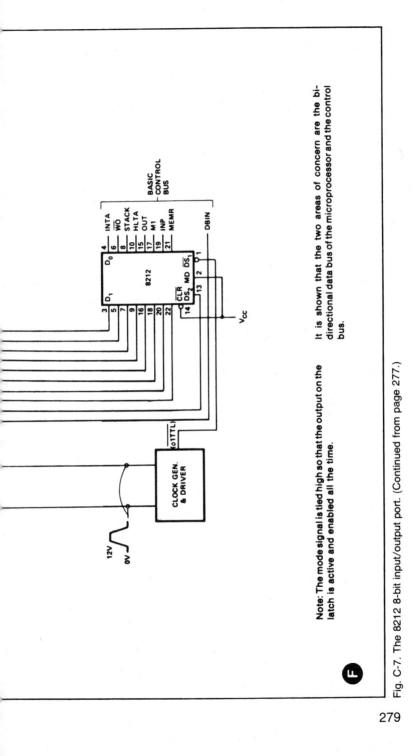

Note: The mode signal is tied high so that the output on the latch is active and enabled all the time.

It is shown that the two areas of concern are the bi-directional data bus of the microprocessor and the control bus.

Fig. C-7. The 8212 8-bit input/output port. (Continued from page 277.)

279

TYPICAL CHARACTERISTICS

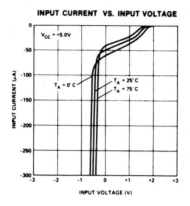

INPUT CURRENT VS. INPUT VOLTAGE

OUTPUT CURRENT VS. OUTPUT "LOW" VOLTAGE

OUTPUT CURRENT VS. OUTPUT "HIGH" VOLTAGE

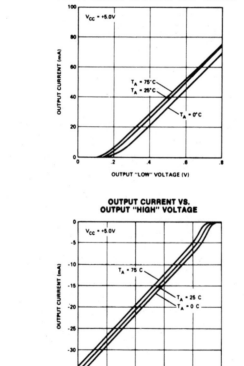

Fig. C-7. The 8212 8-bit input/output port. (Continued from page 279.)

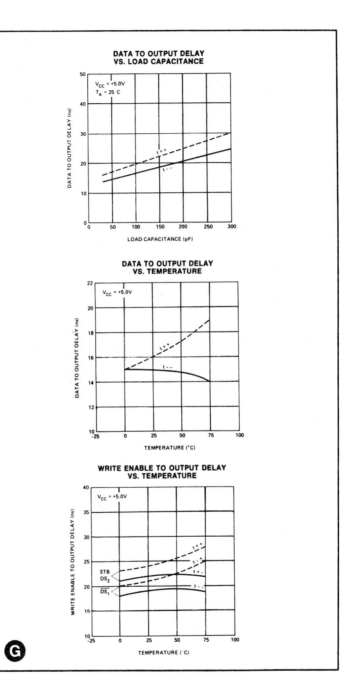

**DATA TO OUTPUT DELAY
VS. LOAD CAPACITANCE**

V_{CC} = +5.0V
T_A = 25 C

DATA TO OUTPUT DELAY (ns)

LOAD CAPACITANCE (pF)

t + +

t - -

**DATA TO OUTPUT DELAY
VS. TEMPERATURE**

V_{CC} = +5.0V

DATA TO OUTPUT DELAY (ns)

TEMPERATURE (°C)

t + +

t - -

**WRITE ENABLE TO OUTPUT DELAY
VS. TEMPERATURE**

V_{CC} = +5.0V

WRITE ENABLE TO OUTPUT DELAY (ns)

TEMPERATURE (°C)

STB
DS_2

$\overline{DS_1}$

t + +

t - +

t + -

t - -

G

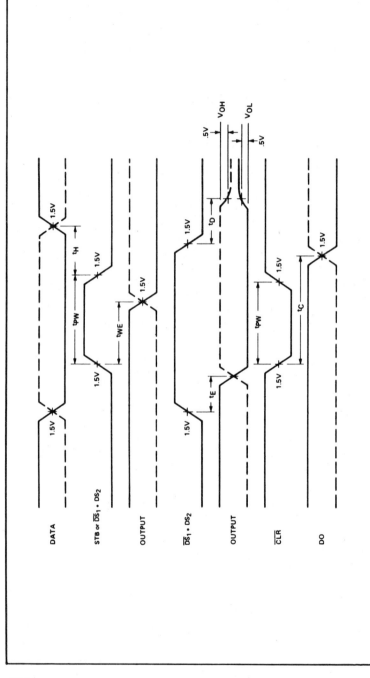

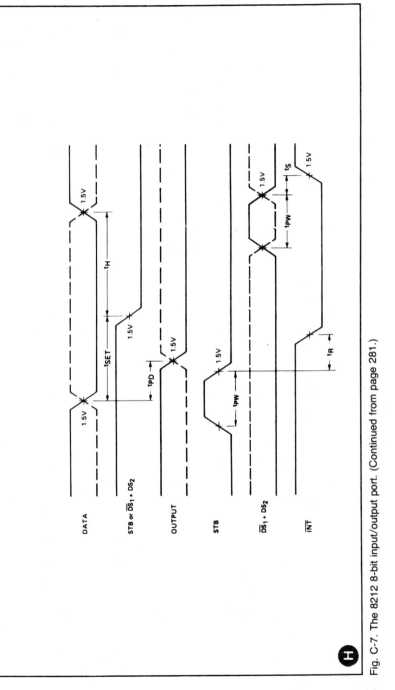

Fig. C-7. The 8212 8-bit input/output port. (Continued from page 281.)

output port. Examples of typical applications are shown in Fig. C-6. The first application reflects the fact that the 8216/8226 were designed for use with the 8080A microprocessor chip. In this case, the 8216/8226 is used as a bus driver/receiver in order to boost the drive capability of the 8080A device. Each 8080A data bus line is capable of driving a single TTL input, but that is totally insufficient for all but the simplest systems. By adding the 8216/8226 devices, the drive capacity is increased to 50 milliamperes, or more than 30 standard TTL loads. For this application the DI and DO lines are connected together, while the DB lines drive the data bus. Since the 8080A is an eight-bit microprocessor chip, a pair of 8216/8226 devices are needed to successfully drive the data bus (each contains only four bits).

INTEL 8212 8-BIT INPUT/OUTPUT PORT

Another Intel device is shown in Fig. C-7. This is the 8212 8-bit I/O port device. The 8212 device is somewhat more complex than the 8216/8226 devices, but operates on much the same principle. Unlike the 8216/8226 devices, however, the 8212 provides for a latched output capability. Again, the original intent was to provide an interface chip for the 8080A microprocessor, but other devices can be just as easily accommodated.

The internal circuitry is shown in block form in Fig. C-7A, along with the device pin-outs. Incidentally, the figure numbers contained within each figure of this appendix are the original figure numbers used in the Intel manual, from which these illustrations were obtained with the permission of Intel. The DI terminals are data in, the DO terminals are data output, the DS terminals are for device select, MD for mode, STB for strobe, $\overline{INT}$ for interrupt and the $\overline{CLR}$ for clear. The descriptions of these terminals are given in Fig. C-7B.

SERIAL OUTPUT PORTS

The input/output ports discussed thus far have been parallel, i.e., there is one output line for each bit of the data word length. Thus, for an eight-bit data bus a total of not less than eight independent lines are required (plus a ground if the port is not in the same cabinet or same printed wiring board as the microcomputer!). This arrangement allows the fastest transfer of data, but it also very costly in some cases. Wherever the data must be transferred over a telecommunications link (radio or telephone wires), or, wherever

284

the peripheral device is more than a few meters from the computer, the serial communications method might be best.

In a serial communications system, the data bits are transmitted sequentially one after another. There are several ways we can make a serial output port. The "software" method involves using a single bit of a parallel output port, and then creating certain software strategies that will cause the data stored in the accumulator to be transmitted out one at a time. There are a couple of different software tactics that are used, but both involve shifting accumulator data one step at a time and then outputting the bit. In one scenario, we will output the word stored in the accumulator, and monitor, say, bit-0 for HIGH or LOW. Then shift left one step and repeat the procedure. Alternatively, we could monitor the carry flag (C-flag) in a processor status register, and output a HIGH if the C-flag is HIGH, and a LOW if the C-flag is LOW. We could also use an n-bit shift register. The shift register is treated as an output port in which the computer can repetitively shift data left to right.

Another method is to use the universal asynchronous receiver/transmitter (UART). The UART is a special LSI integrated circuit that contains independent data receiver and data transmitter stages. The transmitter accepts n-bit parallel format data and transmits it in serial format. The receiver performs exactly the inverse function, namely, it will receive serial format data and reconvert it into parallel format. Since the receiver and the transmitter are independent, the single UART device will serve both sides of a modem or other serial data application. The principal advantage of the UART is that it simplifies the design of serial transmit/receive data ports. Asynchronous transmission is used instead of synchronous because it is not necessary to keep track of the clock pulses at each end of the system when asynchronous transmission is used.

Appendix D
Low-Voltage Dc Power
Supplies for Computers

The dc power supply used with a computer is often overlooked when the design is determined. The typical procedure in some companies is to assign the design of the power supply to the youngest, greenest engineer in the place. Little thought goes to the dc supply. In most cases, this is a reasonable procedure because the design of power supplies is well known for most cases. In this appendix, we will examine some of the reasonable designs for power supplies of 1 ampere, 3-amperes, 5-amperes at 5-volts, ±12-volts at 1-ampere and an S-100 power supply of +8-volts at 20-amperes.

S-100 POWER SUPPLY

The S-100, or *"Altair,"* microcomputer was, perhaps, the first microcomputer on the market. It was the mainline microcomputer for several years, and no other was even considered by many microcomputerists until the *Apple* came along. The bus on the S-100 microcomputer carries an unregulated +8 volts dc at a high current (10 amperes or more). The individual printed wiring boards that plug into the sockets on the motherboard each carry its own +5 volt low-current regulator. Each card will have from one to five 750-mA to 1-ampere three-terminal IC regulators. Most S-100 computers will have their own built-in power supply, but those people who build their own from pieces and parts will have to supply their own. Figure D-1 shows a circuit for an S-100 dc power supply that will

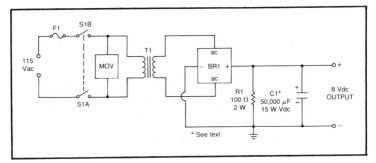

Fig. D-1. S-100 8-volt power supply.

generate +8 volts at currents up to 20-amperes (25-amperes if the correct transformer is used).

The transformer in Fig. D-1 is rated at 6.3 Vac at a current of 20-amperes ; *Triad* makes a suitable type. This rating is "pushed" a little bit because a power supply with a bridge rectifier can only draw fifty-percent of the rated current if the transformer was originally intended for fullwave rectification with a center-tapped transformer secondary. This can be overcome in many cases, however, by using a blower to cool the transformer . . . something that is needed anyway for the rectifier.

Another way to overcome the problem is to use either signal tranformers (a special case) or rectifier transformers intended for battery eliminator applications. Those transformers are routinely rated for bridge service instead of center-tapped service, so they can easily handle the load.

The rectifier can be either bought as a stack or built from individual stud-mounted rectifier diodes. The rating of the diode or bridge stack is 50-volts (PIV) at 25-amperes, or more. Despite whether or not the bridge stack is used, the rectifier(s) should be mounted on a small heatsink and placed in the stream of a blower fan. This is necessary to cool the rectifier and thereby keep the reliability high.

The filter capacitor, C1, is a very high value type. Based on a *minimum* rating of $2,000 \mu F$/ampere, the minimum rating should be $40,000 \mu F$ for a 20-amp supply and $50,000 \mu F$ for a 25-ampere power supply. I recommend that even greater capacitances be used, up to $100,000 \mu F$. The working voltage rating should be 15 WVdc or more.

Connected in parallel across the filter capacitor is a 100-ohm, 2-watt resistor. The purpose of this resistor is to place a minimum load across the rectifier, and to keep the voltage within bounds when the main load is disconnected. Otherwise, an excessive voltage will appear across the filter capacitor.

The device marked "MOV" in Fig. D-1 is a *metal-oxide varistor*. This device is needed to suppress the high-voltage transient "glitches" that arrive on the ac power lines. The MOV is essentially passive at voltages less than the trip-point voltage, but will become a low impedance at higher voltages. Thus, the MOV will be invisible to normal ac potentials, but present a low impedance to greater than 180 volt peaks. In essence, the MOV behaves much like it were a pair of back-to-back 180-volt zener diodes.

The fuse is connected into the ac primary circuit. In normal situations, the fuse will have a rating of about twice the normal flow of current, and should be a slow-blow type (the current is normally quite a bit higher at the onset than a few seconds later). It is good practice to connect the fuse in the hot side of the ac line, rather than the neutral. The switch in this project is a double-pole-single-throw (DPST, DPDT is also usable), and must have a current rating high enough to be happy with the primary current.

±5-VOLT AT 3-AMPERES DC POWER SUPPLY

The dc power supply shown in Fig. D-2 is capable of powering a small computer which requires less than 3-amperes of current at +5 volts. The transformer is rated at 6.3 Vac at a current of 3 to 5 amperes. If the lower of these figures is used, the transformer will run hot and may need a blower to keep it safely cool. When rectified and filtered, the output of the transformer translates to +8 volts unregulated, which is the voltage required (as a minimum) at the input of a voltage regulator device. Use of higher input voltages will increase the power dissipation of the regulator, hence reduce reliability.

The rectifier is rated at a current of 3-amperes or more. In most cases, this means a rating of 6-amperes since 3-ampere rectifier stacks are a little harder to find. The voltage rating should be 50-volts (PIV), or greater.

There are four capacitors in the circuit. Capacitor C1 is the main filter capacitor, and is rated at 1000-μF/ampere to 2000-μF/ampere; since 5000-μF is a relatively easy "standard" value, it is specified here. Capacitor C1 should have a voltage rating of 15 WVdc or more. It is relatively easy to obtain 5000-μF capacitors in 35 WVdc and 50 WVdc ratings. Capacitors C2 and C3 are 0.1-μF units that are used to reduce the effect of noise transients on the voltage regulator (IC1). These capacitors must be mounted as close

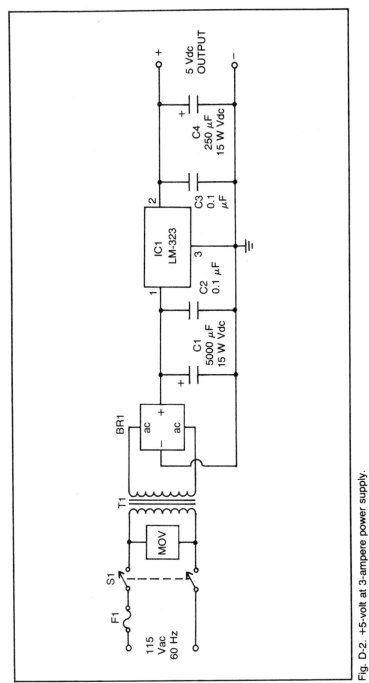

Fig. D-2. +5-volt at 3-ampere power supply.

as possible to the body of the regulator. In most cases, it is possible to mount these capacitors directly to the body of the regulator device. Finally, capacitor C4 is optional, but will improve the transient response of the voltage regulator. If a sudden increase in current demand occurs, the regulator may not catch up with it immediately, but instead will momentarily reduce its output voltage—creating a kind of glitch. The capacitor across the output will store a small reservoir of charge that is dumped into the circuit under this circumstance. The value of the capacitor is 50- to 150-μF per ampere.

The voltage regulator, IC1, is a three-terminal IC voltage regulator of fixed (+5 volts dc) output. The LM-323K is capable of supplying up to 3-amperes. This voltage regulator device comes in a TO-3 power transistor package, and should be heatsinked for best success.

If you want to make a 1-ampere power supply from this circuit, then replace the transformer with a 6.3 Vac at 1-2 ampere type, the rectifier with a 50 volt PIV at 1-ampere type, and the voltage regulator with one of the following devices: 7805, LM-340K-5, LM-340T-5 (if heatsinked), or a LM-309K.

+5-VOLTS AT 5-AMPERES DC POWER SUPPLY

Figure D-3 shows the circuit for a dc power supply that will produce +5-volts dc at a current of 5-amperes. The circuit is the same as in Fig. D-2 except that the components are heavier. The transformer must have a secondary current rating of 5 to 10 amperes (a *Triad* model rated at 6.3 Vac at 8-amperes is particularly inviting), and the rectifier must be rated at 5-amperes or more (preferably more). In many cases, project builders will opt for 25-ampere models because they are so common. The filter capacitor is selected according to the 2000-μF/ampere criteria.

The voltage regulator, IC1, is a *Lambda Electronics, Inc.* type LAS-1905. This device is rated at a current of 5-amperes. There is also an 8-ampere model available.

KILLING THE "GLITCH WITCH"

High voltage transients appearing on the ac power line can have a devastating effect on microcomputers and computer-based instruments. These transients are propagated into the computer and wreak all kinds of havoc, disrupting program execution and so forth. Many of the unexplained "bomb-outs" experienced by com-

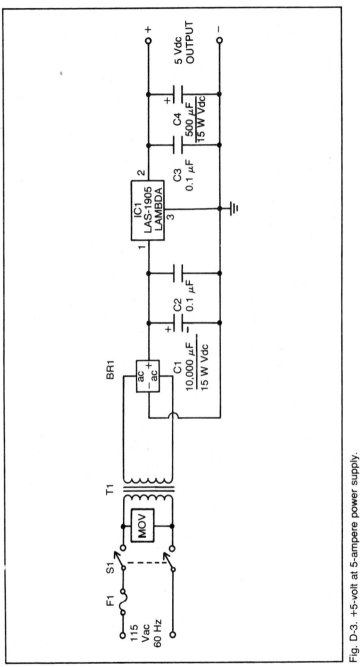

Fig. D-3. +5-volt at 5-ampere power supply.

puters are actually the result of these high voltage transients. There are several ways to suppress these pulses.

One method for killing these glitches is to use an isolation transformer between the computer and the ac power mains. The transformer used must be designed for this application, and will have the ability to suppress high voltage, short duration pulses (such pulses have a high frequency content). Unfortunately, these transformers are both bulky and expensive, so are not always the best solution. Another method is the simple MOV devices used in the power supply projects found earlier in this appendix. This method will work wonders in many cases. Unfortunately, there are still many cases where some stronger medicine is needed.

The circuit of Fig. D-4 combines at least two techniques. There are, for example, three different MOV devices (all identical). The MOV devices are connected as follows:

1. One between hot and neutral;
2. One between neutral and ground;
3. One between hot and ground.

There is also an LC filter installed in this circuit. The filter, FL1, is a low-pass filter, so will pass the 60 Hertz ac power mains signal with ease, but will suppress the high frequency pulses. The filter consists of two inductors, L1 and L2, co-wound on the same ferrite form and three capacitors (C1 - C3). These filters are available in commercial form, and need not be built. Some commercial models are available that have J1 (the ac power mains connector) built-in.

±12-VOLT DC AT 1-AMPERE DC POWER SUPPLY

Some microcomputers and many microcomputer-based instruments will require a low-voltage power supply for such devices as operational amplifiers (and other components of the analog subsystem) and CMOS logic elements. One of the more popular forms of the low-voltage dc power supply is the ±12-volt at 1-ampere supply shown in Fig. D-5. The design of this power supply is essentially the same as the 5-volt supplies shown earlier. The components are selected according to the same rules.

The transformer is rated at 25.6 Vac center-tapped at 2-amperes or more. The rectifier is any 50-volt (PIV) 1-ampere rectifier. In this case, incidentally, the rectifier is used as a pair of half-wave bridges inside the same package rather than as a fullwave bridge rectifier. The voltage regulators are selected as follows:

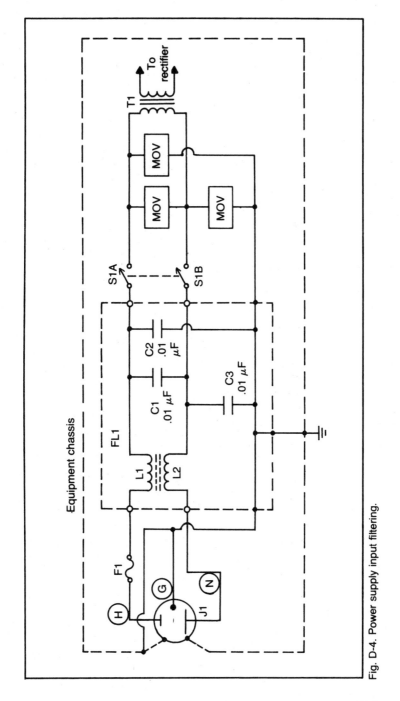

Fig. D-4. Power supply input filtering.

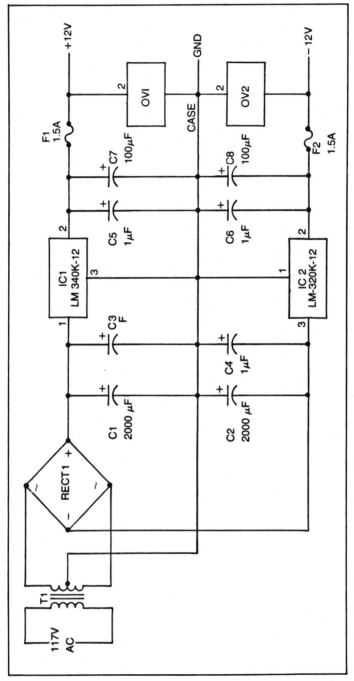

Fig. D-5. ± 12-volt at 1-ampere power supply.

Positive supply
7812
LM-340K-12
LM-340T-12 (if heatsinking is used, otherwise limit current to 750 mA)

Negative supply
7912
LM-320K-12
LM-320T-12 (see LM-340T-12 above)

Index

Edited by Roland S. Phelps